Financing a College Education
How It Works, How It's Changing

Edited by
Jacqueline E. King

AMERICAN COUNCIL ON EDUCATION ★
ORYX PRESS ★
Series on Higher Education
1999

The rare Arabian Oryx is believed to have inspired the myth of the unicorn. This desert antelope became virtually extinct in the early 1960s. At that time, several groups of international conservationists arranged to have nine animals sent to the Phoenix Zoo to be the nucleus of a captive breeding herd. Today, the Oryx population is over 1,000, and over 500 have been returned to the Middle East.

© 1999, 2002 by The American Council on Education and The Oryx Press
88 Post Road West, Westport, CT 06881
An imprint of Greenwood Publishing Group, Inc.
www.greenwood.com

Chapter 2
© 1999 by Gordon C. Winston

Published simultaneously in Canada
Printed and bound in the United States of America

∞ The paper used in this publication meets the minimum requirements of American National Standard for Information Science—Permanence of Paper for Printed Library Materials, ANSI Z39.48, 1984.

10 9 8 7 6 5 4 3

Library of Congress Cataloging-in-Publication Data

Financing a college education : how it works, how it's changing / edited by Jacqueline E. King.
    p. cm. —(American Council on Education/Oryx Press series on higher education)
    Includes bibliographical references (p.) and index.
    ISBN 1-57356-177-0 (alk. paper)   ISBN 1-57356-534-2 (pbk.)
    1. Student aid—United States. 2. College costs—United States.
3. Student loan funds—United States. 4. Parents—United
States—Finance, Personal. 5. Students—United States—Finance,
Personal I. King, Jacqueline E. (Jacqueline Elizabeth) II. Series.
    LB2337.4 .F565   1999
    378.3'0973—dc21   98-55785
                                                          CIP

In order to keep this title in print and available to the academic community, this edition was produced using digital reprint technology in a relatively short print run. This would not have been attainable using traditional methods. Although the cover has been changed from its original appearance, the text remains the same and all materials and methods used still conform to the highest book-making standards.

Part Two. How Financing a College Education Is Changing

CONTENTS

LIST OF FIGURES

LIST OF TABLES

PREFACE

Today, everywhere you turn, people are talking about paying for college. In a recent public opinion poll sponsored by the American Council on Education (ACE), Americans put affording a college education for their children near the top of their list of worries as parents (Ikenberry and Hartle 1998). The only concern parents named more often was fear of their children using illegal drugs; the price of college was cited more often than worries about crime, health care, or the quality of public schools. Media stories about the rapidly rising price of college, and corresponding increases in student indebtedness, abound. Advertisements for mutual funds and brokerage firms almost always point to the high price of college as a reason to save and invest. In 1997, in an attempt to respond to the public's increasing anxiety about this issue, Congress created the National Commission on the Cost of Higher Education and, based on that commission's recommendations, included a new cost study and additional requirements for reporting price and student aid information in the 1998 reauthorization of the Higher Education Act. Clearly, college affordability is an issue of major—and rising—national importance.

Given the concern that policymakers and the American public express about college affordability, it is remarkable that so little is understood—both by the general public and by those on college and university campuses—about what colleges cost, how colleges are financed, and how the student financial aid system functions. The ACE survey found that even people with children in college grossly overestimated both tuition charges and the total price of attendance, hazarding guesses that are double and even triple the actual national averages. Similarly, survey respondents underestimated the amount of financial aid available.

It is obvious that efforts must be stepped up to help the public close their knowledge gap about paying for college. Indeed, the National Commission on the Cost of Higher Education called on the higher education community to launch a national public information campaign about college prices and financial aid. ACE, along with many other higher education associations, has launched such an effort. "College Is Possible" is a multi-year effort, involving over 1,200 colleges and universities, to improve public understanding of the range of college prices and the amount of student aid available.

But what about the knowledge gap on college campuses? Many faculty members and administrators who do not have direct responsibility for institutional finances or student financial aid pay little attention to how their institutions are financed, what they charge, and how students pay those charges. These personnel often are seen as insulated from fiscal realities and indifferent to the difficulties students and families face in paying for college. While this depiction certainly is an exaggeration, it is true that most of us in higher education know less than we should about college financing.

Financing a College Education addresses that problem. Readers who are familiar with higher education but have little or no background in institutional finance or student aid policy will gain a valuable understanding of how the financing system works. However, this book is not merely a descriptive overview. College financing is a complex and contentious policy arena with goals that often conflict, involving numerous stakeholders, each with a separate agenda. Such a realm cannot be described accurately without going into detail. Further, without a basic understanding of the major parameters of this arena—in terms both of policies and of stakeholders—the current policy debates make little sense. Thus, this volume takes a close look at both the parameters of the system and the current issues. Even those who are well versed in college financing will find much in these chapters that is new, noteworthy, and provocative.

OVERVIEW OF THE BOOK

Financing a College Education begins with an introductory chapter by D. Bruce Johnstone, in which he asserts that the basic principles and goals that have formed the fabric of student aid policy in the United States are unraveling. The goal to increase college access for students from the lowest-income households, which animated public policy in this area for over three decades, has been replaced with the objective of making college more affordable for middle-income students and families.

The main body of the book is presented in two sections. The chapters in Part One, "How Financing a College Education Works," describe the major parameters of the college financing system of federal, state, private, and institutional programs, policies, and practices. In truth, there is no real system of college financing because policy is made on numerous levels, both inside and outside of government, with little or no coordination among the various parties. Nonetheless, there are several content areas with which one must be familiar in order to understand the major college financing issues that confront policymakers and campus officials. Part One navigates the reader through these areas. In Chapter 1, John B. Lee provides general background and context for all that follows, summarizing the most recent data on who goes to college, what colleges charge, and the funds that students and families use to meet those charges. In Chapter 2, Gordon C. Winston explains how colleges are financed, what that means for tuition charges, and why our common sense leads us to all the wrong conclusions about the nature of college prices. In Chapter 3, Sandy Baum describes the methods used by governmental agencies and higher education institutions to award need-based student financial aid, outlining the many decisions and trade-offs made between equity, efficiency, and clarity. In Chapter 4, Michael Mumper describes an important and little-examined part of the student aid system—the labyrinth of for-profit and nonprofit companies and organizations that administer student loans, provide technical and managerial support to campus student aid offices, and counsel students and families on how best to "work" the system. These organizations have a great deal of formal and informal influence over both public and institutional student aid policy. In Chapter 5, Kenneth E. Redd describes the programs that provide over half of all student aid—federal student loans. He outlines the major policy changes that have affected those programs in the 1990s and analyzes how those policy decisions have changed the characteristics of undergraduate borrowers.

The chapters in Part Two, "How Financing a College Education Is Changing," explore specific issues that currently are high on the national agenda. In Chapter 6, A. Clayton Spencer analyzes the changing political landscape faced by higher education, especially with regard to student aid. In Chapter 7, Joseph D. Creech and Jerry Sheehan Davis explain need-based and merit-based criteria for awarding student aid, and analyze the recent trend of refocusing state grant programs on merit-based criteria. In Chapter 8, Thomas J. Kane takes a close look at new federal tax provisions designed to help families pay for college, including the Hope tax credit, and evaluates how these programs will augment, or detract from, traditional student aid. In Chapter 9, Kristin D. Conklin and Joni E. Finney examine the new tax provisions from the perspective of state policy and put forward several recommendations for how state higher education policy might complement the new benefits for middle-income families. In Chapter 10, I analyze newly available data to determine whether recent large increases in student borrowing are signs of a true crisis of college affordability or are more a matter of convenience borrowing by middle-income students. In Chapter 11, Lawrence E. Gladieux and Watson Scott Swail evaluate how well student aid has equalized educational opportunity and make the case that student aid alone never can close the achievement gap for disadvantaged students.

In a concluding chapter, I identify some of the reasons that the central goal of student aid policy has shifted from access to affordability, and I propose steps that could be taken to help preserve the programs that serve low-income students.

• • •

Although no one book can provide a comprehensive picture of such a complex topic, *Financing a College Education* covers most of the important aspects of financing a college education. This volume should help faculty, administrators, and students gain a much better understanding of the massive and unwieldy—but vitally important—system of policies and practices that determines, in large part, how institutions are financed and how Americans gain access to higher education.

Jacqueline E. King

REFERENCE

Ikenberry, S. O., and T. W. Hartle. 1998. *Too Little Knowledge Is a Dangerous Thing: What the Public Thinks and Knows about Paying for College.* Washington, DC: American Council on Education.

CONTRIBUTORS

Sandy Baum is a professor of economics and director of the Law and Society program at Skidmore College. Recent publications include articles on financing graduate and professional education, the relationship between student loans and tuition levels, the distribution of subsidies to postsecondary students, and student debt burdens, as well as *A Primer on Economics for Financial Aid Professionals* (National Association of Student Financial Aid Administrators and the College Board, 1996). In 1996, she received the NASFAA Golden Quill Award for Outstanding Contributions to the Literature on Student Aid. Prior to joining the faculty at Skidmore College, Baum taught at Northeastern University and Wellesley College. Baum earned a B.A. with honors in sociology from Bryn Mawr in 1973 and a Ph.D. in economics from Columbia University in 1981.

Kristin D. Conklin is director of the Washington, DC, office of the National Center for Public Policy and Higher Education. The Center is an independent nonpartisan organization, created by national foundations, to ensure educational opportunity, affordability, and quality higher education; it focuses on both state and national higher education policy. Before joining the Center, Conklin was responsible for planning and coordinating research and evaluation efforts of the School-to-Work Opportunities Act of 1994 for the U.S. Departments of Education and Labor. Conklin received a bachelor's degree in political science from California Polytechnic State University, San Luis Obispo, and a master's degree in public policy from Georgetown University.

Joseph D. Creech is director of educational policies at the Southern Regional Education Board (SREB). Prior to joining SREB, Creech was assistant vice-chancellor for academic affairs at Western Carolina University. Creech has been involved in financial aid administration since 1961. He was study director for the Georgia Financial Aid Study and a member of the study staffs for financial aid studies conducted in Florida, Kentucky, and North Carolina. For 15 years, he served as a faculty member at the summer institute on college admissions, placement, and student financial aid sponsored by the College Board and the University of North Carolina at Chapel Hill. Creech received a B.A. in history from Wake Forest University in 1960 and an M.A. in teaching from Duke University in 1961.

Jerry Sheehan Davis is director, education and student loan research, at Sallie Mae, a position he has held since 1994. In 1997, he became vice president for research at the Sallie Mae Education Institute and continues to hold positions in both organizations. Before joining Sallie Mae, he was vice president for research and policy analysis at the Pennsylvania Higher Education Assistance Agency for 13 years. Davis has conducted research in student financial aid and related matters for more than 30 years and has published numerous monographs, research reports, and articles on these and other topics in higher education. For 12 years, he compiled and wrote an annual report on state student aid programs. His research, writing, and contributions to the literature of student aid were recognized by a NASFAA Golden Quill Award, which he received in 1992. Davis has a bachelor's degree and a master's degree in political science, and he received a doctorate in higher education from the University of Georgia.

Joni E. Finney is vice president of the newly founded National Center for Public Policy and Higher Education, in San Jose, CA, and Washington, DC. She was formerly associate director of the California Higher Education Policy Center and director of policy studies for the Education Commission of the States in Denver, CO, where she directed national projects related to public policy and higher education. Finney is an editor and author of *Public and Private Financing of Higher Education: Shaping Public Policy for the Future* (ACE/Oryx Press, 1997) and is currently co-authoring a book on higher education governance. She has authored several policy reports on enrollment and fiscal projections for higher education, teacher education, assessment and accountability, and minority achievement. A frequent keynote speaker and presenter, she recently appeared before the U.S. House of Representatives Committee on Economic and Educational Opportunities, the California Citizens' Commission for Higher Education, the Tennessee Governor's Council on Excellence in Higher Education, and the National Conference of State Legislators.

Lawrence E. Gladieux is executive director for policy analysis of the College Board. He has authored or co-authored articles appearing in numerous education journals, as well as in the popular press. Recent publications include *Memory, Reason, and Imagination: A Quarter Century of Pell Grants* (College Board, 1998) and *The College Aid Quandary: Access, Quality, and the Federal Role* (Brookings Institution, 1995). In 1997, he received the NASFAA Golden Quill Award. Gladieux received a bachelor's degree in government from Oberlin College and a master's degree in public and international affairs from Princeton University. Before joining the College Board, he served as legislative assistant to former congressman John Brademas of Indiana and on the staff of the council of federal relations of the Association of American Universities.

D. Bruce Johnstone is University Professor of Higher and Comparative Education at the State University of New York at Buffalo, where he specializes in higher education finance, governance, and policy formation, and in international comparative higher education. He directs the Learning Productivity Network, a foundation-supported program of communication about, and research into, measures to enhance higher education's productivity on the output, or learning, side. His current research is on college-level learning in high school and international comparative tuition and financial assistance policies. Johnstone has held posts of vice president for administration at the University of Pennsylvania, president of the State University College at Buffalo, and chancellor of the State University of New York, the latter from 1988 through 1994.

Thomas J. Kane is an associate professor of public policy at the Kennedy School of Government at Harvard University. In addition to teaching at the Kennedy School, Kane has been a visiting fellow at the Brown Center on Educational Policy at the Brookings Institution and has served as the senior economist for labor, education, and welfare issues on President Bill Clinton's Council of Economic Advisers. In his research, he has focused on a number of issues related to higher education: the labor market payoff to a community college degree, price responsiveness of students to tuition and financial aid, and affirmative action in college admissions. Kane received a bachelor's degree in economics from the University of Notre Dame, a master's degree in economics from the University of Michigan, and a Ph.D. in public policy from Harvard University.

Jacqueline E. King is director of federal policy analysis at the American Council on Education (ACE). ACE is the umbrella association for higher education, representing 1,800 two- and four-year colleges, research universities, and national and regional education associations. Prior to joining ACE, she was associate director for policy analysis at the College Board. King is the author or co-author of numerous reports, articles, and book chapters on financing higher education, access to postsecondary education, and college admissions. She was named as one of the 40 "young leaders of the academy" by *Change* magazine. King holds a Ph.D. in higher education from the University of Maryland, College Park; a master's degree from Teachers College, Columbia University; and a bachelor's degree from the University of California, Berkeley.

John B. Lee is president of JBL Associates, Inc., in Bethesda, MD, a consulting firm specializing in higher education policy research. His career includes postsecondary policy research at the state and national level. Since 1975, he has published dozens of reports on different aspects of student aid policy. Currently, he and his staff are producing reports on postsecondary-related topics for the National Center for Education Statistics of the U.S. Department of Education and the National Education Association, among others. Before founding JBL Associates, Lee worked for the Education and Labor Committee of the U.S. House of Representatives, the Education Commission of the States, and Stanford Research International, among others. He earned a B.A. and an M.A. from California State University at Sacramento, and a doctoral degree in postsecondary administration from the University of California, Berkeley.

Michael Mumper is a professor of political science at Ohio University. His research interests include the politics of college affordability and the evaluation of federal and state student aid programs. His book, *Removing College Price Barriers: What Government Has Done and Why It Hasn't Worked*, was published by the State University of New York Press in 1996. His articles have appeared in *The Review of Higher Education*, *The Journal of Higher Education*, *The Journal of Education Finance*, *The Journal of Student Financial Aid*, and the 1998 edition of *Higher Education: A Handbook of Theory and Research*. He holds a Ph.D. in government and politics from the University of Maryland and an M.A. in political science from Arizona State University.

Kenneth E. Redd is senior research associate for education and student loan research at Sallie Mae and senior research associate for the Sallie Mae Education Institute. Previously, he has held positions as a researcher and policy analyst at the American Association of State Colleges and Universities, the National Association of Independent Colleges and Universities, and the Pennsylvania Higher Education Assistance Agency. He has published several reports, articles, and book chapters on federal and state student financial aid, college enrollment and achievement, and college financing. Redd has a bachelor's degree from Tufts University and a master's degree from the University of Minnesota.

A. Clayton Spencer is associate vice president for higher education policy at Harvard University. From June 1993 through January 1997, Spencer served as chief education counsel (Majority 1993–94; Minority 1995–97) for the U.S. Senate Committee on Labor and Human Resources. In that role, she was responsible for staffing Senator Ted Kennedy on education legislation and policy, including student aid, education budget and appropriations, technology for education, science and research policy, and regulation of colleges and universities. Previously, Spencer was an associate in the law firm of Ropes and Gray and an assistant United States attorney in Boston. She earned a B.A. from Williams College, master's degrees from Oxford University and Harvard University, and a J.D. from Yale Law School.

Watson Scott Swail is associate director for policy analysis of the College Board, where he provides data and analysis on issues relating to academic preparation, access to college, and postsecondary success. Recent publications include "The Virtual University and Educational Opportunity: Panacea or False Hope" (with Lawrence E. Gladieux), and the College Board's annual *Trends in Student Aid* and *Trends in College Pricing* reports. A former middle-school teacher, Swail now teaches in an adjunct capacity at The George Washington University where he received a doctorate in educational policy. He received a master's degree from Old Dominion University and a bachelor's degree in education from the University of Manitoba, in Winnipeg, Canada.

Gordon C. Winston is the Orrin Sage Professor of Political Economy at Williams College and co-founder and director of the Williams Project on the Economics of Higher Education. He has been chair of Williams's economics department and provost of the college. Winston has held positions as Ford Foundation adviser in Pakistan; member of the Institute for Advanced Study in Princeton; visiting scholar at the Institute for International Economic Studies, Stockholm; and consultant to colleges and universities and to the Mellon Foundation and the National Commission on the Cost of Higher Education. He has written books and articles on economic theory and on the economics of higher education including issues of faculty tenure, "global" accounting, competition, the Cost-Price-Subsidy-Hierarchy model, measuring college costs, peer effects, capital costs, and pricing and financial aid. His work on higher education has been supported by the Andrew W. Mellon Foundation through the Williams Project. He received a B.A. from Whitman College and a Ph.D. in economics from Stanford University.

INTRODUCTION

D. Bruce Johnstone

n the preface, Jacqueline King rightly calls college financing a "complex and contentious policy arena." Politicians, members of the press, and a great many citizens are concerned and even angry about what they believe to be excessive college costs—or is their concern really about high *prices,* the portion of costs passed on to the student and family? (Or, as Gordon C. Winston discusses in Chapter 2, is it really about *net prices*—that is, tuition and other expenses after financial aid grants?)

Many college and university leaders believe this criticism—whether directed at costs, or at prices, or at net prices—is a bad rap. They point to the fact that most undergraduates are in low-cost, relatively lean, and arguably efficient public community and comprehensive colleges, with the portion of costs that is passed on to students (the tuition) subsidized by government funding and made easily affordable with a part-time job, a subsidized loan, a little parental assistance, and a government grant (in the case of low-income students). The low-cost, minimally endowed, moderately priced private colleges (which are numerous) are similarly lean and reasonably affordable. Administrators and faculty of such colleges (many of which have experienced budget cuts to the point of major losses in faculty and professional staff, underinvestment in technology, and seriously deferred maintenance, all the while accepting low-income students, many of whom need academic remediation) are puzzled and distressed when accusations of waste, profligacy, and insufficient attention to the public's interest seem directed at them.

The very-high-priced colleges may be another matter. But widespread price discounting makes the tuition sticker price, for most, more symbolic than

1

substantive. More significantly, the most expensive of these colleges have students clamoring to gain admission.

But the contention and confusion are there, giving those of us who study college finance and public policy another chance in this volume to grapple with these issues and perhaps even to propose some solutions. We approach this task with considerable humility.

In the first place, the issues are indeed complex, and most simple explanations and simple solutions are just that: simplistic and likely to be wrong. The complexity begins with the vast array of U.S. colleges and universities that differ not only in programs and purposes, but in underlying wealth (mainly in the form of endowments); in relationship to, and dependence on, government at different levels; and in prestige, selectivity, and market niches. Differing from systems in the rest of the world, U.S. higher education is particularly complicated because of the presence of a private sector that itself contains great variation: from the well-endowed and internationally prestigious institutions, serving the very brightest (along with a few, still, of the well born), to the small, lean, vocationally oriented, and virtually unendowed colleges, serving anyone who can pay and highly dependent on the availability of federal financial aid for their students.

"Policy" is further complicated by the fact that the federal government, while a significant player in the provision of financial assistance—and thus in the priority accorded to the goal of access—has virtually nothing to do with the operation of American colleges and universities. Public funding and governmental control of colleges and universities, public or private, is a prerogative of the 50 states, not of the federal government. Accreditation, or the continual monitoring for quality control, is left in the U.S. to private, voluntary associations essentially controlled by the institutions already accredited. The allocation of missions and programs among a state's public institutions is mainly the responsibility of its multi-campus systems or quasi-public coordinating boards. The curricula, methods of instruction, academic standards, selection of students, appointment and tenuring of faculty, and subjects of faculty scholarship are matters of "shared governance," with faculty voice paramount. And now, additionally, state governments are involved in student and parent financing of college, with grants, loans, savings, and tuition prepayment plans (see Chapter 7)—to the considerable further muddling of the higher education finance waters.

Into this stew—containing in 1998 almost 3,700 institutions educating nearly 15 million students and consuming some $200 billion—federal and state governments have pursued a largely uncoordinated and unarticulated policy of distributing the costs of college among parents, students, institutions, and taxpayers. The overarching goal has been to maximize access to public and private institutions alike, with the least expenditure of public (especially federal) dollars and with minimal governmental interference in the operations of higher education institutions.

Toward that end, and in support of the $60 billion (College Board 1998) edifice of student financial assistance that has been built since the 1960s, the following have been guiding principles:

1. Parents should contribute toward the expense of their child's higher education, to the limit of their financial ability, at least through the baccalaureate degree or until the child is independent.
2. Government—mainly, the federal government through the Pell Grant program—should make up in grants for shortfalls in students' resources that are due to the very low income of parents (but only to make possible the lowest-cost public education).
3. Students should contribute toward the expense of their higher education, through earnings, student loans, or both.
4. Loans should be made available to all students without regard to creditworthiness.
5. Neither form of governmental student assistance—loans or grants—should take into account (other than minimally) the academic preparedness or academic performance (i.e., the "merit") of the student, the field of study, or the stature or "worthiness" of the college or university.

These principles are, however, under serious strain as we approach the turning of the century. The strain is partly technical: aspects of the former system do not seem to work as well as they used to. Or perhaps the inconsistencies, "bugs," and political irritations that always have been there have simply gotten more difficult to ignore. The strain is also ideological. The nation (at least the electorate) seems to have grown weary of the old agendas of increasing access, expanding opportunities, implementing affirmative action, and providing second (or third, or even more) chances at postsecondary academic success. Some would say that the technical and the ideological cannot be so easily separated; that the goal of equal opportunity to higher education is as compelling as ever, but that faith has been lost in the ability of government programs, government regulations, and taxpayer dollars to achieve it.

Whatever the causes, the fabric of the American "system" of financial assistance and tuition policy seems to be unraveling. This volume explores some of the causes for this unraveling and discusses what may lie ahead for government and institutional policies surrounding the cost of college.

For example, the fundamental principle of the "expected family contribution," while extraordinarily important and financially impossible for the system to jettison, is becoming increasingly irrelevant and/or vexingly complicated for more and more students: older and otherwise independent students, students dependent on a noncustodial parent, or students from one- or two-parent families below the minimum income for a positive expected family contribution.

Furthermore, the expected family contribution for most students, especially those facing the higher expenses of private higher education, will be more than is likely to be available from parents' current income alone, generally necessitating borrowing or the use of savings. Attempting to impact parental savings behavior is becoming increasingly attractive politically, as discussed in Chapters 7, 8, and 9. Such savings-incentive plans address what is a clear problem: inadequate savings by parents for their children's higher education. These plans also appeal to the middle and upper middle classes (who are more likely to vote than the poor); they allow participation by states, with considerable political fanfare; and best of all, they cost very little—and what they do cost (or might cost) can largely be either put off to the future (as with some of the state tuition-prepayment plans) or shifted to the tax expenditure (or revenue loss) side of the state's budget, in relative obscurity.

Sandy Baum points out in Chapter 3 the significance—and the further complexity—of the degree to which the assessment of "means" or "need" takes into consideration past savings in addition to current earned income. Taking savings or other assets into account when calculating a student's need for financial aid can discourage such savings, or at least honest reporting, as they can be used to reduce the aid to which the family might otherwise be entitled. But to not consider them is to jeopardize the principles of horizontal and vertical equity and to reward some families with more taxpayer-based aid than is arguably needed—and thus to diminish the pool of public aid for students and families with no ability to contribute from their own resources.

Students are a major source in the financing of U.S. higher education. But the problem with students as a revenue source is that it is difficult to know, as a policy matter, where to draw a limit. Already, more than one-fourth of all full-time students are employed for more than 20 hours a week. Some empirical evidence, as well as common sense, suggests that such diversion diminishes students' academic time-on-task and thus their academic achievements.

Even more troubling is determining where to draw the line on student borrowing. The federal government makes loans available to all students without regard to creditworthiness, a policy that requires a taxpayer-backed guarantee. The government also pays the interest on need-based loans while the borrower is a student. Although there are limits or caps on amounts that can be borrowed in each year and in aggregate, these caps seem very loosely based on notions of the amounts that can be repaid by average wage earners at various levels and kinds of higher education. But there are great pressures on Congress to set high loan limits to accommodate the high-priced private colleges and expensive advanced professional education (which is also most likely to pay off in higher earnings). Student borrowing has increased dramatically, but in Chapter 10, Jacqueline King shows that, at least for middle-income and low-income dependent students, the larger amounts borrowed are less a function of greater need than of convenience and the sheer availability of the higher loan limits.

Congress and the American people seem concerned about the high and rising student loan burdens. But loans may also be rising because Congress has effectively reduced the expected contribution from middle- and upper-middle-income parents (especially that previously based on home equity), thus making it easier to qualify as "needy" for guaranteed loans, as well as making it necessary to compensate somehow for the diminished parental contributions.

Under the greatest threat today is the principle that scarce grants and subsidies should respond to "need," defined in a variety of ways, but always carrying the implication that the expenditure of taxpayer resources—and, in general, also the expenditure of higher education's philanthropic resources—should make a difference in enrollment behavior. Basing financial assistance on "merit" has been seen (and still is, by most higher education finance analysts) as spending scarce taxpayer dollars for an objective that is doubtlessly appreciated by "good students" and their parents, and is clearly satisfying to politicians, *but that does nothing to make a difference.* In other words, the assistance rewards, but does not cause, good brains and good study habits. Furthermore, the powerful correlation between "good academic performance" and high family socioeconomic status (and thus with race) means that when aid is based on "merit," the children and young adults most in need of financial assistance to make a college education even possible are the least likely to get a scholarship. Because increases in Pell Grants have fallen far behind increases in tuition and other costs of college, merit-based aid is generally perceived to be coming from the same pot as the already-underfunded need-based aid.

The recent evolution of the U.S. financial aid system (some would say "nonsystem") has been dominated by the interplay of three forces. The first has been the overriding objective of "access"—broadening the participation in postsecondary education—coupled with a minimally funded homage to the nation's private higher education sector and the principle of "student choice." The second has been a political and/or electoral demand to spread the available funds to reach as many middle-income families as possible (i.e., to not concentrate funds on the very poor). The third has been to achieve these objectives within formidable budget constraints. What looks to many like a needlessly complicated nonsystem appears to others (at least to some of us "analyst types") as a very rational response, albeit not a simple one, to the realities of a public higher education system owned, financed, and controlled (minimally) by the states, with a large and diverse private sector, driven by the overarching policy goal of maximizing access (especially, making a difference between enrolling somewhere and not enrolling at all), within a context of federal and state budget constraints.

At the close of the 1990s, the highest-priority policy goal, access, is coming into question. The necessarily complex, predominantly need-based system created and regularly perfected by policymakers and analysts, may have maximized accessibility for the public financial aid dollar. But the electorate— and, not surprisingly, most elected officials—is no longer squarely behind the old principles. Politicians at federal and state levels are determined to recognize—and spend money on—their conceptions of "merit." Public tuition will continue to rise, and private tuition, while perhaps peaking, will increasingly be packaged with discounts in a quest to maximize net tuition revenue— rather than to maximize accessibility, per se.

New public policies are emerging, the contours of which are not yet clear. The chapters in this volume are an attempt to clarify options and to guide us into this future, in which one of the few things that we know for certain is that the stakes will continue to be high.

REFERENCE

College Board. 1998. *Trends in Student Aid: 1988 to 1998.* Washington, DC: College Board.

PART ONE

• • • • • • • • • • • •

How Financing
A College Education
Works

CHAPTER 1

How Do Students and Families Pay for College?

John B. Lee

This chapter describes how students and their families pay for college. Funds for college come from family savings, current income, future income (if the student or the parents use a loan), and grants from public and private sources. The College Board estimates that students received $55.7 billion in student financial aid in 1996–97. The federal government provided over two-thirds of the financial aid awarded in that year, most of it as loans (College Board 1997). States and higher education institutions also provide significant amounts of student financial aid. The remainder comes from employers and other private sources.

The growth of student financial aid represents a huge transformation in the financing of postsecondary education, which began when Congress authorized the first federal student financial aid program in 1965. Financial aid is now the largest source of revenue that funds the postsecondary education system. According to the U.S. Department of Education, states provided $43 billion to higher education institutions in 1995, making them the second largest provider of postsecondary education funds (U.S. Department of Education 1997a, 346). Students and their families now have more postsecondary purchasing power, as a result of student financial aid, than the states.

Figures 1.1 and 1.2 show the percentages of undergraduate and graduate students who received financial aid from different sources in academic year 1995–96. Nearly half of the undergraduate students and 51.9 percent of the graduate students received some form of student financial aid (U.S. Department of Education 1998a).

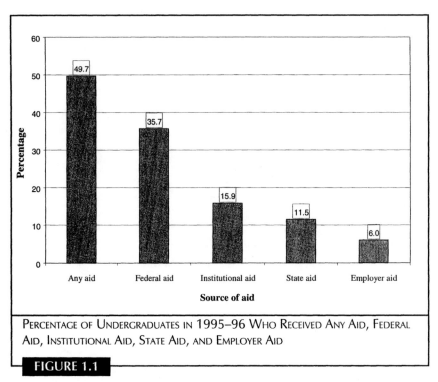

PERCENTAGE OF UNDERGRADUATES IN 1995–96 WHO RECEIVED ANY AID, FEDERAL AID, INSTITUTIONAL AID, STATE AID, AND EMPLOYER AID

FIGURE 1.1

Source: U.S. Department of Education 1998a; analysis by author.

This chapter focuses on undergraduate financial aid. In part, this recognizes the underlying differences in how undergraduates finance their education compared with graduate and first-professional-degree students. Also, most federal and state financial aid programs emphasize undergraduates, and the bulk of government financial aid dollars are spent on these students. However, this does not mean that student financial aid is unimportant for graduate and first-professional students—as noted in Figure 1.2, in 1995–96, over half of the 2.8 million students in postgraduate study received some type of aid (U.S. Department of Education 1998b).

KEY CONCEPTS AND TERMS

The following concepts and terms are key to understanding the information presented in this chapter.

Access and Choice

Important policy questions revolve around the degree to which student financial aid improves institutional access and choice. Families differ in their

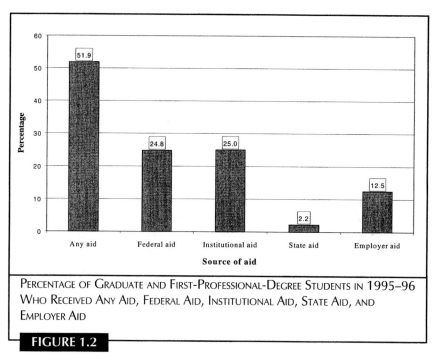

PERCENTAGE OF GRADUATE AND FIRST-PROFESSIONAL-DEGREE STUDENTS IN 1995–96 WHO RECEIVED ANY AID, FEDERAL AID, INSTITUTIONAL AID, STATE AID, AND EMPLOYER AID

FIGURE 1.2

Source: U.S. Department of Education 1998a; analysis by author.

ability to pay for college. Some families have the resources to pay the full price of college on their own, while others lack the discretionary income to pay anything. Most financial aid offices use a need-analysis system to standardize the determination of what a family can afford to pay for college. The U.S. Department of Education requires that certain need-analysis rules be used to award federal grants and loans. Financial need is determined by subtracting the calculated expected family contribution from the institutional cost of attendance. This is determined by a formula that takes the family's wealth and expenses into consideration. No matter what the wealth of the family might be, the need-analysis system generally assumes a minimum contribution from the student.

The primary goal of federal student financial aid, especially grant assistance, is to provide *access* to some type of postsecondary education for students from the lowest-income families. Most federal grants provide aid to the lowest-income students. Other aid providers, such as states and higher education institutions, may award grants to reward merit or to increase enrollment.

A second goal of federal student financial aid is to provide *choice:* to help students afford a college that meets their needs and abilities. Simply providing access to the lowest-priced institution does not necessarily allow low-income students to choose the most appropriate institution for their needs. Middle-income students, too, would have limited institutional choice without student financial aid, often in the form of loans. Unlike federal grants, federal loans are awarded with less consideration of family income. This allows a middle-income student who attends an expensive institution but is ineligible for a federal grant to meet the cost of attendance with a loan.

Cost and Price

Understanding the distinction between the cost of college and the price of college also is important. The *cost* of providing a college or university education usually exceeds the *price* charged to the student as tuition. Tuition is only one source of revenue used by institutions to cover costs. In public institutions, revenue from state and local taxes provide the bulk of income. In private institutions, gifts and income from endowments provide funds. The share of the institutional costs covered by these non-tuition revenue sources varies from almost nothing to nearly 90 percent. One can think of this difference between price and cost as a de facto form of student financial aid. The price—the tuition—charged by an institution can influence both who attends and how students and their families pay for college. Many institutions, especially private colleges and universities, use institutional funds to discount tuition to selected students. These tuition reductions are counted as grants in this chapter.

Distinguishing three kinds of price is also helpful. We call the published tuition plus living expenses the *sticker price.* The price of attendance (tuition and living expenses) after the awarding of student grants is the *net price.* The *out-of-pocket price* is the price of attendance after both grants and loans are subtracted from the sticker price, because loans allow families and students to delay paying the price of college. These three measures provide a systematic way to describe the price of college.

Dependent and Independent Students

Generally, undergraduates are declared to be *independent* if they are more than 24 years of age, a veteran of the U.S. armed forces, a ward of the court, married, or have legal dependents. Those who do not meet these criteria are considered *dependent* on their parents. In most of the tables in this chapter, data are presented for dependent students only, because their circumstances provide an easily defined relationship between family income and student financial aid. Independent students may have low income for many reasons, but their income does not represent their parents' ability to pay for college. Because of these differences, the need-analysis system does not assess the income of independent and dependent students in the same way. Therefore, direct comparisons between dependent and independent undergraduates' income may be misleading.

The exclusion of independent undergraduates does not mean that they are an unimportant part of the student financial aid picture; indeed, full-time independent students received 36.3 percent of the grants and 33.2 percent of the loans awarded to full-time undergraduates in 1995–96 (see Table 1.1). Table 1.1 also shows that 30.6 percent of full-time undergraduates in 1995–96 were independent of their parents' income. Thus, full-time independent undergraduates received a larger share of student financial aid than full-time dependent undergraduates. In part, this is because many full-time independent undergraduates gave up full-time jobs to attend college, which lowered their income substantially and made them eligible for student aid.

TABLE 1.1

PERCENTAGE DISTRIBUTION OF FULL-TIME UNDERGRADUATES, AND GRANTS AND LOANS TO FULL-TIME UNDERGRADUATES, BY DEPENDENCY STATUS, 1995–96

	Dependent	Independent
Percentage of Full-Time, Undergraduate Enrollment	69.4%	30.6%
Share of All Grants Awarded to Full-Time Undergraduates	63.7%	36.3%
Share of All Loans Awarded to Full-Time Undergraduates	66.8%	33.2%

Source: U.S. Department of Education 1998b.

Full-Time and Part-Time Enrollment

In most of the tables in this chapter, data are limited to full-time undergraduates. The inclusion of part-time undergraduates would complicate the analysis: part-time students have more opportunities to work full-time, and their school-related expenses are lower than those of full-time students.

Full-time dependent undergraduates represent the largest single group of undergraduates, but they are not a majority. Table 1.2 shows that full-time dependent undergraduates represent 40.1 percent of the enrolled undergraduates and 45.7 percent of student financial aid recipients. Part-time undergraduates include those who attend full-time for part of the year.

Table 1.2 also shows that a larger proportion of full-time dependent undergraduates received each type of aid compared with their enrollment share. The share of full-time independent undergraduates who received each type of financial aid also exceeded their share of enrollment, with the exception of aid in the form of work-study.[1] It is especially noteworthy that full-time independent undergraduates received 41.8 percent of the unsubsidized loans, although they represent only 21.3 percent of enrollment. This means they were nearly twice as likely to have received an unsubsidized loan as full-time dependent undergraduates.

| TABLE 1.2 |

PERCENTAGE DISTRIBUTION OF UNDERGRADUATES ACCORDING TO DEPENDENCY STATUS AND TYPE OF FINANCIAL AID RECEIVED, 1995–96

Type of Aid	Enrollment and Dependency Status			
	Full-Time Dependent	Part-Time Dependent	Full-Time Independent	Part-Time Independent
Grants	44.5%	4.4%	30.2%	20.9%
Subsidized Loans	52.8%	3.3%	32.9%	11.1%
Unsubsidized Loans	41.9%	3.8%	41.8%	12.5%
Work-Study	73.9%	2.9%	18.8%	4.4%
Financial Aid from Any Source	45.7%	4.7%	28.9%	20.7%
Total Enrollment	40.1%	9.1%	21.3%	29.6%

Source: U.S. Department of Education 1998b.

MEASURES OF ACCESS AND CHOICE

Access

College enrollment rates have grown substantially since World War II. Today, about two out of three high school graduates enroll in a postsecondary institution, in large part because postsecondary education provides an increasingly important gateway to better jobs and an improved quality of life.

A young person's chances of continuing his or her education after high school depend both on ability to pay the price of attendance and on academic achievement. Table 1.3 shows the percentage of 1992 high school graduates who had enrolled in a postsecondary institution by 1994, by socioeconomic status (SES) and quartile on a standard achievement test. Enrollment increases with SES and academic ability. Most (97 percent) of the highest-income/highest-ability students enrolled in college. A student from the highest income quartile and the lowest-tested ability quartile was as likely to have enrolled in a postsecondary institution as a student from the lowest income quartile and the highest-tested ability quartile.

TABLE 1.3

PERCENTAGE OF 1992 HIGH SCHOOL GRADUATES ATTENDING COLLEGE IN 1994, BY
SOCIOECONOMIC STATUS AND ACHIEVEMENT TEST QUARTILE

| | Socioeconomic Status (SES) | | | |
	Lowest Quartile SES	Middle Two Quartiles SES	Highest Quartile SES	Average
Lowest Quartile on Achievement Test	36%	49%	77%	47%
Second Quartile on Achievement Test	50%	66%	85%	66%
Third Quartile on Achievement Test	63%	79%	90%	80%
Highest Quartile on Achievement Test	78%	89%	97%	93%
Average	49%	71%	91%	72%

Source: U.S. Department of Education 1996.

Equal access to college for students from low-income families remains an elusive goal. In a given achievement test quartile, students from lower SES quartiles are less likely to continue their education compared with students in higher SES quartiles. This result suggests that student financial aid and outreach programs have not succeeded in equalizing educational opportunity. Other factors, such as cultural attitudes, inadequate information about college opportunities, and geographic barriers may play additional roles in reducing the chances of a low-income student attending college.

Choice

Families and students can choose among postsecondary institutions offering different sticker prices. Table 1.4 shows the average sticker prices students faced in 1995–96. Tuition accounts for more of the variation in price than living expenses. Living expenses were estimated by using resident student expenses in four-year colleges and commuter student expenses in two-year public and proprietary schools.[2] Living expenses accounted for the largest share of the sticker price in public institutions. Tuition was the major component in the sticker price for private and proprietary institutions.

Contrary to popular perception, most—two-thirds—of all full-time undergraduates were charged less than $5,000 a year for tuition in 1995–96. Tuition charges of less than $5,000 were faced by 82.8 percent of full-time undergraduates attending public four-year institutions, and nearly all the full-time students in two-year public colleges. Less than 20 percent of full-time undergraduates attended colleges with tuition of $10,000 or above. Table 1.5 shows the distribution of students by the tuition they were charged in each institutional sector.

TABLE 1.4

AVERAGE STICKER PRICES FOR FULL-TIME UNDERGRADUATES, 1995–96

	Type of Institution			
	Public Two-Year	Public Four-Year	Private Four-Year	Proprietary
Tuition	$1,394	$2,966	$12,823	$6,496
Living Expenses	$4,516	$6,682	$7,538	$4,516
Total (Sticker Price)	$5,910	$9,648	$20,361	$11,012

Source: College Board 1996.

TABLE 1.5

PERCENTAGE DISTRIBUTION OF FULL-TIME UNDERGRADUATES, BY TUITION AND INSTITUTION TYPE, 1995–96

Institution Type	Tuition					
	Less Than $1,000	$1,001–$2,500	$2,501–$5,000	$5,001–$7,500	$7,501–$10,000	$10,001 or More
Public Four-Year	0.9%	35.8%	46.1%	8.3%	5.3%	3.7%
Public Two-Year	38.2%	52.7%	8.9%	0.2%	0.1%	0.0%
Private Four-Year	0.0%	1.9%	9.1%	7.1%	12.3%	69.6%
Proprietary	0.9%	5.1%	15.9%	38.7%	29.5%	10.0%
All Institutions	8.8%	29.5%	27.4%	8.1%	7.0%	19.2%

Note: Rows may not total to 100 percent because of rounding.

Source: U.S. Department of Education 1998a; analysis by author.

Table 1.6 shows the distribution of dependent full-time undergraduates by their college sticker price and family income. This distribution helps show the relationship between family income and institution choice. The table shows that the largest difference in the distribution of undergraduates occurs at the extremes of sticker price and income. Undergraduates with the lowest income predominate in institutions with the lowest sticker prices and the highest-income students prevail at institutions with the highest sticker prices. The results suggest that choice lessened for low- and middle-income students when the sticker price reached $15,000. At that level, undergraduates from families with incomes of $70,000 or more represent a larger share of the enrollment and those with income below $30,000 account for smaller share. This suggests that low-income students were not likely to attend the most expensive institutions, but probably still could choose among most colleges and universities.

TABLE 1.6

PERCENTAGE DISTRIBUTION OF FULL-TIME, DEPENDENT UNDERGRADUATES, BY FAMILY INCOME AND STICKER PRICE, 1995–96

Sticker Price (Tuition plus Living Expenses)	Family Income				
	Less Than $20,000	$20,000– $29,999	$30,000– $49,999	$50,000– $69,999	$70,000 or More
Less Than $4,999	40.6%	13.7%	22.3%	14.6%	8.7%
$5,000–$9,999	18.5%	13.3%	25.1%	21.5%	21.7%
$10,000–$14,999	18.0%	10.4%	21.1%	20.4%	30.1%
$15,000–$24,999	13.2%	10.2%	20.5%	21.1%	35.0%
$25,000 or More	14.5%	7.1%	15.8%	18.1%	44.4%
Average	17.8%	11.5%	22.5%	20.8%	27.4%

Note: Columns may not total to 100 percent because of rounding.

Source: U.S. Department of Education 1998a; analysis by author.

WHERE DOES THE MONEY COME FROM TO PAY FOR COLLEGE?

Half of undergraduates and their families do not use student financial aid to pay for college. The other half receive student financial aid in the form of grants, loans, or work assistance. Most students work while they attend college and their families help pay their expenses. Even the lowest-income students who receive student financial aid are expected to pay part of the price of attendance. This section provides information on the sources of student funding.

Loans

As Figure 1.3 shows, in 1970–71, grants constituted 70 percent and loans 30 percent of all financial aid awarded to students. In 1984–85, the two sources were about equal. By 1996–97, loans provided 59 percent of all financial aid awarded—an all-time high.

Policymakers are ambivalent about the expanding use of student loans. On one hand, loans help students pay the expenses associated with attending a postsecondary education institution. On the other hand, borrowers may burden themselves far into the future by excessive borrowing. The burden may be highest for those undergraduates who borrow but do not finish their education.

The federal government provides nearly all of the loans available to students. According to the College Board, students borrowed $30.1 billion in

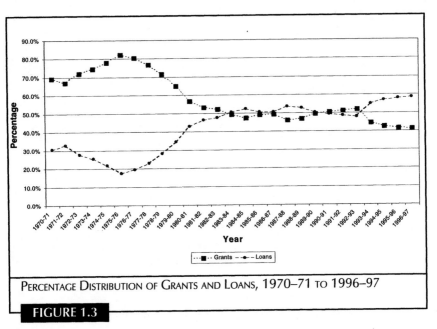

PERCENTAGE DISTRIBUTION OF GRANTS AND LOANS, 1970–71 TO 1996–97

FIGURE 1.3

Source: College Board 1997.

1996–97 (see Table 1.7). Loans help students pay for college by deferring the payments until they start working. Borrowers can take up to 10 years, and sometimes more, to repay their loans. Parents often pick up some of this debt, and the rest is students' liability.

There are two main types of federal student loan programs, which should be analyzed separately: subsidized loans and unsubsidized loans. Subsidized loans accrue no interest while a borrower is in school. Federal subsidized loans can be awarded only to students with financial need. Almost 60 percent of all student loans made in 1996–97 were subsidized. Unsubsidized loans do not require a student to prove financial need. Interest accrues on unsubsidized loans from the time the loan is made. A smaller subsidized loan program for students with financial need is the Federal Perkins Loan Program, which is financed with federal funds and some institutional matching money. Postsecondary institutions select the recipients and are responsible for collecting the payments.

Parents are eligible for federal PLUS loans if they are creditworthy. Parents can use PLUS loans to pay their expected share of college expenses. These loans are characterized as unsubsidized loans in this chapter. Technically, they are not student loans, but they are included in reports of total aid.

TABLE 1.7

FEDERAL STUDENT LOANS AWARDED IN FY 1996

Type of Loan	Volume (Billions of Dollars)	Number (Millions of Loans)
Subsidized	$17.1	4.9
Perkins*	$1.0	0.7
Unsubsidized	$9.4	2.6
PLUS	$2.6	0.4
Total	$30.1	8.7
* Subsidized.		

Sources: U.S. Department of Education 1997a; College Board 1997.

If loans improve choice, then the mean loan amount per undergraduate should increase as the price of attendance increases. Dividing the total amount of loan aid by the number of undergraduates determines the mean loan amount received by undergraduates. The denominator includes all undergraduates, both those who received a loan and those who did not. As seen in Table 1.8, the mean loan amount increases as the price of attendance increases until the sticker price reaches $25,000.

The mean loan amount does not change as much with family income as it does with the price of attendance. The results in Table 1.8 suggest that middle-income dependent undergraduates, defined as those with a family income between $20,000 and $49,999, depend more on loans than undergraduates from other income groups. Students in this middle-income group may be too wealthy to receive need-based grants, but lack the resources to pay the sticker price out of their own pockets. As was shown in Table 1.6, higher-income students attended higher-price institutions and may use loans to pay for that choice.

Student Grants

Student grants provided $22.1 billion to students and their families in 1996–97 (College Board 1997). Thirty-nine percent of undergraduates received a grant in that year from federal, state, institutional, and private sources. Table 1.9 shows that institutions provide the largest share of grant assistance. Private colleges provide much of it, although many public institutions provide tuition remission to students. Institutional aid may be used to increase the diversity of the student body or to help enroll enough students to fill the class. Some institutions provide institutional grants out of special endowments or

TABLE 1.8

MEAN LOAN AMOUNT RECEIVED BY FULL-TIME DEPENDENT UNDERGRADUATES, BY
FAMILY INCOME AND STICKER PRICE, 1995–96

Sticker Price (Tuition plus Living Expenses)	Family Income					
	Less Than $20,000	$20,000–$29,999	$30,000–$49,999	$50,000–$69,999	$70,000 or More	Average Mean Loan
Less Than $4,999	$111	$24	$425	*	*	$272
$5,000–$9,999	$1,000	$1,153	$1,073	$795	$439	$873
$10,000–$14,999	$2,172	$2,210	$2,239	$1,569	$866	$1,673
$15,000–$24,999	$3,116	$3,237	$3,026	$2,529	$1,439	$2,400
$25,000 or More	$2,539	$3,692	$2,975	$2,009	$1,454	$2,112
Average Mean Loan	$1,629	$1,811	$1,770	$1,415	$918	$1,442
*Too few cases to report.						

Source: U.S. Department of Education 1998a; analysis by author.

TABLE 1.9

STUDENT GRANTS AWARDED BY SOURCE, 1996–97

	Volume (Millions of Dollars)	Percent (Share of Total Grants)
Federal Grants	$8.389	37.9%
State Grants	$3.190	14.4%
Grants from Higher Education Institutions and Other Private Sources	$10.569	47.7%
Total	$22.148	100.0%

Source: College Board 1997.

private contributions; for others, these awards represent a loss of tuition revenue.

The federal government does not dominate in the awarding of grant aid as they do in loans. Pell Grants, the biggest federal student grant program, provide about two-thirds of the federal share of grants and one-quarter of the total share of grant assistance awarded to students in 1996–97. Pell Grants, along with most other federal grants, are awarded to students based on their financial need. State, institutional, and private grants may be awarded to students based on criteria including financial need; academic achievement; or special status, such as being a veteran, disabled, or having membership in a particular religious or service organization.

If grants improve access for low-income students, the mean award should decrease as income increases. As shown in Table 1.10, lower-income full-time dependent undergraduates received larger mean awards than those with higher income in 1995–96. The mean grant amount also increased as the sticker price increased. The evidence suggests that grants are sensitive to income and reduce the net price of attendance more for low-income undergraduates than for higher-income undergraduates. Mean grants were calculated using the same method as was used to calculate mean loans (see Table 1.8).

TABLE 1.10

MEAN GRANT AMOUNT RECEIVED BY FULL-TIME DEPENDENT UNDERGRADUATES, BY FAMILY INCOME AND STICKER PRICE, 1995–96

Sticker Price (Tuition plus Living Expenses)	Family Income					Average Mean Grant
	Less Than $20,000	$20,000–$29,999	$30,000–$49,999	$50,000–$69,999	$70,000 or More	
Less Than $4,999	$1,596	$851	$425	*	*	$847
$5,000–$9,999	$1,901	$1,250	$627	$344	$240	$816
$10,000–$14,999	$3,008	$2,258	$1,421	$798	$474	$1,434
$15,000–$24,999	$5,798	$5,708	$4,922	$3,404	$1,858	$3,747
$25,000 or more	$9,546	$12,594	$9,927	$5,149	$2,331	$5,865
Average Mean Grant	$3,068	$2,642	$1,971	$1,279	$900	$1,828

*Too few cases to report.

Source: U.S. Department of Education 1998a; analysis by author.

Work-Study

Work-study is not an equal partner in student financial aid. According to the College Board, this form of aid accounted for less than 2 percent of the total financial aid received by undergraduates in 1996–97. In strict terms, we may think of work-study as aid to the institution, because the college—or other nonprofit employer—can hire work-study students with the federal government paying most of the wages. A work-study job may be more meaningful educationally or more convenient than a private job, but it does not necessarily represent more income than the student could otherwise earn. In fact, because work-study is needs-tested, a student can earn only up to a predefined amount. This may make a work-study job less attractive than other jobs available to the student.

Combinations of Aid

Table 1.11 shows the income distribution of full-time dependent undergraduates who received different types of aid. The distribution of aid across income categories helps evaluate the degree to which student financial aid helps low-income undergraduates. Table 1.11 shows that in 1995–96, half of the dependent undergraduates had a family income of $50,000 or more (20.9 percent between $50,000 and $69,999 and 28.5 percent of $70,000 or more). Although half of the undergraduates had income below $50,000, nearly 70 percent of the grant assistance, 68 percent of the work-study, and 71 percent of the subsidized loans awarded to full-time dependent undergraduates went to those with income less than $50,000. Unsubsidized loans represented the only student financial aid programs in which more than half the aid went to students with family income of more than $50,000. This evidence shows that full-time undergraduates with income below the average for all full-time undergraduates were more likely to receive student financial aid than those with income above the average.

The one type of student financial aid that families above the average income were more likely to receive was an unsubsidized loan. PLUS loans make up a large share of unsubsidized loans for full-time dependent undergraduates. They help creditworthy families and are not limited to families with financial need. It is not surprising that higher-income families use these loans. Only part of the unsubsidized loan volume is reflected in this table because independent undergraduates and graduate students receive a large share.

TABLE 1.11

PERCENTAGE DISTRIBUTION OF FULL-TIME DEPENDENT UNDERGRADUATES, BY TYPE OF FINANCIAL AID RECEIVED AND FAMILY INCOME, 1995– 96

			Type of Aid			
Family Income	Grants	Subsidized Loans	Unsubsidized Loans	Work-Study	Financial Aid from Any Source	Enrollment Distribution
Less Than $20,000	27.4%	23.7%	7.4%	24.2%	23.0%	17.1%
$20,000–$29,999	16.1%	16.5%	6.5%	15.9%	13.9%	11.3%
$30,000–$49,999	25.4%	30.9%	18.6%	27.6%	24.9%	22.2%
$50,000–$69,999	16.0%	18.7%	30.5%	18.0%	19.1%	20.9%
$70,000 or More	15.1%	10.3%	37.0%	14.2%	19.1%	28.5%

Note: Columns may not total to 100 percent because of rounding.

Source: U.S. Department of Education 1998a; analysis by author.

Much of the debate about student financial aid revolves around the share of aid awarded to students in each of the major institutional sectors. Table 1.12 compares the institutional share of enrollment and the share of major aid programs going to students attending institutions in each sector of postsecondary education. The results show that students in some sectors use a large share of aid from specific programs. For example, the 45 percent of dependent, full-time undergraduates enrolled in public four-year institutions received 56.9 percent of the unsubsidized loans and 58 percent of the subsidized loans that went to full-time, dependent undergraduates in 1995–96. Undergraduates in private institutions received a high share of subsidized loans, but their share of unsubsidized loans was nearly the same as their share of enrollment. Families who sent their children to public colleges were more likely to use PLUS loans than those whose children attended private institutions.

Full-time, dependent undergraduates in private four-year institutions re-ceived 62.5 percent of the work-study awards made to this type of student, although they represented 24.3 percent of the full-time dependent under-graduate enrollment in 1995–96. Twenty-seven percent of the full-time de-pendent undergraduates attended public two-year institutions, but they re-ceived only 17 percent of the student financial aid. This is due to the low tuition typically charged by community colleges.

TABLE 1.12

PERCENTAGE DISTRIBUTION OF FULL-TIME UNDERGRADUATES, BY INSTITUTION TYPE AND CONTROL AND BY TYPE OF AID RECEIVED, 1995–96

	Type of Institution			
Type of Aid	Public Four-Year	Public Two-Year	Private Four-Year	Proprietary
Grants	42.0%	17.7%	36.1%	4.3%
Subsidized Loans	58.0%	7.4%	37.6%	7.1%
Unsubsidized Loans	56.9%	11.2%	25.4%	6.5%
Work-Study	31.9%	5.7%	62.5%	0.3%
Financial Aid from Any Source	46.1%	17.2%	31.4%	5.3%
Total Enrollment	45.1%	26.6%	24.3%	4.0%

Note: Rows may not total to 100 percent because of rounding.

Source: U.S. Department of Education 1998b.

Parent Contribution

Parents may use savings, loans, and current income to pay for their child's college expenses. The expectation in student aid policy is that parents will help their dependent children pay for college unless they do not have the financial resources to do so. Table 1.13 shows the mean out-of-pocket prices families pay for children enrolled in each postsecondary-education sector. This price reflects the estimated amount that a family pays after subtracting grants and loans from the sticker price. The expected family contribution guidelines used to award Pell Grants were used to calculate the living ex-

---

TABLE 1.13

Mean Out-of-Pocket Price for Families of Full-Time Dependent
Undergraduates, by Institution Type and Family Income, 1995–96

| | Type of Institution | | | | |
| | Public Two-Year | Public Four-Year | Private Four-Year | All Proprietary | Average Out-of-Pocket Price |
Family Income					
Less Than $20,000	$3,826	$4,828	$8,014	$6,911	$5,403
$20,000–$29,000	$4,718	$5,616	$7,697	$7,102	$5,850
$30,000–$49,999	$5,106	$6,710	$9,643	$8,882	$6,998
$50,000–$69,999	$5,434	$8,181	$12,549	$10,547	$8,524
$70,000 or More	$5,380	$9,857	$17,243	$10,725	$11,220
Average Out-of-Pocket Price	$4,933	$7,517	$12,203	$8,508	$8,036

Source: U.S. Department of Education 1998a; analysis by author.

penses. The actual cash a family might use to pay college expenses may be different from the expected amount, but the estimate does provide a rough approximation of what families typically pay. It shows that, after subtracting all student financial aid, the average family comes up with $8,036 to send a full-time dependent undergraduate to school.

If the student financial aid system helps reduce the out-of-pocket price paid by families, the price should increase in each type of institution as family income increases. The figures in Table 1.13 show that this does happen. On average, families with income of $70,000 or more paid over twice as much out-of-pocket price as families with income less than $20,000—$11,220 compared with $5,403. Two factors may explain this difference in the out-of-pocket price paid by families at different income levels. First, as we have seen, lower-income students are more likely than higher-income students to receive aid to defray their price of attendance. Second, higher-income students are more likely to attend institutions with a higher sticker price than lower-income students.

Another way to look at the distribution of aid is to compare out-of-pocket price with family income. The lowest-income family would have to contribute more than 25 percent of their income to pay the out-of-pocket college price, compared with a maximum of 16 percent for the family with income of more than $70,000. The lower-income family would have to make a much larger effort than the higher-income family to send a child to college, even with the help of student financial aid.

Student Contribution

While going to college, most students work to help pay their expenses. Just under 30 percent of the undergraduates who work classify themselves as employees taking classes. The remaining 50 percent work to help pay their college expenses (U.S. Department of Education 1998a). Student work is an important part of the postsecondary finance picture. The results in Table 1.14 suggest that student work may be the main source of income for students in community colleges, where the average out-of-pocket price was $4,933 (see Table 1.13) and student earnings averaged $6,580 annually. If all the students' earnings went toward their education expenses, very few of their families would have to contribute anything out-of-pocket.

TABLE 1.14

PERCENTAGE OF FULL-TIME DEPENDENT UNDERGRADUATES WHO WORKED WHILE THEY ATTENDED A POSTSECONDARY INSTITUTION, AVERAGE HOURS WORKED, AND AVERAGE EARNINGS WHILE ENROLLED, 1995–96

	Public Two-Year	Public Four-Year	Private Four-Year	Proprietary	Average
Percent of Undergraduates Working	84%	71%	77%	63%	79%
Number of Hours Worked per Week	26 hrs.	21 hrs.	19 hrs.	30 hrs.	22 hrs.
Earnings While Enrolled	$6,580	$4,887	$4,580	$10,484	$5,492

Source: U.S. Department of Education 1998b.

SUMMARY

Student financial aid is the single largest form of funding for postsecondary education today. Half the enrolled students received financial aid in 1995. Over half of the aid—55 percent—was in the form of loans; most of the rest was awarded as grants. The federal government provides the majority of loans, and institutions provide the largest share of grant assistance. Work-study provides assistance to very few undergraduates.

Student financial aid traditionally has had two purposes. The first is to improve access for students from low-income families, and the second is to ensure that students have the opportunity to attend a more expensive institution if it meets their needs. Access remains an elusive goal. Given the same general ability, low-income students are less likely to attend college than those with more wealth. Student financial aid may not be the only answer to this persistent problem.

To clarify the relationships between income and receipt of student financial aid, the analysis in this chapter was limited to full-time dependent undergraduates. However, graduate students and first-professional students, independent undergraduates, and part-time undergraduates all receive student financial aid, too. The issues of access and choice apply to these populations, as well as to full-time dependent undergraduates. However, defining a meaningful measure of success in reaching policy goals for these populations is problematic. Most graduate students and independent undergraduates have very low income by definition because their parents' income does not count and they have given up their own earnings to attend school. Part-time students may have very low income, but their price of attendance is lower than full-time students and their opportunity to earn an income is greater.

The data for full-time dependent undergraduates suggest that the financial aid system's objective to enable student choice of postsecondary institutions has been more fully realized than the goal to increase access. The largest differences in the distribution of undergraduates occur at the extremes of sticker price and income. The lowest-income undergraduates predominate in institutions with the lowest sticker price, and the highest-income students prevail at institutions with the highest sticker price. The distribution of students in the middle-income categories is even until the sticker price hits $15,000. This means that most undergraduates can afford to attend about 80 percent of the colleges in the nation.

Generally, loans improve student choice and grants provide a financial boost to the lowest-income students to ensure that they can afford to enroll. Currently, more loan aid is awarded than grant aid, which raises the possibility that lower-income students may be forced to rely on loans more than is prudent. The data suggest that those with the largest loan burden may be middle-income undergraduates who are just past eligibility for need-based grant aid, but have too little money to pay the college sticker price out of family income.

Considering the fact that different organizations with diverse purposes provide financial aid, it is heartening that it usually goes to lower-income families rather than to those with higher income. This is especially true of grant aid. The only federal program in which this was not true is the unsubsidized student loan program.

This national commitment to equity is reflected in the fact that the mean out-of-pocket price paid by families increased as income increased. The average family with an income below $20,000 paid $5,403 to send a dependent to college after all financial aid was subtracted. Families with income greater than $70,000 paid an out-of-pocket price of $11,220. As disclosed in other chapters of this volume, states, institutions, and even the federal government are awarding an increasing amount of financial aid based on factors other than need. This trend may reduce equity of opportunity because developed academic talent may be an attribute of those with financial advantage.

Even with financial aid, college expenses represent a significant financial burden for most families, especially the lowest-income families. Students themselves also bear a large portion of the price of attending college by working while enrolled and taking out loans they must repay out of future income.

Access and choice remain important considerations for the award of student financial assistance. Too much is at stake both for the future of individuals and the long-term national interest to exclude students from continuing their education because they lack the money. Student aid alone may not be sufficient to reduce the barriers to postsecondary education, but it is a necessary component of that effort.

NOTES

1. Most work-study funding comes from the federal government, but several states have developed their own programs.
2. A proprietary school is any institution with a for-profit tax status.

REFERENCES

College Board. 1996. *Annual Survey of Colleges 1996–97.* New York: College Board.

———. 1997. *Trends in Student Aid: 1987 to 1997.* Washington, DC: College Board.

U.S. Department of Education, National Center for Education Statistics. 1996. *Condition of Education: 1996.* Washington, DC: U.S. Department of Education.

U.S. Department of Education, Office of Postsecondary Education. 1997a. *Federal Student Loan Programs Data Book, FY1994–FY1996.* Washington, DC: Office of Postsecondary Education.

———. 1997b. *Student Financing of Graduate and First-Professional Education, 1995–96.* Washington, DC: U.S. Department of Education.

U.S. Department of Education, National Center for Education Statistics. 1998a. National Postsecondary Student Aid Study, 1995–96. Dataset. Washington, DC: National Center for Education Statistics.

———. 1998b. *Profile of Undergraduates in U.S. Postsecondary Education Institutions: 1995–96.* Washington, DC: U.S. Department of Education.

CHAPTER 2

College Costs

Who Pays and Why It Matters So

Gordon C. Winston

The current national interest in college costs is quite remarkable. In an earlier time, the costs of college would have been seen as a rocky and unfamiliar piece of financial terrain, quite unattractive to much public attention or concern. But three things have changed, making our new and widespread interest easy to understand. The majority of the nation's youth now go to college—and President Bill Clinton has called for making college as universal as high school is today. The economic importance of a college education—in simple terms of lifetime income—has nearly doubled in 20 years. But at the same time, the price of college seems to have risen out of the reach of many, if not most, American families, raising suspicions that costs are out of control.

Using ordinary common sense, college costs are impossible to understand. Our economic intuition is based on the business firms that dominate the economy, but colleges and universities are fundamentally different animals—not more complicated, necessarily, but different: prices have little to do with production costs and they're always *below* those costs; the "customer" is an object of subsidy instead of a source of profit; what a buyer gets for a dollar varies widely among providers; and more "customers" can mean that higher prices are paid for less product. If we don't understand colleges' most basic economic features, it will be hard to avoid bad public policy, bad student choices, and bad management decisions. Luckily, even as national anxiety has increased, so has the understanding of how college economics actually works.

This chapter is an introduction to that understanding and to why it matters to parents, policymakers, and colleges.

The chapter covers four issues, broadly. It describes the economic structure of the typical college or university; it shows, by some very straightforward arithmetic, how that differs from the more familiar economic structure of a business firm; it indicates how little of costs students actually pay; and it suggests why that fact matters so much. It will become clear that business-based intuition distorts our understanding by making us look at the wrong things: we search, for instance, for rising educational costs when they're falling, and we don't look for evidence of falling subsidies because business firms don't pay subsidies.

PRICES, COSTS, SUBSIDIES, AND STRATEGIES: THE ECONOMIC STRUCTURE OF A COLLEGE

The most fundamental anomaly in the economics of higher education is the fact that virtually all U.S. colleges and universities sell their primary product—education—at a price that is far less than the average cost of its production. The subsidy that is given in this way to nearly every college student in the country is neither temporary, nor small, nor granted only by public institutions: student subsidies are a permanent feature of the economics of higher education; they represent a large part of total costs; and on average, they are only slightly smaller in private than in public institutions. In total, student subsidies exceeded $82 billion in 1995.

Subsidies involve a unique set of strategic decisions for colleges and universities—and unique circumstances for public policy—that are familiar neither to for-profit firms nor to the economic theories designed to understand them. In 1995, the average American college produced an $11,967 education that it sold to its students for $3,770, giving them each a subsidy of $8,197 a year (see Table 2.1, row 1, on page 34): it's as if cars that cost the dealer $20,000 to put on the showroom floor were routinely sold for $6,300. We expect normal, for-profit firms to grant *negative* subsidies—that is, to earn a profit—by selling at a price greater than the costs of production. Nonprofit firms don't do that.[1]

It's not that student subsidies have been ignored in the analysis of higher education; they have, indeed, attracted a great deal of attention ever since the 1969 Hansen and Weisbrod study showed that the university system in California subsidized higher-income students at the expense of lower-income taxpayers (Hansen and Weisbrod 1969). But that study also established what has become the conventional framing of the issue of subsidies as a matter of *student* characteristics: Which students, with what characteristics, get how much subsidy? In the recent work reported on here, the focus has shifted to *institutions:* Which colleges grant how much subsidy to their students, and how do they choose to do it? Subsidies are a central part of college and university policies on admissions, quality, and pricing.[2]

The Economic Structure of a College

Since the structure of costs, prices, subsidies, and aid in colleges and universities is no more a part of the familiar logic and vocabulary of for-profit economics and accounting than of the intuition it supports, it is worth a few paragraphs to spell it out.

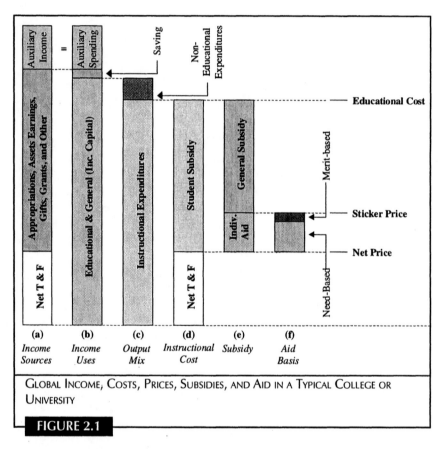

GLOBAL INCOME, COSTS, PRICES, SUBSIDIES, AND AID IN A TYPICAL COLLEGE OR UNIVERSITY

FIGURE 2.1

Figure 2.1 provides a useful if stylized description of the economic structure of a typical college or university. In the first two bars, a school's yearly accounts are pictured as (a) the *sources* of its income and (b) the *uses* of that income. By definition, they are equal. The heights of the bars and their segments represent dollars per student per year, and the proportions are roughly appropriate to the average student at the average college in 1995. Income is inclusive and global—the value of *all* the resources that accrue to the institution in the course of the year—rather than a component of that income, like the operating budget or current fund revenues.[3] For present purposes, not a lot of detail about the sources of income is needed, so in (a), the only income components identified separately are tuition (Net T & F, or net tuition and fees), auxiliary income (room and board, for instance, or hospitals),[4] and what Henry Hansmann (1980) called "donative resources" (government appropriations, asset earnings, gifts, grants, and other). And in column (b), the uses of income can similarly be simplified, described as auxiliary expenditures, educational and general spending (including capital service costs),[5] and saving. Finally, since auxiliary activities are usually expected to break even, we can simplify things at the outset by setting auxiliary income equal to auxiliary expenditures and ignoring them in what follows.

The income sources of interest, then, are tuition income and nontuition income in the form of donative resources. That income is used to cover the costs of production. What's left over is saving. *Income Sources = Income Uses* in any period.

These two broad categories, sources and uses, fully encompass yearly flows in the accounts of a firm. More details would, of course, be needed to answer important questions, but they would simply come from disaggregating bars (a) and (b) to tell where, more specifically, the money came from and where it went. In the typical for-profit firm, income would come largely from the sale of a product. When income is greater than production costs, the firm shows a profit (positive saving); when income is smaller than costs, it shows a loss.

Thus, an additional set of questions, embedded in bars (c) through (f), is introduced by the fact that for a college, only a fraction of its total income is generated by sales proceeds—by the tuition and fees paid by its student "customers." Indeed, in Figure 2.1, the *income sources* bar, (a), shows nontuition income, income from sources other than the sale of educational services, to be a lot greater than tuition income. The *income uses* bar, (b), is more conventional in showing that total income can be used for production costs or, if big enough, that some can be left over as saving.

Together, bars (a) and (b) illustrate the fact that customers of higher education are getting something that costs a lot more to produce than they're paying for it—net tuition and fee (Net T & F) income is a good deal less than the average cost of producing the services that the student gets; therefore, the student is subsidized for the difference.

The next four bars, (c) through (f), frame the key question of how that subsidy is divided up among students: an institution's decision on the sticker price that determines the general subsidy, and on individually targeted financial aid, whether awarded on the basis of need or merit.

Bar (c) recognizes that higher education is "a multi-product industry" that produces a lot of things besides instruction. The college's sale of hotel and restaurant services (room and board), in the form of its auxiliary income, was just noted. Other major products of the university that have little to do directly with its instructional functions are recognized by subtracting out its funded research, public service, and their portion of shared costs, which leaves those costs that pay for a student's instruction.[6]

Bar (d) shows how that instructional cost per student is divided between the part the average student pays in net tuition and fees—his or her price— and the part that represents a subsidy.

Bar (e) describes how that subsidy portion is divided, in turn, between general subsidy and individual student aid: a "general subsidy" is given equally to each student at a college whenever its sticker price is set below production cost, while financial aid[7] is a further price reduction based on individual student characteristics. Bar (f) divides that individual financial aid between the part that is awarded on the basis of a student's economic *need* and the part based on *"merit"*—other characteristics like race or athletic or academic abilities. Since the heights of these columns represent dollars per student, we can indicate, at the far right, the sticker price and net price levels, consistent with the breakdowns shown in (d) through (f).[8]

Strategic Decisions

Figure 2.1 highlights the most important strategic economic decisions facing a college or university. Given its total nontuition income, the school must make the following choices:

- A decision on total enrollment size, which will influence[9] nontuition income *per student*. So, for instance, by restricting its student body to 1,300, Swarthmore has protected its per-student asset income; if it had twice as many students, other things being equal, it would have half as much asset income per student.[10]
- A decision on saving—how much of its nontuition income a school will use to subsidize its current students, and how much it will save and invest in order to subsidize future students. Saving builds the endowment and funds the construction of buildings, which provide asset income that will benefit subsequent generations.
- A decision on cost per student, and hence on net tuition and fees, given its nontuition income and saving. A school's per-student nontuition income fixes the maximum *difference* between costs and price—its maximum subsidy—but it supports *any* combination of costs and price that maintains that difference. So the school must determine, simultaneously, the nature of its educational product and

how much students will have to pay for it. With, say, $10,000 per student to support the subsidy, one school might produce a $15,000-a-year education to be sold at a $5,000 average net tuition, while another might produce a $35,000-a-year education to be sold at a $25,000 net tuition. Per-student subsidy, cost, and price are locked together, arithmetically and relentlessly, by the equation:

$$Subsidy = Cost - Price$$

- A decision on output mix—how much of a school's total spending will go to education. At the highly stylized level of Figure 2.1, that's about all that can be said, but at the finer-grained level on which colleges actually function, this decision involves fundamental questions of identifying an institution's mission and core activities, setting priorities, and increasing the efficiency with which those activities are conducted. Other things remaining the same, the higher the share of instructional costs, the higher the level of student subsidies.
- A decision on sticker price, which divides the subsidy into the general subsidy that goes to all students (74 percent on average in 1995, see Table 2.1 on page 34), and financial aid that goes to those who have specific, desirable characteristics (the remaining 26 percent). The same $10,000 average yearly subsidy can be given in equal amounts to all enrolled students through a sticker price set just $10,000 below instructional costs or—at the other extreme—it can be given through a sticker price set equal to costs, then offset selectively by individually targeted financial aid that averages $10,000 per student. Of course, very few institutions operate at the extremes.
- A decision on financial aid—the division of individually differentiated subsidies—whether it is to be based on the student's economic circumstances (need) or on other characteristics, such as academic or athletic or artistic merit, or race, or anything else (merit).

These are strategic choices that all colleges and universities have to make about output, quality, saving, and pricing. And they simply have no parallel in for-profit firms. In any school, history, too, will matter a great deal—resources can be highly "illiquid," and traditions, cultures, alumni, and faculties can be resistant to change. And some public institutions will have been given limited discretion by legislatures. But Figure 2.1 pictures the underlying economic relationships, in their barest structural form, that define possibilities and set constraints on a college's costs, prices, subsidies, and aid. The magnitude of a school's subsidies is determined by its access to nontuition resources, its saving, and its size, and any student subsidy is exhaustively divided between general subsidies and financial aid based on need or on merit.

TABLE 2.1

SUBSIDIES, COSTS, PRICES, AND AID, BY CONTROL, SUBSIDY SIZE, AND CARNEGIE CLASSIFICATION, IN DOLLARS PER STUDENT (FTE), 1994–95

	Number of Institutions (1)	Average Enrollment (2)	Subsidy $ (3)	Educational Spending $ (4)	Net Tuition and Fees $ (5)	Sticker Price $ (6)	Net Price of Education (7)	General Subsidy $ (8)	Student Aid $ (9)	General Subsidy as % of Total (10)	Financial Aid as % of Total (11)
All Institutions	**2,739**	**3,493**	**8,197**	**11,967**	**3,770**	**5,919**	**31.5%**	**6,048**	**2,149**	**73.8%**	**26.2%**
Public	**1,420**	**5,140**	**8,686**	**9,919**	**1,233**	**2,272**	**12.4%**	**7,648**	**1,038**	**88.0%**	**12.0%**
Private	**1,319**	**1,721**	**7,670**	**14,172**	**6,502**	**9,846**	**45.9%**	**4,326**	**3,344**	**56.4%**	**43.6%**
Public by Subsidy Size											
Decile 1	142	5,316	22,915	24,551	1,636	3,257	6.7%	21,295	1,621	92.9%	7.1%
Decile 2	142	5,695	10,516	11,680	1,163	2,471	10.0%	9,208	1,308	87.6%	12.4%
Decile 3	142	6,060	9,082	10,311	1,229	2,405	11.9%	7,906	1,176	87.0%	13.0%
Decile 4	142	5,310	8,260	9,567	1,307	2,394	13.7%	7,173	1,087	86.8%	13.2%
Decile 5	142	5,294	7,592	8,738	1,145	2,165	13.1%	6,573	1,020	86.6%	13.4%
Decile 6	142	4,816	6,931	8,031	1,101	2,057	13.7%	5,974	956	86.2%	13.8%
Decile 7	142	4,867	6,364	7,448	1,084	1,976	14.6%	5,472	892	86.0%	14.0%
Decile 8	142	4,224	5,810	6,981	1,171	2,032	16.8%	4,950	861	85.2%	14.8%
Decile 9	142	5,304	5,215	6,330	1,115	1,907	17.6%	4,424	792	84.8%	15.2%
Decile 10	142	4,511	4,174	5,555	1,381	2,053	24.9%	3,502	672	83.9%	16.1%
Public by Carnegie Type											
Research	83	21,399	10,569	13,719	3,150	4,571	23.0%	9,148	1,421	86.6%	13.4%
Doctoral	63	11,363	8,780	11,436	2,656	3,776	23.2%	7,660	1,121	87.2%	12.8%
Comprehensive	271	6,428	8,372	10,188	1,816	2,907	17.8%	7,281	1,091	87.0%	13.0%
Liberal Arts	80	2,477	8,090	9,670	1,580	2,857	16.3%	6,813	1,277	84.2%	15.8%
Two-Year	874	3,186	7,494	8,208	714	1,623	8.7%	6,584	910	87.9%	12.1%
Specialized	49	1,672	36,041	37,682	1,640	3,537	4.4%	34,145	1,896	94.7%	5.3%

TABLE 2.1 (continued)

Private by Subsidy Size

Decile 1	132	2,780	22,235	30,325	8,089	13,353	26.7%	16,971	5,264	76.3%	23.7%
Decile 2	132	1,228	12,050	19,095	7,045	11,782	36.9%	7,313	4,737	60.7%	39.3%
Decile 3	132	1,506	9,594	15,961	6,368	10,357	39.9%	5,605	3,989	58.4%	41.6%
Decile 4	132	1,716	7,953	13,824	5,871	9,523	42.5%	4,301	3,652	54.1%	45.9%
Decile 5	132	1,757	6,726	13,094	6,368	9,944	48.6%	3,150	3,576	46.8%	53.2%
Decile 6	132	1,710	5,725	11,758	6,033	9,339	51.3%	2,419	3,307	42.2%	57.8%
Decile 7	132	1,594	4,900	10,946	6,046	9,067	55.2%	1,879	3,021	38.3%	61.7%
Decile 8	132	1,906	3,941	10,466	6,525	9,078	62.3%	1,388	2,553	35.2%	64.8%
Decile 9	132	1,403	2,723	8,835	6,112	8,097	69.2%	737	1,986	27.1%	72.9%
Decile 10	132	1,606	801	7,363	6,562	7,907	89.1%	-544	1,345	-67.9%	167.9%

Private by Carnegie Type

Research	39	11,821	20,950	32,596	11,646	16,975	36.4%	15,621	5,329	74.6%	25.4%
Doctoral	43	5,800	8,094	19,110	11,016	14,417	58.8%	4,694	3,400	58.0%	42.0%
Comprehensive	245	2,460	5,821	13,220	7,399	10,484	57.3%	2,736	3,084	47.0%	53.0%
Liberal Arts	526	1,228	9,526	15,887	6,361	10,505	41.2%	5,382	4,144	56.5%	43.5%
Two-Year	243	572	5,395	10,458	5,063	7,565	49.5%	2,893	2,502	53.6%	46.4%
Specialized	223	771	7,592	13,238	5,646	7,949	43.7%	5,289	2,303	69.7%	30.3%

Source: U.S. Department of Education 1997; analysis by author.

THE FACTS: SUBSIDIES AND STRUCTURE
IN U.S. HIGHER EDUCATION

The purpose of this chapter is not to analyze the role of subsidies, costs, prices, and aid in the structure of U.S. higher education—such analyses have been done at some length elsewhere (Winston and Yen 1995; Winston 1999). But it will be useful, nonetheless, to look briefly at the facts in Table 2.1 with its summary data for 2,739 degree-granting schools in 1995.[11]

In Table 2.1, subsidies—column (3)—are simply educational costs per student (4) *less* what he or she paid the school in net tuition (5). Thus, as noted in the introduction, averaged over all schools, an $11,967 education was sold in 1995 for a price of $3,770, giving each student an $8,197 subsidy. That, subsidy is in part a *general* subsidy to all students (8), given by setting the sticker price (6) lower than educational costs (4), and in part additional *financial aid* to some students (9), given by charging them even less than the sticker price. The "Net Price of Education," column (7), is especially useful: it describes both the share of total cost borne by the student and, when read as cents rather than percents, what the average student pays for a dollar's worth of higher education. Finally, the last two columns show how any given subsidy is distributed between general subsidy and financial aid.

While resisting the temptation to say much about the rich information in Table 2.1, the most important observations to make are: (a) the sheer size of student subsidies, and that subsidies are both (b) ubiquitous, and (c) about the same size in public and private sectors; (d) that subsidies are distributed to students largely in the general form of sticker prices set well under costs, so little of the subsidy is left over to be given as financial aid; (e) that there is a high degree of variety among schools; and (f) that the difference between those giving large subsidies and those giving small ones is very great. These characteristics and differences describe the core economic structure of U.S. higher education.

SO WHAT?
IMPLICATIONS

There are three kinds of answers to the ever-important question, "So what?"

Our Mental Model of Higher Education

Most basically, understanding the structure of costs, prices, subsidies, and aid in and among colleges and universities is essential to understanding the "industry." If our shared conception of the economics of higher education isn't reasonably accurate, we will look for the wrong things and fail to see the importance of the right things. A model built on the facts of Table 2.1 can illuminate the roles of competition, institutional wealth, student quality and selectivity, faculty tenure, and institutional saving, among other factors. And the facts of Table 2.1 are crucial to assessing the likely impact of new technology and the inroads that privatization can make into college and university activities. So, broadly, improved understanding—a better "mental model"—has to be the primary implication of the facts. Other papers from the Williams Project have described such a model.[12]

Understanding Trends and Changes

The information in Table 2.1 also provides a structure with which to monitor changes in higher education—changing circumstances and strategies like those associated with the tax revolt of the 1970s and early 1980s and increased private competition (Winston and Lewis 1997b). Those variables, over time, describe patterns of change in colleges and universities in response to circumstances, opportunities, and pressures. And they make it clear that, among colleges and universities, circumstances and strategies are so very different that adaptation to change will also be very different; to think of "higher education" as a single, monolithic entity is to risk considerable error. Recognizing the fundamental differences among colleges and universities is central to understanding what is happening and why (Winston, Carbone, and Lewis 1998).

Public Policy and Common Sense

The third implication—the focus of the rest of the chapter—is that how clearly the public recognizes the large and ubiquitous student subsidies in higher education means a very great deal both for public understanding and for public policy. The disjunction between the facts and what people "know" to be the facts with regard to prices, costs, and subsidies poses the most serious danger for public attitudes and public policy toward higher education.

PUBLIC POLICY, ECONOMICS, AND BUSINESS INTUITION

Paradoxically, the single most serious factor affecting the understanding of higher education—and hence public attitudes and public policies—may well be common sense. We have, collectively, a well-schooled intuition based on extensive experience with business firms. We have lived with ordinary business firms all our lives, and from them we've absorbed a strong feeling for what makes economic sense and what does not. Anyone who's taken Econ 101 will have had that common sense reinforced by graphs, lectures, quizzes, and a final exam. But unfortunately, the economics of colleges and universities is counterintuitive in these common-sense terms: what's accurate is unfamiliar, and what seems obvious is often just plain wrong.

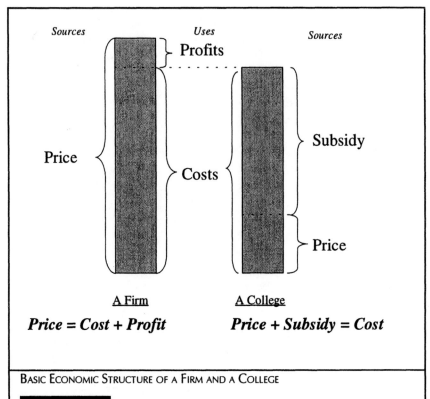

BASIC ECONOMIC STRUCTURE OF A FIRM AND A COLLEGE

FIGURE 2.2

Simple pictures can be used to illustrate two key facts—arithmetic facts—that show the difference between businesses and higher education institutions. The pictures and the facts are highly stylized, but essentially correct.

A business firm's economic structure is represented on the left in Figure 2.2, and that of a college or university is represented on the right. Like Figure 2.1, Figure 2.2 describes sources and uses of funds. The left-hand bar describes a firm's income and what it does with that money—where it comes from and where it goes. A firm's income derives from the sale of the things it produces—their price. That income goes to pay the costs of production and—if costs are less than sales income—what's left over is profit. A car dealer, for instance, earns money from the cars that are sold and pays that money out as costs—the wholesale cost of the cars, salaries, commissions, rent, heating oil—and what's left over is profit. A car sold for $25,000 that costs $23,000 to deliver to the customer means the dealer makes a $2,000 profit. Pretty routine stuff that even my granddaughter has started to learn with a lemonade stand at the age of seven.

The right-hand bar shows the same basic facts for a college or university. But, of course, only a fraction of the income for a higher education institution comes from the sale of its product, from the price its student "customers" pay for the education services the college sells them. Most has to come from somewhere else, from those donative resources from alumni and taxpayers, and from earnings from endowments and the services of expensive buildings and equipment that support that student subsidy. Of course, the primary reason society makes donations to colleges and universities—and doesn't make them to the local Ford dealer—is that higher education is considered to be socially "a good thing," so we encourage people to buy more of it by offering generous subsidies on its purchase.[13] From this, two crucial facts emerge:

1. For a *business firm*, price is always *greater* than production costs, and the difference is profits:

$$Price = Cost + Profit$$

Sell the product for \$5, and if it costs \$4 to make, \$1 is left as profit.

2. For a *college*, price is always *less* than production costs, and any difference is covered by student subsidy:

$$Price + Subsidy = Cost$$

Sell the product for \$1, and if it costs \$4 to make, a \$3 subsidy will have to be obtained from elsewhere.

This simple difference has profound consequences, moreso the less clearly it is recognized.

THROUGH THE LOOKING GLASS

Let me illustrate the dangerous role of business intuition and its accompanying "common sense" with four examples: the confusion of costs, prices, and net prices that enters most discussions of college costs; the difficulties for educational policy based on the business model and its intuition; the popular tuition-relief policies modeled on Georgia's HOPE Scholarship program; and the strange threat posed by increased "sales" in higher education.

Costs, Prices, and Net Prices

A major semantic problem with our national conversation about college costs should be clear from what has been said so far, but the role of business intuition may not be so apparent. We use "college costs" to mean three very different things: (1) *production costs*, the cost of delivering a year of education to a student; (2) *sticker price*, the posted, nominal (and maximum) price that any student pays; and (3) *net price*, what the average student actually pays, after financial aid grants. But we carelessly give them all the same name—*college costs*. To make things worse, Econ 101 goes to great pains in describing competitive for-profit businesses to argue that, in the long run, any business's economic profits will disappear as competitors drive down prices until the price will just cover costs; thus, theoretically at least, price and cost can be treated as the same thing. Intuition and common sense confirm the idea that production costs and prices, if not exactly the same thing, are pretty close. In business, they usually are. In higher education, they usually aren't. But basic economics has told us that there should only be a single price and that it will roughly equal costs.

Economic Policy for Higher Education

The dilemma facing national efforts to make coherent economic policy for higher education is nicely demonstrated by the task of the National Commission on the Cost of Higher Education that was established by Congress in the summer of 1997. The Cost Commission was supposed to figure out why a typical family's costs of higher education (read "net tuition" or "price," of course) had risen so much in the recent past.

From the familiar perspective of the business intuition embedded in *Price = Cost + Profit* that most of us share, the answer looks pretty simple. Since the price has gone up, it has to be because costs went up or because profits went up. Colleges are nonprofit firms, so the place to look is at costs; they must have gone up. And that leads directly to questions about increased waste, rising administrative costs, a less productive faculty, elaborate buildings and equipment, a too-exuberant embrace of expensive technologies, or the costs of increased regulation. This is an agenda right out of *Price = Cost + Profit*, and the solid business intuition it describes. Sensible from that perspective, but guaranteed to obscure the facts.

What *has* been happening in public higher education (which 80 percent of college and university students attend) shows up only when we look at *Price + Subsidy = Cost*, which actually describes a college or university.

There, it's clear that tuition (price) might have gone up because costs went up. But tuition also might have gone up because subsidies went *down*. And that's what the data suggest has happened.[14] The taxpayers' revolt that restricted state appropriations (donative resources) has met an increase in enrollments, and together these factors have reduced student subsidies in public higher education. That, of course, is a very different picture from the one that comes from business intuition. If subsidies go down at a college, it means either that prices have to go up, or that educational spending has to go down, or both. We've seen both. Students in public colleges are paying a higher price in 1995 than in 1987 to get a cheaper education with fewer and larger classes and more TAs and TVs.

It is devoutly to be wished that increased efficiency and cost savings could make it unnecessary to choose between higher prices and lower quality when subsidies are reduced—that colleges and universities could simply produce the same education quality at lower costs through new technology or belt-tightening. But it's not clear that there's much room for that. There is no firm evidence that even for-profit firms operate with a great deal more efficiency than nonprofit firms in producing "products" with complicated characteristics; beyond some early point, less spending means lower quality (Pauly 1987; Oster 1997). New learning technologies appear able to reduce the cost of some of what colleges and universities do, but both the extent of possible cost savings and the impact of technology on education quality are still unknown. The magnitudes involved make it unrealistic to hope that technology-based efficiencies in production could offset either reduced appropriations or increased enrollments.[15]

Thus, it's clearly not the case that what a college spends on educating its students measures the quality of experience students get in any simple way. Different schools with different missions run by different people for different students often will achieve different levels of quality that will be assessed differently by different observers (McPherson and Winston 1993). And even if all that were no problem, the quality of the education a student gets appears heavily dependent on the quality of his or her fellow students or, in other words, on "peer effects" (Winston 1996a; Goethals, Winston, and Zimmerman 1998). So, despite these complications and caveats, colleges are not able to protect educational quality from significant changes in spending per student.

The Promise of Government Tuition Support

A rash of appealing proposals have offered direct government support of family tuition costs in the hope of easing the burden and increasing college enrollments—like President Clinton's Hope tax credit. Business intuition, and its Price = Cost + Profit logic, say those measures make good sense—like food stamps, the government will pick up part of the price, allowing people who can't afford a college education to buy it anyway.

But the reality of higher education, where Price + Subsidy = Cost, leads to a very different picture—one of rising enrollments, declining quality, and rising tuition.

Table 2.1 showed that, over all institutions, students' tuition payments cover only 32 cents of each dollar of their costs. In the public colleges that most students attend, tuition pays 12 cents of each dollar of costs. So, if a student is induced by these subsidies to go to the average public college, for every one dollar she or he brings in new tuition revenues, there will be nine dollars in additional costs. The question is, then, "Who's going to pay the rest?"[16]

The most realistic answer sees two unhappy outcomes. One is that spending per student falls. The other is that, trying to protect educational quality, colleges and universities raise tuition so it covers more of the cost. That, of course, revives the old familiar charge that government efforts to help students always induce colleges to jack up their prices.

Are any colleges and universities winners under tuition-support policies? Yes, ironically. The wealthy and selective schools that restrict enrollments in the face of long queues of would-be students—colleges like Harvard, Stanford, and Swarthmore—won't be induced to expand, so they won't need extra resources. For them and their students, tuition-relief policies will only help pay their often-considerable tuition.

The Worrisome Prospect of Increased Sales

Higher education faces an increase in enrollments over the next decade estimated at 10 to 30 percent. That kind of demand increase would be cause for dancing in the streets in any for-profit industry. But for higher education, it is cause, instead, for genuine panic. If it comes to pass that 3 million more students enter U.S. colleges and universities, they will bring with them an additional $11.3 billion in net tuition revenues, but they will also generate an additional $35.9 billion in costs—if educational spending and quality is to be maintained at 1995 levels—and that will require $24.6 billion of additional nontuition resources. Our for-profit economic intuition doesn't prepare us for a dilemma like that.

Cross-Subsidies

In business firms, a product is cross-subsidized if profits from another product or activity are used to offset losses on that one. For example, new car sales are cross-subsidized if profits from the service department are needed to offset losses on selling new cars. But in a college or university, things are more complicated. That's frustrating, because we'd like very much to understand cross-subsidies in higher education—to find that the rich students subsidize the poor ones, or that undergraduate education subsidizes faculty research or Ph.D. programs, or that football subsidizes classics courses.

But cross-subsidies are much harder to measure in a university than in a business firm. Because *all* activities taken together are heavily subsidized, it's difficult to tell the difference between a genuine cross-subsidy—where one activity supports another (e.g., football supporting women's ice hockey)—and simple *differences* in the amount of subsidy given to two well-subsidized activities. "Robinhooding" is a popular case in point. It is sometimes asserted (Larson 1997) that colleges make a profit by charging their rich students high prices in order to subsidize their poor students. But we've seen in Table 2.1

that, except at the very bottom of the pecking order (in the bottom decile of private colleges), the fact is that the rich kids may get a smaller subsidy than the poor kids, but they all get subsidized, even those who pay the full sticker price.

More basic is the fact that nobody knows how much a college's activities actually cost, since there's only the vaguest recognition of the costs of the capital services—the services of the buildings and computers and libraries and stadiums used in those activities. Yet we do know that facilities account for 20 to 30 percent of the total production costs of a college education (Winston and Lewis 1997a). Those large and important cost elements can be estimated for a single school with a great deal of work and a great deal of cooperation from its accountants and facilities managers, but that hasn't been done widely and, until it is, any estimate of the magnitude of cross-subsidies in schools' activities can only be a guess.

STUDENTS, PARENTS, AND OPTIONS

One last issue: what does this increased understanding of higher education do for parents and students? Its main effect should be, I think, reassurance. If Table 2.1 says anything, it says that there is tremendous variety in U.S. higher education and that the differences among institutions are not at all superficial—they go deep to include what students pay and what they get. Those differences say, above all, that within "higher education," there are so many very different schools that there's something for everybody.

But even more to the point, since college prices and costs aren't the same thing, the wise buyer of a college education will pay attention to both prices *and* costs. To some extent, this notion is captured in the persistent advice to learn about financial aid—not everyone pays the announced sticker prices that attract the headlines. But more basically, since nearly 75 percent of the average school's student subsidy takes the form not of financial aid but of a sticker price set well below costs, careful buyers will look both at what they'll pay—their net price or tuition after financial aid—*and* at what they'll get—the resources devoted to their education. In raw dollars, average yearly per-student subsidies range from $800 in the poorest 10 percent of private schools to nearly $23,000 in the richest decile of public institutions, and in some private colleges, they rise to more than $40,000 a year. Even more dramatically, perhaps, the *share* of his or her costs that the average student pays ranges from nearly 90 percent in the poorest private institutions to less than 7 percent in the top public schools. And in Table 2.1, it's clear that the biggest bargains—both in dollars and in price relative to cost—are typically found in the schools that spend the *most* on a student's education.

If that's good news to the average student, the wealthiest students—who are more likely to pay the full sticker price—may be reassured to know that they will rarely be the source of money to pay someone else's college costs. On average, a student charged the full sticker price covers only half of the costs of her *own* education, so there's certainly nothing left over for anyone else. Only in the bottom 10 percent of private schools is there evidence of robinhooding— of sticker prices that cover a student's own costs plus extra left over for someone else's financial aid. In the top 10 percent of private colleges and universities, tuition is $13,400, but it buys an education that costs more than $30,000 to produce.

CONCLUSION

Colleges and universities are very different, in fundamental *economic* ways, from the for-profit businesses on which our intuitions and economic theories are based. Sometimes those differences don't much matter. But too often they matter very fundamentally, and policies based on common sense can produce results that are puzzling, unintended, and damaging. No task is more difficult than convincing people that what makes good common sense is likely to be wrong, and what's right is flatly counterintuitive. But that's the challenge facing those who would understand higher education. Mosquitoes, it was said with confidence in 1904, couldn't possibly cause malaria and yellow fever. The idea that they could was implausible, counterintuitive, and, of course, entirely correct.

NOTES

This chapter is similar to a paper written for the National Commission on the Cost of Higher Education and discussed with them in Boston in November 1997 (National Commission on the Cost of Higher Education 1998). It relies heavily on "Costs, Prices, Subsidies, and Aid in U.S. Higher Education" (Winston and Yen 1995). The Andrew W. Mellon Foundation has generously supported the ongoing research that informs this work. This chapter has benefited a great deal from the comments of Henry Bruton, Jared Carbone, Clare Cotton, Stuart Crampton, Al Goethals, Jacqueline King, Jim Kolesar, Mike McPherson, Hank Payne, Clayton Spencer, and the members of the Cost Commission.

1. The fundamental legal and economic characteristic of nonprofit firms is that any "profits" they earn—any saving as surplus of current income over current spending— cannot be distributed. See the seminal paper by Henry Hansmann (1980).

2. The core studies are reported in a series of discussion papers of the Williams Project on the Economics of Higher Education: Winston (1994) on colleges' economic information; Winston and Yen (1995) on the structural economic facts summarized here; Winston and Lewis (1997a) on the large role of capital services in college costs; Winston (1996a) on the model of higher education implied by these facts; and Winston and Lewis (1997b) on changes in these circumstances, strategy, and perfor-

mance over time. All Williams Project discussion papers are available on the Internet at <http://www.williams.edu/mellon> and can be downloaded.

3. See Winston (1996b) for more details on global accounting. The new FASB 117 accounting standards go a good distance toward an economically coherent description of a college or university (Winston 1994).

4. Including hospitals and independent operations.

5. Note that current spending is net of institutional grant aid, so financial aid is treated as a price discount rather than a cost of education. See Winston 1998.

6. It would be useful, too, to pull out all the other primary noninstructional products of the university and their costs—like television programming through athletics—but these can't always be disentangled from strictly instructional costs, either in individual school accounts or in financial information aggregated over all of higher education, so they aren't segregated here. Fortunately, some of the largest, like hospitals and independent operations, can be identified and removed from the subsidy calculation. More subtle judgments about the "necessity" or "appropriateness" of particular components of spending are beyond the scope of this chapter. While there is undoubtedly some gilding of the lily, not only are data unavailable, but it would be hard to get agreement on which part of spending is "too much," an issue made even more complicated by the role of subsidies in increasing student demand and selectivity (Winston 1996a).

7. Lee and Sango-Jordan (1989) call these "institutional subsidies" and "student subsidies."

8. a. Income Sources = Net Tuition and Fees + Non-tuition Income + Auxiliary Income

   b. Income Uses = Auxiliary Expenditures + Saving + Educational and General Spending (E&G&K)

   c. E&G&K = Instructional E&G&K + Research + Service

   d. Instructional E&G&K = Net Tuition and Fees + Subsidy

   e. Subsidy = General Aid + Individual Aid

   f. Individual Aid = Need-Based Aid + Merit-Based Aid

   So—

   g. Income = Net Tuition and Fees + Auxiliary Expenditures + Saving + Need-Based Aid + Merit-Based Aid + General Aid + Research + Service

   Educational and General Spending is augmented with recognition of the yearly cost of using buildings, equipment, and land, hence "E&G&K."

9. For a private institution with subsidy resources that are fixed over long periods without regard to enrollment—like physical assets and endowment—size *determines* per-student resources.

10. Size enters importantly, too, as a determinant of student selectivity, but that is a subject of other papers (Winston 1996a; 1997).

11. Based on 1995 IPEDS data (Integrated Postsecondary Educational Data System, published yearly by the Department of Education's National Center for Educational Statistics) for the colleges and universities in the 50 states that reported positive expenditures, FTE enrollments of more than 100 students, of whom 20 percent or more were undergraduates.

12. See Note 2.

13. The past decade (regrettably) has seen this emphasis on the economic and civic virtues of an educated citizenry largely replaced by attention to individuals' occupational and financial gains from higher education. But even that narrow view supports the ideals of distributional equity and access.

14. It's worth noting that the National Commission on the Cost of Higher Education used national data that hid this fact by looking only at endpoints—1986–87 and estimated figures for 1995–96—missing the decline and recovery of national subsidy support that took place in between. Thus, they felt that there was no solid evidence that a decline in subsidies had caused rising net prices in the public sector, though evidence was there (Winston, Carbone, and Lewis 1998).

15. The idea—delivered with energy in Econ 101—that marginal cost is less than average cost, and marginal cost is what really counts, runs into a difficult problem of quality when applied to a college. Those neat diagrams on the blackboard always assume that output of the product could be expanded without affecting its quality, but that's wrong for higher education, where adding more students with the same faculty and facilities inevitably degrades quality unless schools are operating with generous excess capacity, which is not often the case.

16. The GI Bill, too, channeled funds to the student, rather than the college, but that was in a climate where expansion of public sector schools was supported with increased appropriations (donative resources). Private schools, with their limited non-tuition resources, resisted expansion. So the answer to "who's going to pay the rest?" was "taxpayers" or "society," willingly.

REFERENCES

Goethals, G. R., G. C. Winston, and D. J. Zimmerman. 1998. "Students Educating Students: The Emerging Role of Peer Effects in Higher Education." Paper presented at the Forum for the Future of Higher Education, Aspen, CO, September 29.

Hansen, W. L., and B. Weisbrod. 1969. *Benefits, Costs and Finance of Higher Education.* Chicago: Markham Publishing.

Hansmann, H. 1980. "The Role of Nonprofit Enterprise." *Yale Law Journal* 89(5): 835–901.

Larson, E. 1997. "Why Colleges Cost Too Much." *Time* March 17.

Lee, J. B., and M. Sango-Jordan. 1989. *Further Exploration of the Distribution of Higher Education Subsidies.* Bethesda, MD: JBL Associates, Inc.

McPherson, M. S., and G. C. Winston. 1993. "The Economics of Cost, Price, and Quality in U.S. Higher Education." Chapter 4 in *Paying the Piper: Productivity, Incentives, and Financing in U.S. Higher Education,* by M. S. McPherson, M. Schapiro, and G. C. Winston. Ann Arbor: The University of Michigan Press.

National Commission on the Cost of Higher Education. 1998. *Straight Talk about College Costs and Prices: The Report of the National Commission on the Cost of Higher Education.* Phoenix: Oryx Press.

Oster, S. 1997. "An Analytical Framework for Thinking about the Use of For-Profit Structures for University Services and Activities." Paper presented at the Forum for the Future of Higher Education, The Aspen Institute, September 22.

Pauly, M. 1987. "Nonprofit Firms in Medical Markets." *American Economic Review* 77: 257–62.

U.S. Department of Education, National Center for Education Statistics. 1997. Integrated Postsecondary Education Data System. Dataset. Washington, DC: National Center for Education Statistics.

Winston, G. C. 1994. "A Note on the Logic and Structure of Global Accounting." Williams Project on the Economics of Higher Education, Discussion Paper No. 23. Williamstown, MA: Williams College.

————. 1996a. "The Economic Structure of Higher Education: Subsidies, Customer-Inputs, and Hierarchy." Williams Project on the Economics of Higher Education, Discussion Paper No. 40. Williamstown, MA: Williams College.

————. 1996b. "Global Accounting." In *Resource Allocation in Higher Education*, edited by W. F. Massey. Ann Arbor: The University of Michigan Press.

————. 1997. "Why Can't a College Be More Like a Firm?" *Change* September/October.

————. 1998. "A Guide to Measuring College Costs." Williams Project on the Economics of Higher Education, Discussion Paper No. 46. Williamstown, MA: Williams College.

————. 1999. "Subsidies, Hierarchy, and Peers: The Awkward Economics of Higher Education." *The Journal of Economic Perspectives* 13(1) Winter.

Winston, G. C., J. C. Carbone, and E. C. Lewis. 1998. "What's Been Happening to Higher Education, 1986–87 to 1994–95: A Reference Manual." Williams Project on the Economics of Higher Education, Discussion Paper No. 47. Williamstown, MA: Williams College.

Winston, G. C., and E. G. Lewis. 1997a. "Physical Capital and Capital Service Costs in U.S. Colleges and Universities: 1993." *Eastern Economic Journal* 23(2) Spring.

————. 1997b. "Subsidies, Costs, Tuition, and Aid in U.S. Higher Education, 1986–87 to 1993–94." Williams Project on the Economics of Higher Education, Discussion Paper No. 41. Williamstown, MA: Williams College.

Winston, G. C., and I. C. Yen. 1995. "Costs, Prices, Subsidies, and Aid in U.S. Higher Education." Williams Project on the Economics of Higher Education, Discussion Paper No. 32. Williamstown, MA: Williams College.

CHAPTER 3

Need Analysis
How We Decide Who Gets What

Sandy Baum

SUBSIDIZING STUDENTS

Providing access to higher education regardless of ability to pay has been a primary motivation behind the dedication of large amounts of both public and private funds to subsidizing college students. Subsidies take two basic forms—public or private funding of institutions, which reduces tuition across the board, and direct aid to individual students. Direct aid based on financial need is the subject of this discussion of financial aid policy. It is noteworthy, however, that the funding of institutions actually constitutes the largest portion of the subsidies students receive, a fact that makes the distribution of total subsidies, particularly public subsidies, much less progressive.

Few students pay the full cost of their college education. Most students attend public institutions, which are heavily subsidized by state governments. For these students, tuition and fees cover less than one-quarter of the cost of education. But even students at private colleges and universities, where the price of attendance now averages about $20,000, are heavily subsidized by institutional funds. This difference between the cost of education and the "sticker price" is an indirect subsidy received by all students who attend a particular college. The subsidies do not depend on any of the characteristics of the individual students—their financial circumstances, academic qualifications, or any other characteristics that might influence the institution's eagerness to enroll them.

This does not mean that there is no systematic distribution of these indirect subsidies. More-affluent students and those with stronger academic qualifications are likely to enjoy the largest indirect subsidies because they are more likely to attend high-cost selective private colleges, which (thanks to ample endowments) usually can afford hefty indirect subsidies to all students. However, there is no conscious effort to use these subsidies to differentiate among students.

DIRECT AID TO STUDENTS

Direct student aid is a very different phenomenon. Since the federal government began its active role in promoting college attendance in the 1960s and 1970s, both grant and loan policies have been focused primarily on individual students, rather than on educational institutions. Because of the stated goal of ensuring access to higher education regardless of ability to pay, federal aid has purportedly been need based, and formulas based on the financial resources available to each student financial aid applicant have been used to allocate limited federal dollars.

Similarly, institutions have devoted considerable resources to need-based aid. While athletic and academic scholarships have always existed, a high proportion of institutional funds, particularly in the private nonprofit sector, have been devoted to enabling students with inadequate means to enroll.

This broad-based commitment to need-based financial aid has weakened considerably in recent years. The federal government has been more responsive to the political voice of the middle class as stagnating incomes have become inadequate to keep up with spiraling college prices. The recent implementation by Congress of tax credits for students, while not divorced from financial circumstances, is a movement away from focusing aid on the neediest students. Institutions, which took up much of the slack when federal grant aid diminished in real terms in the 1980s and early 1990s, are also focusing less on the neediest students, turning increasingly to academic qualifications as the basis for allocating aid dollars. Stiff competition for enrollments and declining willingness to pay have pushed colleges away from an agenda based on creating access to higher education and toward a policy of using financial aid to maximize net revenues and craft entering classes. In this age of enrollment management, schools are using fewer of their scarce aid dollars to increase the diversity of their student bodies or to provide access to low-income students. Instead, they are using aid strategically to increase the average academic qualifications of incoming students and to attract students whose families can afford to make considerable contributions to their children's education.

Still, the majority of institutional aid and about $24 billion per year of federal aid are allocated through the use of need-analysis formulas. The strength of the competing demands for the limited dollars available for student subsidies suggests two fundamental questions about the equity of the student aid distribution system. The first is whether an adequate portion of the subsidy is allocated based on financial need. The second is whether the way financial need is determined is reasonable. Beginning from the premise that a significant amount of subsidy must be need based if our education system is to continue to fulfill its role of providing opportunity for upward mobility in American society, this chapter looks more closely at how that need-based aid is distributed.

MEASURING ABILITY TO PAY

Student need is generally defined as the difference between the cost of attendance and ability to pay. The amount a family is deemed able to pay is known as the expected family contribution (EFC). The basic idea behind any need-analysis system is that knowledge of the financial resources available to students can yield reasonable estimates of their ability to pay for college. Students whose ability to pay is less than the cost of the college they wish to attend will need some sort of assistance to enable them to enroll.

There are a variety of formulas currently in use to calculate the expected family contribution. The Federal Methodology (FM), legislated by Congress during the 1992 reauthorization of the Higher Education Act, is the mandated allocation formula for federal student aid. It represents the second iteration of the congressional attempt to legislate a need-analysis system, the Congressional Methodology (CM) having been in effect from 1988 through 1992. Before 1988, colleges and universities were allowed to distribute aid based on the formula of their choice; commonly, the Uniform Methodology (UM), developed by the member institutions of the College Board and American College Testing (ACT), in cooperation with the U.S. Department of Education. FM contains many of the features that were part of UM, but it differs in fundamental ways. In fact, because it does not incorporate sufficient information about applicants' financial circumstances, FM has become more an eligibility index than a true measure of financial capacity.

Institutions that have little more than federal funds are obligated to rely exclusively on FM. But other colleges and universities, primarily in the private nonprofit sector, have significant institutional funds to distribute. Many of them rely on a nonfederal formula, such as the College Board's Institutional Methodology (IM), or some modification of that formula. This formula resembles the earlier UM and CM. Unlike FM, it considers both current income and assets for all families, and it assumes a minimum contribution from all students. It has, however, been modified in a variety of ways in recent years.

No formula will ever be devised that can provide a perfect ranking of families and students in terms of ability to pay or a precise determination of the subsidy required to make paying for college manageable for every student. Numerous subjective judgments about what is fair must inevitably be made, and for a variety of issues, there is tension between what seems fair and the incentives or disincentives generated by the formula for allocating aid dollars.

In other words, at times there is a trade-off between equity and efficiency, between treating people fairly and encouraging people to behave responsibly. But the two may also be complementary. Even in a system for determining ability to pay, which is primarily designed to ensure equity, paying attention to the incentive effects, the behavioral responses, and the impact of a policy on market outcomes is vital. In rough terms, if we waste a lot of money trying to help people in ways that end up being counterproductive, we will find ourselves with lower levels of overall resources, unable to attain our most basic goals. If the need-analysis system punishes people for certain choices or behaviors—such as saving—those behaviors will be discouraged and we will end up with fewer dollars to distribute to those most in need.

EQUITY

It is tempting for students and families to consider the aid distribution system unfair if it provides them with less funding than they would like. A more sophisticated concept of fairness is based on the ideas of horizontal and vertical equity. Horizontal equity refers to the equal treatment of people in similar circumstances, while vertical equity involves treating people in different circumstances in appropriately different ways. These concepts are, to a considerable degree, subjective; there is no definitive way to measure the equity of any particular policy.

It is easy to say that two families in similar circumstances should be judged to have the same ability to pay. But judging equal circumstances is not always straightforward. If two families have the same family income, but one includes two adults working full time, while the other consists of one worker and one stay-at-home parent, it is not clear that their financial situations should be considered equal. If one family has twins who have to go through college at the same time, but another has two children four years apart, only one of whom has to be educated immediately, their circumstances may be more similar than they appear at first glance.

One of the most common horizontal equity quandaries in designing a need-analysis system is determining whether or not to give similar treatment to families with similar incomes who have, for a variety of reasons, made different choices. If two families have equal incomes, but one has chosen to save while the other has chosen to consume, should they have equal expected family contributions because they had equal opportunities, or should the family with savings pay more because their accumulated savings increases their capacity to pay?

Vertical equity is even harder to identify than horizontal equity, both because there is considerable room for disagreement on defining the types of differences in circumstances that should correspond to different treatments, and because there is not one right answer to how different the treatments should be. We have a progressive federal income tax, under which those with higher incomes pay a higher percentage of their income in tax than do those with lower incomes, because there is a general sense that this constitutes appropriately different treatment of people whose circumstances are different. But extensive efforts by many great minds have been unable to prove that a progressive tax is fair, much less develop any objective standard for the optimal degree of progressivity.

The need-analysis system, like the federal income tax, uses a graduated rate structure, combined with the exemption of some amount of income, in order to create a progressive system. There is no way to determine, however, whether the existing rate structure is more vertically equitable than any alternative rate structure would be. This is a judgment on which reasonable people will always differ.

The subjective nature of equity considerations means that there is no absolute standard against which a need-analysis formula can be measured. Different institutions have different mandates, different resources, and different student bodies, so they face a wide variety of problems and options. No single aid-allocation mechanism would be suitable for all institutions, much less for all funds, public and private. Nonetheless, it is possible to examine need-based allocation methods against the backdrop of generally acceptable concepts of equity.

THE STRUCTURE OF A NEED-ANALYSIS FORMULA

Income

Any formula measuring ability to pay in order to determine a student's need for financial assistance must begin by defining income and assets. Then the formula must determine which components of income and assets should be taxed[1] to determine expected contributions, as well as the appropriate tax rates. The starting point for determining how much assistance a student or family needs to make college a feasible option is to determine their level of discretionary income. It is tempting to argue that a certain amount is required for necessities and that we should be able to agree on a percentage of discretionary income to be devoted to paying for education. But defining necessities is not simple. Clearly, everyone needs basic goods—food, clothing, and shelter. But how many families contemplating higher education for their children really define necessities so narrowly? Is owning a television set a necessity? Is buying new sneakers when the old ones begin to tear a necessity? Is occasionally ordering pizza a luxury that we should expect families to forego? What about a second car?

The need-analysis formula taxes income above the level of allowances provided. These include an income protection allowance (IPA), designed to make sure no contribution is expected from the first dollars of family income, over which the family has little or no discretion because of basic needs. Both aid administrators and parents frequently complain that the income protection allowance is too low because it is not enough for the family to live on. In fact, the need-analysis system does not incorporate the idea that the IPA is the family's living allowance. The idea is that up to the level of the IPA, a family's income is so low that they have virtually no discretion about how to spend their money. No one expects families to spend all of their money above the level of the IPA on college. Rather, some fraction of those dollars must be devoted to college. Allowances are also provided for the payment of both income taxes and state and local taxes.

The impossibility of precisely defining "necessities" is sufficient to make the determination of need subjective. But the difficulty of ranking people according to capacity to pay is an even more serious impediment to constructing the optimal need-analysis system. We have equivalency scales to approximate the difference that family size makes in living standards, but these scales are clearly imprecise. For example, they do not adequately differentiate between families with two adults and one child, and those with one adult and two children. Geographical differences in the cost of living present another problem. While regional adjustments might be possible, it would add considerable complexity to also correct for the urban/rural/suburban differences, which vary across the country.

Moreover, it is not obvious which circumstances should be taken into consideration as affecting ability to pay. Should people who choose to work part-time receive larger subsidies than those with similar skills who hold down two jobs? How does the status of a family that owns its own home but has high mortgage interest payments compare to the status of a family that rents? How do liquid and nonliquid assets affect a family's ability to finance college?

The Snapshot Approach

At its inception, need analysis was grounded in several basic principles. One was the idea that aid applicants should be taken as they appear at the time of application. In other words, a family's past options and choices should not be taken into consideration or judged. The need-analysis system would simply look at applicants' current income and assets and determine the amount they were able to pay in that year. This view became deeply ingrained in the financial aid profession, but it has been brought into question in recent years by the focus on education as an investment and the recognition that few families can afford to pay for college without planning over time, saving, and borrowing.

The logic behind the "snapshot" approach is both pragmatic and philosophical. The purpose of the aid system is to allow potential students who do not have adequate financial resources to attend college. Punishing students whose parents chose to travel extensively or buy expensive cars instead of saving for college would violate the principle of providing access to all, regardless of ability to pay. Moreover, from a practical perspective, no amount of reprimanding or denial of aid can make a family change its past behavior, so denying aid because of poor planning will simply deny access, it will not change behavior.

But the arguments against this principle appear much stronger, now that the cost of college is significantly higher relative to family incomes than it was at the time the original formula was devised. It is clear to anyone comparing expected family contributions to incomes that few families will be able to pay these contributions out of current income and liquid assets. Education is an investment in human capital, not a consumption good like restaurant meals or trips to Disney World. While some of the most important benefits are nonpecuniary, it is very clear that a college education significantly increases expected future earnings. Given the reality that education is an investment with long-term benefits—one that can and should be anticipated and planned for—the narrowly defined snapshot view is not satisfactory from an economic perspective. Economic theory suggests that modifying the snapshot approach could diminish the savings disincentive problem currently embedded in the need-analysis system. It would help to encourage families and students to think of education as an investment that must be paid for over time. Perhaps if collecting multiple years of income data becomes feasible because of improvements in technology and/or the involvement of the Internal Revenue Service, taking a longer-term view of financial capacity will become more widely accepted.

As a direct result of the snapshot approach, the current practice is to calculate the amount a family can be expected to pay and then to divide that amount over the number of college students in the family. The logic here is that need analysis should determine the amount the family can reasonably be expected to pay in a given year. Asking them for more money than they can afford because they have two students to educate would, from this perspective, be unreasonable.

This practice, however, results in a serious horizontal inequity. The spacing of a family's children has a dramatic effect on the total cost of educating those children. A family with twins going through four years of college simultaneously will end up paying a total of four parental contributions (PCs).[2] A family with two children born four years apart will pay a total of eight PCs.

Many people believe that, while families with two children in college should be expected to make larger contributions than similar families with one child in college, the contribution should be less than twice as large. There is, unfortunately, no precise way to determine the appropriate ratio. This debate is likely to continue for the foreseeable future, and although the principle of horizontal equity dictates a change from current practices, it does not provide a perfect solution.

Another complication arises from the reality that parents are sometimes in college at the same time as their children. Under the current system for determining federal aid eligibility, this practice can significantly increase the subsidy a family receives. The problem is that parents who work to help their children through college and postpone their own studies are penalized for that behavior.

Parents and Students

Some students are considered by the need-analysis system to be independent and are responsible for financing their own education, while others are required to use both their own resources and the resources of their parents. Students have the incentive to declare themselves independent if at all possible, since this significantly increases their eligibility for financial aid. According to federal rules, graduate and professional students, married students, veterans, orphans, wards of the court, individuals with legal dependents, and students over the age of 24 are automatically considered independent. Other students are considered dependent unless determined otherwise by financial aid officers.

For dependent students, the income and assets of both parents and students are taken into consideration. However, student resources are taxed at higher rates than parent resources. The logic behind this distinction is that students' primary responsibility is to pay for their education, whereas parents, who are not the primary beneficiaries of the investment in education, have other responsibilities.

The distinction between parent and student income makes sense, but it is not the only reasonable approach. For many families, especially those with low incomes, children's income supplements parents' income to fund general family expenses. Under these circumstances, it would make more sense to tax family income as a whole.

The case of divorced or separated parents poses a more serious question about how the income of different individuals is relevant to ability to pay. Under FM, the income of the noncustodial parent is not considered. IM does allow for the incomes of both natural parents to be considered, but the question of how to treat noncustodial parents and the spouses of custodial parents is one to which there are almost as many answers as there are financial aid offices. Economic reasoning cannot solve this ethical and social dilemma, but it can focus attention on the possible incentive and distributional effects of various practices. Affluent parents should not be able to reduce their responsibilities by getting divorced, so the FM solution of ignoring the noncustodial parent would seem to be the least equitable and the least efficient. Taxing the income of step-parents creates a disincentive for remarriage. On the other hand, ignoring that income may seriously underestimate the financial resources available to some students.

Assets

Both income and assets contribute to a household's financial strength. Income is the flow of dollars coming into the household over a particular period. Assets are the stock of resources that have been accumulated over time. Households with higher incomes are likely to have an easier time accumulating assets because they may be able to save more. Nonetheless, the correlation between income and assets among households is far from perfect.

About one-sixth of the filers in the lowest-income quarter of those who apply for aid through the College Board fall into the highest 30 percent according to net worth. About 30 percent of the filers in the highest fifth according to income fall into the lowest third according to assets (Baum 1996, 47). Some of the households with low income and large assets are undergoing temporarily difficult experiences such as unemployment; some are retired; some are small-business owners with cash flow problems; but others are affluent people who, for tax purposes (or for the purpose of manipulating the student aid system) are able to disguise their income.

Households with high income and low asset levels may have had a recent large increase in income, or they may have faced unusual circumstances, such as special-needs children or high medical expenditures, which prevented them from saving or depleted their assets. But they also may simply have made lifestyle choices leading to high levels of current consumption and little planning for the future.

The extent to which assets contribute to ability to pay and whether or not different types of assets should be treated differently have been ongoing issues in the need-analysis system. Current practices vary widely. FM ignores all assets for many families with income under $50,000. The College Board's IM taxes a much broader base of assets—it considers assets for all filers and includes both liquid and nonliquid assets, including home equity.

Very different philosophies underlie these two approaches. FM relies on the principle that homes and family farms are nonliquid assets, the taxing of which would require families to disrupt their lives in unacceptable ways in order to finance college. It also assumes that families with low and moderate income either do not have significant assets—and therefore there is little benefit of having those assets reported—or cannot afford to tap those assets because of their low current income.

Formulas that pay more attention to assets rest on the principle that assets and income contribute independently to financial strength. This approach, aside from its solid grounding in economic realities, eases the allocation of limited resources, since a contribution from assets is expected to supplement the contribution from current income, reducing calculated need. Home equity constitutes the largest part of assets for many families who apply for financial aid.

The logic behind FM not taking home equity into account under any circumstances is primarily political. During the 1980s, home prices in many parts of the country increased dramatically. For many homeowners, home equity skyrocketed, reaching levels totally out of proportion with their income. Families found themselves living in homes they could not possibly afford to buy at their current income levels. This increase in net worth did not have any meaningful impact on consumption opportunities, since if they sold their houses to realize the capital gains, they would not be able to find cheaper housing without diminishing their standard of living considerably. However, since the need-analysis system taxed home equity like other assets, an increasing proportion of expected family contributions was attributable to assets, as opposed to income. Families whose homes had dramatically increased in value were not able to borrow against their home equity because of limited cash flow. The difficulties created by these circumstances created considerable political pressure from the middle class to modify the need-analysis system.

The problem being addressed was a very real one, but the solution adopted by Congress was inconsistent with economic principles of both equity and efficiency. Choosing to ignore home equity entirely in the newly designed FM of the 1992 reauthorization of the Higher Education Act created significant horizontal inequities, as well as making it difficult to distinguish among families in very different circumstances. While it may not have been reasonable to expect families with artificially inflated home equity to come up with the contributions prescribed by the old formula, the new formula totally ignored the reality that their assets gave them considerable financial strength relative to non-homeowners. Moreover, there is a fundamental problem with treating different forms of assets differently. As long as people have choices about the form in which to hold their assets, differential treatment will create incentives for people to alter their asset holdings in response to the need-analysis system.

Many private institutions relying on their own funds to meet the need of accepted candidates could not ignore home equity without creating huge gaps between measured need and available aid. Some schools continued to treat home equity as they always had—like any other asset. Others adopted a compromise approach, capping home value at three times annual income. Families with home equity in excess of this amount are likely to have been the beneficiaries of this temporary housing market bubble.

The compromise approach recognizes that homeowners have greater ability to pay than renters with similar incomes. At the same time, it recognizes the reality that inflated home prices could generate levels of expected contribution that families may be unable to finance or that could lead them into precarious financial situations if they deplete home equity, which may be quickly dissipated by the vicissitudes of the housing market.

Princeton University, the institution with the highest per-capita endowment in the country, recently made news by announcing that it, too, will begin to ignore home equity in calculating family ability to pay (Gose 1998). Because of its wealth, Princeton can, at least in the short run, provide larger grants to middle- and upper-middle-income families who hold significant wealth in their homes without reducing the aid they award to needier students. Nonetheless, they will lose the ability to differentiate between students who truly lack the wherewithal to pay for college and those for whom paying is an inconvenience.

Yale University responded to Princeton's action by announcing that it would ignore the first $150,000 of assets for all applicants, regardless of the form in which those assets are held. This policy is both more equitable and more efficient than Princeton's because it does not discriminate against renters or provide artificial incentives for families to change the form of their savings.

If other, less-well-endowed schools follow Princeton's lead in order to remain competitive in the market for qualified students, they soon will be redirecting significant amounts of aid away from those who need it most. Failing to measure financial capacity will, by definition, lead away from the long-standing practice of using scarce funds to compensate for inadequate family resources.

Ignoring home equity while taxing other forms of assets may be the most glaring example of the problem of treating assets differently depending on the form in which they are held. Other problems with differential treatment of assets are common to both FM and IM. It is widely recognized that the differential treatment of student assets, which are taxed at a rate of 35 percent, and parent assets, which are taxed at rates ranging from 2.6 to 5.6 percent, has created fertile ground for private financial advisers. Taxing parent and student assets at different rates may make sense on its face but, given the ease of transferring assets from one family member to another, there is little logical basis for this provision. The difficulty of making a meaningful separation of the assets held by different family members also brings into question the practice of ignoring assets held in the names of siblings. An alternative to the current approach, which might solve these problems, would be to collect data on assets held by all family members and tax them all at the same rate. While it might create some new problems, this would eliminate the horizontal inequity based on the arbitrariness of the names on many savings vehicles.

Perhaps the most widely recognized shortcoming of the need-analysis system is the disincentive it creates against saving. This is an effect of the snapshot view on which the need-analysis system has historically rested. Families who have chosen to save for college end up having to pay more than those who have not. If long-term income were the foundation for measuring financial capacity, assets accrued through foregoing consumption of current income would be irrelevant. Only assets accumulated through inheritance, capital gains, and other "windfalls" would differentiate families.

The idea that assets increase ability to pay collides with the idea that families should be free to choose whether to save in advance, to cut deeply into current consumption, or to borrow. Two families with identical income histories should, according to principles of horizontal equity, be asked for identical contributions (at least if they are choosing equally priced education options). But ignoring assets makes it impossible to accurately rank families.

There is, of course, no perfect solution to this dilemma. Financial aid administrators tend to focus on the fact that a family with $10,000 of college savings will pay a maximum of $560 more in one year than a similar family with no savings. The family with the $10,000 will have a much easier time financing their expected contribution and will, in the long run, be better off than the family that depends on borrowing and suffers the effects of compound interest.

There is, however, a clear perception among the public that savers are chasing a moving target. Every dollar they save in an attempt to be prepared for the daunting expected contributions they will face increases the amount colleges will expect them to contribute. Economists also complain about the savings disincentive in the need-analysis system (Dick and Edlin 1997). The combined effects of the income tax system and the need-analysis system on the marginal tax rates on income and on savings may discourage significant amounts of saving. A family applying for aid that chooses to save may pay 28 percent of the interest in federal income taxes, 5 percent in state income taxes, and then another 47 percent of the after-tax interest in increased expected family contribution from income. Interest income of $100 would then generate only about $34 to help pay the expected family contribution.

The need-analysis system taxes both the interest generated by assets and the accumulated asset. The contribution expected from a family over four years of college would increase by about 20 percent of the amount originally saved. This means that a family that had saved the anticipated amount to avoid having to make excessive sacrifices in consumption out of income during the college years might find itself with inadequate resources despite their efforts. Their savings would cover the expected contribution based on their income, but not the additional contribution generated by the existence of the assets they saved. For families with more than one child, the situation is even more extreme.

Clearly there is a trade-off between reducing the savings disincentive in the need-analysis system and recognizing the reality that assets increase ability to pay. But it seems reasonable to assume that assets that have been saved in order to finance expected contributions will be used up entirely when those contributions are paid. From this perspective, it is not logical to raise the expected contribution because of the existence of the assets required to pay it.

Instituting an educational savings protection allowance, which would protect an appropriate amount of savings from taxation under the need-analysis system, would be a step in the direction of an efficient and equitable solution to the problem of how to treat savings. Ideally, it would be possible to differentiate college savings from other assets. Since this is impossible, it would be a mistake to treat assets in particular savings instruments favorably. Rather, allowing an amount related to the family's expected contribution from income to be ignored by the formula would prevent families from being penalized for saving.

One form of asset about which omission from need analysis has generated considerable controversy is pension assets. The reality is that families with pension assets have less need to save than similar families without those assets. A perfectly equitable need-analysis system would accurately assess pension assets and tax them at a rate identical to the rate applied to other assets. The practical problem is that measuring those assets is extremely difficult, particularly in the case of defined benefit plans, under which the beneficiary can expect a certain monthly benefit upon retirement. Assessing all pension plans except defined benefit plans would be a significant horizontal inequity.

Existing need-analysis formulas incorporate an asset protection allowance, designed to protect some parental assets for retirement. Parental assets are protected to the extent that they are required to generate income in retirement that will supplement the average Social Security benefit, allowing the family to live at an agreed-upon income standard for people over the age of 65.

While this allowance is not directly related to college savings, it is important to note that a significant quantity of family assets are exempt from taxation. Only families with assets above this level are expected to contribute anything from them to pay for their children's education.

Tax Rates

Perhaps the most misunderstood facet of the need-analysis formulas is the role of marginal tax rates. People tend to think that it is the overall fraction of income or assets that is the most important measure of the impact of a tax. However, it is the marginal rate, the percentage of the last dollar that has to be paid, that matters most in terms of incentives. Even if the first $30,000 of income were exempt, a marginal tax rate of 80 percent on dollars over this amount would cause anyone with earning capacity in the taxable range to think twice about extra work effort. Similarly, if students are asked to contribute 35 percent of their assets each year, even with some sort of asset protection, many will find that accumulating assets in anticipation of paying for college is not worth the effort. This means that although high marginal tax rates may be appealing, because people with large amounts of discretionary income should be willing to spend a large portion of it on their own or their children's education, the negative incentive effects must be considered in determining the appropriate assessment rate schedule.

The current marginal tax rate of 50 percent on the after-tax incomes of both dependent students and independent students without dependents probably discourages some students from working to earn more than the income set-aside allowed in FM or the minimum student contribution required by some schools allocating their own funds. It is understandable that some professional schools choose to apply even higher marginal tax rates to the incomes of independent students whose future income prospects are very promising. Nonetheless, this practice is likely to significantly diminish student work effort.

THE FUTURE OF NEED ANALYSIS

This discussion of the components of the aid-allocation system is not exhaustive. It does, however, suggest that there are many imperfections in the system, some fairly easily corrected, but many others the inevitable results of incompatible goals. In fact, considerable thought goes into the development of need-analysis systems. Despite the ease with which they can be criticized, the practices developed by most institutions to allocate their need-based funds are reasonably equitable. These institutions deserve considerable credit for their attempts to increase student opportunities. It is too easy to forget that need analysis is a system for allocating subsidies, not an involuntary tax imposed on potential students. Still, an equitable and efficient system for allocating student aid requires continued vigilance and creative thinking about ways to improve the formula.

Need-based aid is likely to come under increasing scrutiny and pressure as enrollment management tensions mount. In an environment where public sympathy for income redistribution and affirmative action is considerably weaker than it has been over most of the last two decades, immediate financial pressures are likely to take center stage. Those making public policy are unlikely to sacrifice middle-class support in the interest of those at the lower end of the income scale. On college campuses, even where the commitment to increased opportunity is strong, enrolling students who do not need large institutional subsidies is frequently the only feasible response to fiscal exigencies.

The shrinking role of need-based student aid does not diminish the importance of ensuring the appropriate distribution of funds intended to allow people from all segments of American society access to costly higher education. In fact, the equity and efficiency of systems designed to allocate need-based aid may be even more vital in an era where need-based aid must constantly be justified. If need-analysis formulas create notable inequities or create significant negative incentives, relying on them will be considerably less compelling.

Moreover, students with the least capacity to pay should be assured that aid will, in fact, be available and sufficient to allow them to enroll in college. If the system is too unpredictable or too difficult to decipher, the students most at risk are likely to believe that they are unable to pay and therefore will effectively be denied access to higher education. So, in addition to equity and efficiency, those who design need-analysis systems also must strive for clarity and continuity. Clearly, this is no small task. Compromises and concessions are inevitable.

It behooves those who are committed to access and choice in higher education to continue to strive for the best possible allocation systems. Any need-analysis formula will be arbitrary in some respects and will face trade-offs between measuring financial capacity and creating disincentives, as well as between equity and simplicity. Those involved in designing and administering these systems should concentrate both on improving them and on explaining their importance and their logic to the public.

NOTES

1. The aid system "taxes" income and assets in the sense that it requires that a fraction of each additional dollar be contributed to pay for education. Only people who choose to apply for aid are subject to this tax, which is really a reduction of subsidy, not a payment out of income or assets.

2. The expected family contribution (EFC) includes both the parental contribution (PC) and the student's own contribution.

REFERENCES

Baum, S. 1996. *A Primer on Economics for Financial Aid Professionals*. Washington, DC: College Board and the National Association of Financial Aid Administrators.

Dick, A., and A. Edlin. 1997. "The Implicit Taxes from College Financial Aid." *Journal of Public Economics* 65(3).

Gose, B. 1998. "Recent Shifts on Aid by Elite Colleges Signal New Push to Help the Middle Class." *Academe Today*, electronic news service of the *Chronicle of Higher Education*, March 6.

CHAPTER

The Student Aid Industry

Michael Mumper

O ver the past 30 years, federal and state governments have provided billions of dollars in financial aid to college students. An increasingly large and complex implementation system has emerged to award, distribute, and monitor that aid. In addition to the U.S. Department of Education and campus financial aid offices, an elaborate and lucrative student aid industry has developed to facilitate the flow of funds from government to students. There is no question that elements of this industry have helped to make the student aid process more efficient and have reduced levels of fraud in the programs. Indeed, important aspects of the student aid process could not operate without the participation of this private industry. At the same time, it has brought additional layers of participants to the student aid process, which have resulted in greater complexity and new costs for taxpayers and students.

This chapter sorts out and describes some of the major components of the student aid industry. A large portion of this industry developed around the guaranteed student loan program. Because of its design, this program requires the participation of private lenders for its successful operation. The guaranteed student loan program has also encouraged the development of loan servicers, secondary markets, and guaranty agencies, both to attract broader lender participation and to ensure compliance with the program's regulations. But the student aid industry now extends far beyond these financial intermediaries. Today, a vast array of companies, consultants, publishers, and advisers are available to assist in every aspect of the student aid process. They help students apply for aid. They assist campuses in managing and disbursing that aid. They contract with the Department of Education to determine student eligibility, to collect outstanding loans, and to ensure that campuses are in compliance with federal regulations in the implementation of the programs. There are even consultants who offer assistance to campuses in preparing for the audits and compliance reviews conducted by the contractors hired by the Department of Education.

The increasing complexity of the administration of student aid, and the growth of the student aid industry, have received relatively little public attention. This is, at least in part, because these developments have occurred without the awareness of most students and their families. In many ways, from the student's perspective, the financial aid process has become more simple over the years. Today, after completing the federal financial aid form, the entire process is managed for them by the campus financial aid office. These offices are responsible for translating the complexity of numerous aid programs into language that will be easily understandable to their students. At the same time, they must transform aid funds and an uneven and often overwhelming flow of regulations into a smooth and legal disbursement process. Paradoxically, the development of the student aid industry has made the job of the campus financial aid office substantially more complex, while at the same time providing services that help them cope with that complexity.

THE RISE OF THE GUARANTEED STUDENT LOAN INDUSTRY

The birth of today's student aid industry can be traced to the design of the federal guaranteed student loan program. The original ancestor of that program is found in Title IV of the Higher Education Act of 1965. President Lyndon Johnson wanted to develop a low-cost way to ensure that middle-income students could borrow the money they needed for college. But rather than set up a system of direct federal loans, it was decided instead to use federal money to encourage private lenders to originate student loans. In this system, participating lenders received subsidies and guarantees in return for making student loans. This structure was thought to be cheaper and involve less risk for the federal government.

In the early years of the guaranteed student loan program, now called the Federal Family Education Loan Program (FFELP), its major problem was attracting sufficient participation (McPherson 1989). Many needy students were hesitant to borrow. Lenders, wary of high administrative costs and uncertain returns, were reluctant to lend. And states, who were to administer the program, also had little to gain from participation. The result was that relatively few loans were made—a disturbingly small percentage of which went to minority and disadvantaged students.

In order to address these problems, the federal guaranteed student loan program was changed in several ways to make it more attractive to all sides. In the mid-1970s, the government began to hold the program's interest rate well below market rates to make the loans more appealing to students. But this made making the loans less attractive to banks. The government then began to pay lenders a series of fees and subsidies to allow them to keep rates low, cover administrative costs, and still make a profit. The federal government also helped set up an agency in each state to monitor and oversee student loans. These new organizations, called state guaranty agencies, also received federal payments to cover their administrative costs and to enable them to encourage lending in their state.

These financial incentives led to substantial increases in lending. In 1970, federally guaranteed student loans amounted to slightly more than $1 billion. By 1980, loan volume had increased to $4 billion. By 1990, it was $13 billion. In 1996–97, more than five million students borrowed in excess of $20 billion to pay for higher education (College Board 1997). This complex arrangement has been remarkably successful at making low-interest capital available to the vast majority of students enrolled in postsecondary education. Over the past 30 years, the various federal programs have made more than $250 billion in loans to students. But the expansion of the system has been bought at a high cost to the taxpayers. In 1997, the federal government paid nearly $4 billion in servicing fees to the loan industry. During the past 30 years, the government has paid more than $50 billion in fees to the loan industry and an additional $30 billion to cover the costs of defaulted loans (Strauss 1997). There is little doubt that without the availability of these loans, millions of students would be unable to afford the tuition charged at the institutions they attend. And without the participation of the federal government and the student loan industry, the vast majority of these loans might never be made. At the same time, these government payments have generated substantial profits for the student loan industry. Along the way, the industry has become a powerful force in the process of making and modifying the policies that govern student lending.

COMPONENTS OF THE STUDENT AID INDUSTRY

As presently constructed, the allocation of federal student aid involves a wide variety of tasks, and a substantial industry has developed around each activity. The guaranteed student loan program, for example, comprises four distinct components: lenders, loan servicers, secondary markets, and guaranty agencies. But the industry is not limited to the loan programs. An additional array of publishers, consultants, lawyers, and technicians has developed to help students and institutions navigate the student aid system. These businesses often provide important, sometimes essential, services. At the same time, their existence adds new costs to the program. Moreover, they further complicate the student aid process, making it more difficult for an institution or a student to get by without them.

It is important to note that, although these conceptual categories may be distinct, many companies are fully involved in the entire range of activity. USA Group, for example, administers an $11.6 billion portfolio of education loans on behalf of 150 private lenders; owns USA Funds, which guaranteed nearly 1.5 million loans totaling more than $6 billion; operates a secondary loan market; and includes the Noel-Levitz consulting company, which offers a wide range of management services to colleges and universities (USA Group 1997). USA Group is thus in a position to make money from assisting in a wide range of student aid activities. As such, the various sectors of the industry more often find themselves sharing a common interest than actively competing with one another.

Banks and Lenders

Today, more than 5,000 lenders originate student loans in the federal program known as FFELP. It is easy to see why lenders are so willing to participate. The changes made during the 1970s and 1980s have made the program extremely lucrative for lenders. While some of those benefits have been reduced in the 1990s, student loans still remain a highly profitable business. First, lenders are paid a subsidy in addition to the interest charged as students repay their loans. Second, student loans are largely protected from default risk by a federal guarantee. From the perspective of the industry, student loans are a virtually risk-free source of revenue. It is the federal government that shoulders the responsibilities for borrowers who fail to repay their loans.

For a commercial bank, a savings and loan association, or a credit union, whose main liabilities are short-term deposits, federally guaranteed student loans offer significant protection from interest rate risk, especially when compared with longer-term commercial lending. A 1991 study of lender profitability concluded that

> student lending has been a consistently profitable activity for lenders. Moreover, it has been shown that student lending has generally been more profitable than other important lending activities such as mortgage and automobile lending. The relatively high level of student loan profitability is due to their low level of credit and liquidity risk. (Jenkins 1991)

Finally, such loans also offer lenders virtually no liquidity risk. Indeed, many banks do not hold the loans but sell them in secondary markets. Through purchase commitments and warehousing arrangements, government-created secondary markets make it easy for lenders to originate and maintain student loans without changing the profitability of their balance sheets.

The Secondary Loan Market

During the 1970s, in order to encourage lenders to participate in the program, Congress authorized the creation of a secondary loan market for student loans. Operating through nonprofit agencies or large banks, secondary markets provide a place for lenders to sell their student loans. This facilitates the free movement of capital and easy entrance and exit from the student loan market. The players in the secondary market raise capital by issuing (usually tax-exempt) stock or selling shares in pools of loans. They are able to service and collect the loans, and still make a profit, by taking advantage of interest rate spreads.

Today, there are more than 40 secondary markets for student loans. The largest of these, the Student Loan Marketing Association, or Sallie Mae, began as a federally chartered company. It was created in 1972 to reduce the risk of student loans to banks and encourage their participation in the student loan program. Sallie Mae has grown rapidly since its creation. In 1976, it accounted for about $200 million in student loans and generated a profit of less than $3 million. By 1982, it accounted for more than $3 billion in student loans and generated more than $38 million in profits (Quint 1983). In 1997, Sallie Mae was fully privatized. It is now a privately owned and operated company that is active in nearly every aspect of student loans. It services nearly four million such loans, or one-quarter of all loans backed by FFELP (Sallie Mae 1997). In return for these services, Sallie Mae was paid $575 million last year by the government in interest payments on the loans it held (Strauss 1997).

Guaranty Agencies and Loan Servicers

The third component of the student loan industry is the guaranty agency. Also created by Congress in the 1970s, guaranty agencies assist the government in tracking and collecting student loans. This was originally thought to be necessary because student loan default rates were alarmingly high, and lenders and the government had an abysmal record in collecting these loans. In 1981, former secretary of Health, Education, and Welfare (HEW) Joseph Califano recalled that, as recently as 1978, government records for guaranteed student loans in some locations

> were kept on index cards in shoeboxes; in others, what little computer training existed was woefully inadequate to the task of collection. The backlog of alleged fraud cases in this program alone equaled three

years of work for the available HEW investigative staff. (Califano 1981, 310)

It was in this context that guaranty agencies were created to take over the monitoring and collection functions from HEW. Each state was required to establish its own agency, or to designate a not-for-profit agency, to insure and service their student loans. Today, these agencies review all student loans to ensure student eligibility and monitor the students, lenders, and postsecondary institutions to make sure that all parties are complying with federal regulations. They also monitor lenders to make sure that they are diligent in collecting on delinquent loans. In the end, they are also responsible for collecting defaulted student loans and paying the holder of a defaulted loan any unpaid principal and interest. In return for these services, agencies are funded by an administrative cost allowance paid by the federal government, and they receive a percent of all defaulted student loans collected (Cronin 1989).

As the volume of student loans has grown, guaranty agencies have grown into a full-scale industry. In 1996, for example, they took in $775 million from the guaranteed student loan program. Eighty percent of that came in the form of fees from the federal government and the remaining 20 percent as fees from borrowers (Strauss 1997). While they are designated as nonprofit agencies for tax purposes, the industry has been criticized for the high salaries and generous perks paid to its executives. A *Washington Post* exposé noted that in 1996 USA Group earned more than $200 million in fees for processing and collecting student loans. It paid its chief executive more than $1 million and four other executives at least $300,000 a year. Its guaranty agency, USA Funds, reported "an 'excess'—the non-profit word for profits—on its latest tax return of more than $67 million" (Babcock 1997).

In recent years, these guaranty agencies have generated a great deal of controversy. A growing number of critics claim that these agencies have outlived their usefulness. They argue that technological advances in the tracking and administration of loans have eliminated the need for these intermediaries. Assistant Secretary of Education David Longanecker described them as "dinosaurs" and has urged their elimination (Babcock 1997). The Clinton administration recently put forth a proposal that would make the government, rather than guaranty agencies, the sole insurer of student loans. If enacted, it would eliminate the major function of guaranty agencies (Burd 1997b).

Of course, most guaranty agencies strongly oppose efforts to replace them with the Department of Education. They argue that their investment in computers and data-processing technology justifies their continued existence. By reducing defaults and lowering administrative costs, guaranty agencies argue that they are actually saving the government money. They point out that Congress has reduced the fees paid to banks and guaranty agencies in recent years and contend that their revenue is high because of the huge increase in student loan volume, not because of high fees (Goodling 1994).

But as the necessity for these guaranty agencies is increasingly called into question, a few have sought to stake out a new role for themselves in the loan process, focusing on the task of preventing students from defaulting on their loans. Richard Johnson of the Great Lakes Higher Education Corporation describes the new role this way: "In the guaranteed-student loan program, there is a perverse incentive for guaranty agencies to wait to collect loans until after they have gone into default. What we should be doing is preventing students from going into default" (Burd 1997c). Paul Combs of the American Student Assistance Guarantor echoes that view: "Our mission should be to keep students from getting into trouble" (Burd 1997c). Such a position may allow the guaranty agencies to continue to receive federal funds, even if they are replaced as the program's sole insurer.

The Alternative Loan Industry

Under FFELP, a student can borrow the cost of attendance minus other financial aid up to the maximum loan amount. But more and more students are finding these limits to be too low and are seeking ways to borrow additional funds. While these loans are used for higher education, they are originated, serviced, and collected entirely by the student loan industry. These "alternative" loans, which are available only through private lenders, are now being offered by such mainstays of the student loan industry as Sallie Mae (Signature loans), CitiBank (the CitiAssist loan), and The Money Store (the Educaid loan). The College Board (1997) estimates that these loans amount to $1.5 billion. While this is an increase of almost 20 percent from 1996 to 1997, it remains only a small portion of student borrowing.

Today, dozens of lenders encourage students to take out alternative loans in addition to, or even in place of, traditional federal loans. The pioneer in the field is EduCap, which aggressively markets alternative loans directly to students. EduCap, which describes itself as the nation's "largest provider of affordable credit-based education financing," made more than $300 million in loans last year. In order to make these loans, they sell bonds, use the proceeds to make loans, and then use the interest paid on those loans to repay the bonds and underwrite company operations. And it is all done with no government guarantees or subsidies. It is also done without the direct participation of campus financial aid offices.

The alternative loan industry has been criticized for their high costs to students. While interest rates vary widely, they are always higher than federal loans and often higher than regular commercial loans offered by banks. EduCap's PLATO loan, for example, charges an annual percentage rate of more than 12 percent. But the alternative loan from the Sallie Mae Signature Education Loan Program charges only 9.17 percent (Strauss 1997). Some observers are worried that borrowers who are familiar with the FFELP program, where rates are the same from one lender to another, may not understand the importance of shopping around for the best rate on an alternative loan.

Consultants, Publishers, and Computer Technology Vendors

The complex and fluid nature of the student loan industry has, itself, spawned new and profitable industries. Students and families, bewildered by the rising costs of higher education and the wide range of financing options, have sought help in navigating the process. Dozens of books and software packages are now sold that claim to help decipher that process. Financial planners and consultants offer individualized preparation sessions and group seminars. Some of these services are offered directly by a potential lender or service provider. But many seek to sell nothing more than advice about how and where to get the best financial aid package.

Similarly, many campus financial aid offices have sought consultants and technical experts to aid them in managing FFELP, as well as other federal, state, and institutional aid programs. A part of this, of course, is driven by rapid changes in technology, which have forced financial aid officers to continually upgrade their data-processing capabilities. The options available to the financial aid office are now enormous and expensive. For example, AFSA Data Corporation provides institutions with comprehensive loan billing and collection services. Datatel offers integrated management systems for everything from financial aid to human resources and alumni affairs. EduServ Technologies provides management systems, student billing, and financial aid services to more than 1,200 lenders and schools. PeopleSoft, KPMG Peat Marwick, and Sigma Systems all aggressively market products and services that assist campus leaders in effectively operating their loan programs.

One of the largest and most comprehensive of the financial aid consulting firms is Mitchell Sweet and Associates. It offers an extensive array of services to help campuses cope with the financial aid system. Its staff provide training and technical support to campus staff in the financial aid and controllers' offices. They publish newsletters and provide telephone hotlines to keep colleges informed about changes in the aid programs and help them solve problems. They aid in generating exception and verification reports. They even offer assistance in preparing for audits and program reviews. Without the size and complexity of the federal student aid system, it is likely that far fewer of these consulting and data-processing activities would be necessary.

THE CHALLENGE OF DIRECT LENDING

In the early 1990s, the entire system of federally guaranteed and subsidized student loans faced a drumbeat of criticism. Opponents charged that the system was unnecessarily complex and far too profitable for the student loan industry. Stephen Waldman describes the system as "so jumbled, that Rube Goldberg himself would have needed an efficiency consultant to figure it out" (Waldman 1995, 53). Lawrence Gladieux echoes that view when he states:

> If somehow we could start over, few independent observers would argue for anything much like the structure for student loans that has evolved. Layers of legislative revision, accumulated regulations, changed economic circumstances, and quick fixes under pressure have disheveled what should seemingly be a straightforward transaction. (Gladieux 1989, 36)

In the early 1990s, a different system of lending was proposed that would provide direct federal loans to students as a replacement for the guaranteed student loan program. Under "direct lending," the federal government provides capital to participating schools that would, in turn, originate student loans. The U.S. Treasury sells government securities to meet the capital requirements of the program. The Department of Education then services the loans through private sector contracts, including management of a national data system, servicing, collecting, and consolidating loans. The direct lending approach represented a fundamental challenge to the student loan industry. Across-the-board adoption of direct lending would have led to the virtual elimination of the student loan industry. There would no longer have been a need for private lenders, secondary markets, or guaranty agencies.

In 1993, in the face of strong opposition from the student loan industry, Congress enacted the William Ford Direct Loan program. But they did not eliminate the FFELP, as President Bill Clinton and many advocates of direct lending had hoped. Instead, they allowed the two programs to operate side by side. Individual campuses would be left to choose between the two. As shown in Table 4.1, direct lending has reduced the number of FFELP borrowers from about 6.5 million in 1993–94 to 5.4 million in 1996–97. While there were no direct loans in 1993–94, more than 2.7 million students were borrowing through the program in 1996–97. In those three years, the student loan industry had more than one-third of its business simply taken away.

TABLE 4.1

RECENT GROWTH IN THE COMPETING FEDERAL LOAN PROGRAMS

	1993–94		1996–97	
	Total Loan Volume (Millions)	Number of Loans	Total Loan Volume (Millions)	Number of Loans
Federal Family Education Loan Program (FFELP)	$21,177	6.5 million	$20,177	5.4 million
William Ford Direct Loan Program	—	—	$9,797	2.7 million

Source: College Board 1997, 10.

The enactment of the direct loan compromise was a major political upset for the student loan industry. How could a powerful and well-represented industry suffer such a stunning defeat on such an important issue? Certainly, President Clinton was largely responsible for pushing the reform forward. The president, working with William Ford in the House of Representatives and Paul Simon in the Senate, spent a great deal of political capital to enact the new program (Ford 1994). But he was aided by some unexpected good fortune. The lobbying clout of the student loan industry, which was used aggressively against direct lending, turned out to be more of a liability than an advantage. As Deputy Secretary of Education Madeleine Kunin described it:

> Contrary to the customary political dynamic of Washington, where the powerful usually prevail, in this case the powerful withdrew because their financial success could be interpreted as greed which made members of Congress squeamish about any linkage between their interests and the banks and Sallie Mae. (Kunin 1994, 96)

The fact that the student loan industry lost an important battle in 1993 should not be taken as an indication that it is no longer an influential player in student aid policymaking. Between 1993–94 and 1995–96, direct lending grew rapidly at the expense of the FFELP and the student loan industry. But since 1995–96, the percentage of total loan volume made by direct lending has remained stable at about 33 percent. This has created concern among supporters of direct lending, who had anticipated that the new program would quickly grow to over half of the total loan volume by 1997–98 (Burd 1997a). This slowing of growth in direct lending can be traced to two sources. First, many institutions remain concerned about the ability of the Department of Education to effectively manage the full range of activities required by the program. These schools thus feel safer waiting until the government has a proven track record before they sign on.

A second reason for the slowing growth is that the competition between the two programs has forced the student loan industry to provide better, and less expensive, services. Lenders and servicers have made great strides in speeding up the delivery of loans and reducing the number of complaints by students and institutions. In addition to improved service, many FFELP lenders now offer reduced interest rates to borrowers who repay their loans consistently. With these rebates, guaranteed loans actually cost students less than direct loans. Under its newly created Great Rewards Program, Sallie Mae reduces borrowers' interest rates by one percentage point after the first 48 scheduled payments. Borrowers who enroll in automated payment plans get an additional 0.25 percent reduction. As a consequence, several institutions that were frustrated with the performance of the student loan industry in FFELP now find it serves them well.

Direct loan supporters are sharply critical of these bonuses. They claim that the student loan industry is using tax-exempt funds to finance these discounts. Thomas Butts, associate vice-provost for university relations at the University of Michigan, argues that lenders are giving some students benefits at taxpayer expense (Burd 1997c). Phyllis Hooyman of Hope College contends that "excess profits in the student loan program should be used to benefit all students and not just a select few" (Burd 1997a). Loan industry officials counter that they are able to provide these benefits for diligent behavior because it is so much less costly to administer on-time borrowers.

ASSESSING THE INFLUENCE OF THE INDUSTRY

In assessing the influence of the student loan industry, a few things are clear. Each student loan produces a steady flow of revenue to some element of the industry from the day the loan is made until the day it is fully repaid. As such, lenders, loan servicers, secondary markets, and guaranty agencies all have a substantial financial interest in the continued expansion of the FFELP. Direct loans, on the other hand, produce no revenue for lenders, secondary markets, or guaranty agencies. Only those select companies that have a contract with the Department of Education to service direct loans make any money at all. Accordingly, the loan industry has a substantial financial stake in limiting, or even eliminating, the direct loan program.

As they seek to advance these interests, the student loan industry can exercise influence in several ways. Every aspect of the industry is organized to ensure that their voice is heard in the arenas of national policymaking. One organization that speaks directly for their interests is the Consumer Bankers Association (CBA), which represents more than 500 banks with a direct stake in the federal student aid program. To be sure, the CBA is involved in a broad spectrum of issues other than student loans, but it has a substantial financial interest in maintaining the profitability of the federal guaranteed student loan program. In addition to its own office of government relations in Washington, DC, the CBA has hired John Dean of the Washington law firm Dean, Blakey, and Moskowitz to lobby for it in student loan matters. Similarly, the National Council of Higher Education Loan Programs represents the guaranty agencies.

The influence of the student loan industry is not restricted to the direct role it plays in Washington. The thousands of lenders and servicers are spread across every congressional district in the country. Bank presidents and credit union directors serve on the boards of trustees of hundreds of colleges. They are respected civic leaders, many of whom are active in the local chambers of commerce or other community groups, and they are often generous contributors to campus capital campaigns. They are thus able to have their voices heard on campus and, in turn, to have campus leaders act as advocates for their interests in their national associations and directly in Washington policymaking.

By contributing to congressional campaigns, the industry can also ensure that the doors of policymakers remain open to them. A 1996 study by Citizen Action reported that the 100 banks that make the most guaranteed student loans contributed more than $2.3 million to lawmakers in 1995 and 1996. Many argue that these contributions are made to reward opponents of direct lending and help to ensure the continued profitability of the student loan industry. Five senators, including Alfonse D'Amato (R-NY) and Phil Gramm (R-TX), each received more than $27,000 from those banks. Five members of the House each received contributions of more than $30,000. It should be no surprise that all 10 voted in 1996 to eliminate direct lending (Burd 1996).

But how effectively the student loan industry is able to translate their interests into influence in the policy process is less clear. Certainly, the industry has a clear motive, opportunity, and the resources to advance its interests. Through their direct and indirect activities, the student loan industry has reaped substantial benefits over the years. The expansion of guaranteed student loans in the 1960, 1970s, and 1980s was accomplished by ever larger payments of public funds to the loan industry. By the early 1990s, the industry was thought to be among the most powerful actors in student aid policymaking.

Yet in 1993, the industry clearly lacked the power to fend off the enactment of direct lending. Despite an intense lobbying effort from all elements of the industry, a substantial portion of their business was taken away and given over to direct lending. Against the specter of total elimination of the FFELP, the industry was forced to slash their fees and alter their conventional patterns of operation. This is hardly evidence of an all-powerful industry. Since their dramatic defeat in 1993, however, the loan industry has struggled to regroup and find ways to reassert influence. Its efforts seem to be working. The number of colleges leaving FFELP for direct lending has slowed to a trickle. Several highly visible schools that had initially planned to switch to direct lending have opted instead to stick with FFELP (Burd 1997a). The industry continues to control two-thirds of government loans, as well as the entire alternative loan business.

Further, in 1998, the industry fared very well in a prolonged dispute about a scheduled reduction in the interest rate on direct and FFELP loans. Interest rates were reduced, but not by as much as planned, and lenders won a new government subsidy. In addition, lenders blocked the Department of Education from charging the original scheduled rate, which would have made direct loans much less expensive for students than FFELP.

But the influence of the student aid industry may not be measured simply by the portion of the student loan business they receive. The very high financial rewards at stake make it difficult for policymakers to focus on anything else. Thomas Butts, for example, argues that

> there is so much money at stake for the industry that we never get to talk about the really important issues such as the amount of debt a student should reasonably be expected to bear and whether low-income students will have the resources for college. (Babcock 1997, 6)

Indeed, today's debate over student aid policy simply assumes there will be massive borrowing. That debate focuses narrowly on such topics as the merits of direct lending, the maximum amount students should be allowed to borrow, and the proper role for the guaranty agencies. As a consequence, the more fundamental question—whether all this borrowing really serves the interests of students, colleges, and the American public—is almost never asked.

Finally, the highly charged struggle between the two loan programs can produce the false impression that full implementation of direct lending would lead to significant reduction in the scope and scale of the student aid industry. There is little to support this view. As long as the federal government writes complex regulations, campuses will continue to hire consultants to ensure that they are in compliance. As long as the campus financial aid office continues to be the main point of contact between the government and the student, aid staff will continue to need training and will require technical assistance. As such, significant segments of the student aid industry seem likely to continue to thrive, regardless of who originates, administers, and collects student loans.

REFERENCES

Babcock, C. 1997. "Majoring in Money." *Washington Post: National Weekly Edition* December 8: 6–7.

Burd, S. 1996. "Foes of Direct Lending Are Backed by Banks, Study Finds." *Chronicle of Higher Education* September 20: A35.

———. 1997a. "Despite an Apparent Cease-Fire, the Battle over Student Loans Rages On." *Chronicle of Higher Education* January 24: A19.

———. 1997b. "A Rift Forms among Loan-Guarantee Agencies." *Chronicle of Higher Education* March 18: A42.

———. 1997c. "Staying Put." *Chronicle of Higher Education* April 18: A32.

Califano, J. 1981. *Governing America*. New York: Simon and Schuster.

College Board. 1997. *Trends in Student Aid: 1987–1997*. Washington, DC: College Board.

Cronin, J. 1989. "Improving the Guaranteed Student Loan Program." In *Radical Reform or Incremental Change?* edited by L. Gladieux. Washington, DC: College Board.

Ford, W. 1994. "The Direct Student Loan Program: Acknowledging the Future." In *National Issues in Education*, edited by J. Jennings. Bloomington, IN: Phi Delta Kappa.

Gladieux, L. 1989. "The Student Loan Quandary." *Change* May/June: 35–41.

Goodling, W. 1994. "Direct Student Loans: A Questionable Public Policy Decision." In *National Issues in Education*, edited by J. Jennings. Bloomington, IN: Phi Delta Kappa.

Jenkins, S. 1991. *Lender Profitability in the Student Loan Program*. Washington, DC: U.S. Department of Education.

Kunin, M. 1994. "Student Loan Reform Act of 1993." In *National Issues in Education*, edited by J. Jennings. Bloomington, IN: Phi Delta Kappa.

McPherson, M. 1989. "Appearance and Reality in the Guaranteed Student Loan Program." In *Radical Reform or Incremental Change?* edited by L. Gladieux. Washington, DC: College Board.

Quint, M. 1983. "Sallie Mae at 10: Profitable and Competitive." *New York Times* March 20, A8.

Sallie Mae. 1997. *Annual Report: 1997*. Washington, DC: Sallie Mae.

Strauss, V. 1997. "One Student Loan Company's Profitable Experience." *Washington Post: National Weekly Edition* December 8: 8–9.

USA Group. 1997. *Annual Report 1997*. Indianapolis, IN: USA Group.

Waldman, S. 1995. *The Bill*. New York: Viking Press.

CHATER

The Changing Characteristics Of Undergraduate Borrowers

Kenneth E. Redd

Existing student loan programs have, in most cases, been quite success-ful. The scope of their assistance, however, is limited . . . College costs in this country have now spiraled to a point at which it is not just the very needy who require financial aid. Many students from middle-income families are also finding it difficult to meet the constantly increasing costs of a college education. (House Report Number 89-621, as cited in Clohan 1985)

W ith these words, Congress authorized the Guaranteed Student Loan Program (later renamed the Stafford Subsidized Loan Pro-gram) in Title IV, Part B, of the Higher Education Act of 1965. This program provides federally subsidized low-interest loans to undergradu-ate, graduate, and first-professional-degree students who attend postsecondary education institutions. Unlike most private commercial loans, these loans are guaranteed by the federal government; lenders are reimbursed for the loans if borrowers default, die, declare bankruptcy, or become disabled. Loan recipi-ents are not required to pay the interest on the loans while they are enrolled in higher education, nor do they have to undergo credit checks or use their financial assets as collateral in order to receive the funds.

In addition to Stafford loans, the Higher Education Act also authorizes the Federal Perkins Loan Program. This program provides low-interest (5 percent interest rate) loans to undergraduate and graduate/first-professional students who have exceptional financial need. The loans are administered on the campuses of participating institutions, which receive federal funds to provide the loans to students. An institution must match at least 33 percent of its federal allocation. Interest on the loans does not begin to accrue until borrowers leave their postsecondary institutions (Santiago 1997).

Lawmakers clearly intended that the loan programs help students from low- and middle-income families pay their higher education expenses. Congress also intended for recipients of these subsidized loans to have financial need for the aid. As the Senate report for the Higher Education Act of 1965 states:

> The committee believes this program provides a final line of financial defense for families and students from all levels of income . . . A family of mid-level income can utilize this source of assistance to survive . . . mishaps without crippling interruption of family life. The most essential feature is that in emergencies this credit resource can be depended on, a condition not unusually known by low- and middle-income families. (Senate Report Number 89-673, as cited in Clohan 1985)

Since 1965, rising college prices have continued to be a great concern, particularly to middle-income families. According to the U.S. Department of Education (1997a), the average tuition and fee charges at public four-year colleges and universities rose by more than 80 percent in inflation-adjusted value between 1976 and 1996, while charges at private colleges grew by 90 percent. In the same period, median family income rose by just 10 percent (U.S. Bureau of the Census 1998). The public now ranks their concerns about paying for postsecondary education with paying for health care and for the care for an elderly relative (National Commission on the Cost of Higher Education 1998).

In the 1970s and 1980s, Congress responded to these concerns by raising the maximum amounts that students could receive in the subsidized loan program and, most important, by increasing the number of students from middle-income families who were eligible to receive need-based Stafford loans. This expansion was accomplished by raising the income ceiling to qualify for the loans. In 1992, Congress further expanded access to subsidized loans; additionally, it authorized a new, non-need-based loan program, the Stafford Unsubsidized Loan Program, which made it possible for all students, regardless of their income or financial need, to receive federal student loans.

The 1992 changes in the federal loan program have led to a surge in borrowing; in four years, the amount students received under the Stafford loan programs jumped by 118 percent, from $13.5 billion in fiscal year (FY) 1993 to $29.4 billion in FY 1997 (U.S. Department of Education 1997b; 1998a). The new law also has led to eligibility changes in the income levels and financial need levels of undergraduates who are allowed to receive loans, and it has influenced the number and types of loans that are included in students' financial aid packages.

This chapter provides an overview of the recent trends in undergraduate borrowing in the federal student loan programs. It reviews some of the changes made in the processes used to determine eligibility for federal student loans and shows how these changes have affected the amounts students borrow. The chapter also reviews the changes in the income levels, financial need levels, financial aid packages, and cumulative debt of loan recipients in 1992–93 and 1995–96. The information on the borrowers' characteristics comes from the 1993 and 1996 National Postsecondary Student Aid Studies (U.S. Department of Education 1998b; 1998c).

CHANGES IN FEDERAL NEED ANALYSIS

Need analysis is the process used to determine eligibility for student financial aid. For need analysis, federal program administrators collect information on income and financial assets from students and their families to estimate the students' need for financial assistance. Financial need is the difference between students' total costs of education and their estimated family contributions (EFCs), the estimated amount students and their families can afford to pay for college. Costs, EFCs, and financial need are determined when students and their families apply for federal student aid. Need analysis is used to determine eligibility for Stafford loans, federal Perkins loans, and the other student assistance programs authorized under Title IV of the Higher Education Act.

Need analysis also is used to determine students' financial dependency status. Undergraduates who are financially *dependent* are those whose parents are expected to pay at least a portion of their costs of attending postsecondary education. *Independent* students—generally, those who are 24 years old or older, or married, or have dependents other than a spouse—are not dependent on their parents to pay any of their college costs. Independent students usually have lower income and lower EFCs than dependent students.

Throughout the history of the Stafford Subsidized Loan Program, Congress has made changes in the need-analysis system to expand access to these need-based loans by undergraduates from middle-income families. In 1965, an annual income of $15,000 was the eligibility ceiling for these loans; that is, all applicants with family income of less than $15,000 were automatically eligible for assistance. Those with income above this ceiling had to establish financial need in order to receive the loans. The 1976 reauthorization of the Higher Education Act raised the income ceiling to $25,000. Just two years later, Congress passed the Middle Income Student Assistance Act (MISAA), which removed the income ceiling entirely. Thus all students, regardless of family income or financial need, could receive the loans (Clohan 1985).

Congress hoped that MISAA would "provide renewed access to student loans for middle income families whose higher incomes by the late 1970s had placed them beyond the range of the existing need test requirements, but who were apparently finding it difficult to meet higher education costs" (Clohan 1985). However, MISAA greatly increased federal program costs. In 1981, MISAA was repealed by the Omnibus Budget Reconciliation Act, which established a financial-need test for subsidized student loan applicants whose annual income exceeded $30,000.

However, the most substantial changes in need analysis occurred with the passage of the Higher Education Act amendments of 1992. This law instituted a new need-analysis system to be used for federal student aid programs. Under the new system, called Federal Methodology (FM), all aid applicants were allowed to exclude their home and family farm equity from consideration for eligibility. The FM also included a new "simplified needs test," which allowed all applicants with income of less than $50,000 to exclude all of their families' assets from consideration (Redd 1994).

The 1992 amendments also increased the maximum amounts of subsidized loans that undergraduates could receive. The loan limit for those in their second year of study was raised from $2,625 to $3,500, and the maximum amount for those in their third years or higher grew from $4,000 to $5,500.

Additionally, the 1992 law authorized the Stafford Unsubsidized Loan Program, which replaced the Supplemental Loans for Students (SLS) Program. SLS loans had generally been limited to financially independent undergraduates and to graduate and first-professional students (Sallie Mae 1996). Dependent undergraduates who received SLS loans usually had exceptionally high financial need. Under the new Stafford Unsubsidized Loan Program, all students—regardless of their income, financial need, dependency status, or academic grade level—could be eligible. Independent borrowers were allowed to receive both unsubsidized and subsidized loans in the same academic year.[1] However, unlike the subsidized loan program, SLS and Stafford unsubsidized loan borrowers were responsible for the interest on their loans while enrolled in postsecondary education. Students could pay the interest on the loans while still in school, or they could have it capitalized (added to the principal balance of the loans, thus increasing the total debt).

RECENT TRENDS IN LOAN VOLUME AND FEDERAL GRANT AID

Members of Congress hoped the 1992 changes in the need-analysis procedure would further expand eligibility for federal financial aid programs to middle-income students (U.S. Congress 1992). Most of this expansion has come in the new Stafford Unsubsidized Loan Program. As Table 5.1 shows, from FY 1992 to FY 1996, the number of unsubsidized borrowers grew by nearly 269 percent, and the amount of loans jumped by 324 percent in inflation-adjusted value—from $2.2 billion to $9.4 billion. At the same time, the number of subsidized loan borrowers increased by just 27 percent, and the amount borrowed rose by only 35 percent. In just five years, the unsubsidized loans grew from just 15 percent of combined Stafford/SLS Loan volume to nearly 36 percent.

Table 5.1 also shows that the number of Perkins loan borrowers grew by less than 1 percent, and the amount borrowed rose by only 2 percent. Several changes made in the Perkins Loan Program during the 1990s may have made it more difficult for some institutions to continue to participate in the program, and may have caused the slow growth in borrowers. First, the federal appropriation for new Perkins loans fell by 14 percent, from $183 million in FY 1989 to $93 million in FY 1996. Second, in the 1992 Higher Education Act amendments, the institutional matching fund requirement was increased from 11 percent of federal allocations for new loans to 33 percent. And third, institutions with Perkins loan cohort default rates of 20 percent or more were assessed penalties that reduced their federal allocation (U.S. Department of Education 1998d). Due, in part, to these program changes, the number of institutions that participated in the Perkins Loan Program fell from 3,097 in FY 1989 to 2,216 in FY 1996 (U.S. Department of Education 1990; 1998d).

TABLE 5.1

NUMBER OF BORROWERS AND AMOUNTS BORROWED IN THE FEDERAL STUDENT LOAN PROGRAMS, FY 1992 TO FY 1996

	Number of Borrowers in FY 1992 (Thousands)	Number of Borrowers in FY 1996 (Thousands)	Percent Change	Amount Borrowed in FY 1992 (Millions)	Amount Borrowed in FY 1996 (Millions)	Percent Change
Perkins Loans	669	674	0.7%	$997	$1,022	2.5%
Stafford Subsidized Loans	3,103	3,940	27.0%	$12,581	$16,944	34.6%
SLS/Stafford Unsubsidized Loans*	573	2,114	268.9%	$2,207	$9,355	323.9%

* Data for FY 1992 are for the Supplemental Loans for Students (SLS) Program. Data for FY 1996 are for the Stafford Unsubsidized Loan Program. FY 1992 loan amounts are adjusted for inflation (U.S. Bureau of Labor Statistics 1998).

Sources: U.S. Department of Education 1997b, Tables 6, 7, 9, 11, pp. 30, 33, 39, 45; U.S. Department of Education 1997d, Section 1, p. 4.

While the amount of Stafford loan borrowing increased substantially, funding for federal Pell Grants, the largest federal grant program for undergraduate students, declined by 8 percent in inflation-adjusted value, from $6.1 billion in FY 1993 to $5.6 billion in FY 1996 (College Board 1997). One reason Pell Grant funding fell was that the maximum allowable grant, which is set annually by Congress, was reduced from $2,400 in FY 1992 to $2,300 in FY 1993 (U.S. Department of Education 1997c). This loss in funding likely caused more undergraduates, particularly low-income students, to borrow through the expanded Stafford loan programs.

INCOME LEVELS OF LOAN RECIPIENTS

The changes in the federal need-analysis procedure, combined with increases in loan limits and the decline in Pell Grant aid, helped boost the number of undergraduates who received federal student loans from 3.5 million in 1992–93 to 4.2 million in 1995–96. Figure 5.1 shows that the percentage of undergraduates who received federal loans rose from 19 percent in 1992–93 to 25 percent in 1995–96. The largest increase occurred in the non-need-based loan programs. In 1992–93, only 2.5 percent of undergraduates received an SLS loan, but in 1995–96, 10 percent received a Stafford unsubsidized loan. The proportion of students who received a subsidized loan grew from about 18 percent to nearly 22 percent, while the percentage who were awarded Perkins loans remained at about 3 percent.

The need-analysis changes also appear to have had a great effect on the income levels of borrowers who received federal student loans. The proportion of financially dependent undergraduate borrowers from families with adjusted gross income (AGI) [2] of $80,000 or more increased from just 2 percent of borrowers in 1992–93 to 10 percent in 1995–96 (see Table 5.2). But the proportion of financially dependent borrowers from families with AGI of less than $20,000 *fell* from nearly 31 percent to just under 23 percent, and the percentage of borrowers from families with income between $20,000 and $39,999 dropped from about 40 percent to about 28 percent.

These results indicate that the changes in need analysis helped more upper-income borrowers become eligible for federal loans. The number of borrowers from upper-income families grew faster than the number of those with lower AGI. Thus, a much greater proportion of the borrowers came from upper-income families.

Most of these new upper-income borrowers received non-need-based loans. In 1995–96, about half of all Stafford unsubsidized loan borrowers came from families with AGI of $60,000 or higher, compared with just 16 percent of subsidized loan recipients. However, the need-based loan programs also have seen increases in the proportion of dependent borrowers from upper-income families. Collectively, the proportion of borrowers from families with AGI of

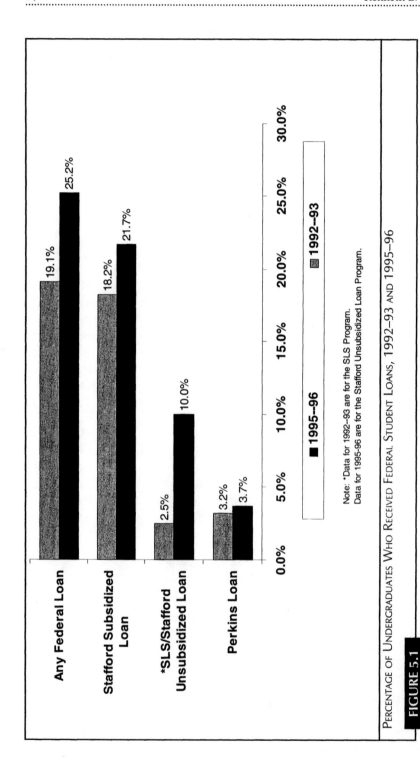

PERCENTAGE OF UNDERGRADUATES WHO RECEIVED FEDERAL STUDENT LOANS, 1992–93 AND 1995–96

FIGURE 5.1

Sources: U.S. Department of Education 1998b; 1998c.

TABLE 5.2

ADJUSTED GROSS INCOME LEVELS OF FINANCIALLY DEPENDENT UNDERGRADUATE
FEDERAL STUDENT LOAN BORROWERS, 1992–93 AND 1995–96

AGI*	1992–93**	1995–96
All Federal Student Loan Borrowers		
Less Than $20,000	30.6%	22.9%
$20,000 to $39,999	39.6%	28.2%
$40,000 to $59,999	21.3%	24.0%
$60,000 to $79,999	6.4%	14.9%
$80,000 and Over	2.1%	10.0%
Stafford Subsidized Loan Borrowers		
Less Than $20,000	30.2%	26.6%
$20,000 to $39,999	39.3%	32.1%
$40,000 to $59,999	21.7%	24.9%
$60,000 to $79,999	6.5%	11.6%
$80,000 and Over	2.2%	4.9%
Stafford Unsubsidized Loan Borrowers		
Less Than $20,000	n/a	8.0%
$20,000 to $39,999	n/a	15.9%
$40,000 to $59,999	n/a	26.1%
$60,000 to $79,999	n/a	27.4%
$80,000 and Over	n/a	22.5%
Perkins Loan Borrowers		
Less Than $20,000	32.5%	30.5%
$20,000 to $39,999	42.6%	35.0%
$40,000 to $59,999	19.2%	22.4%
$60,000 to $79,999	5.7%	8.5%
$80,000 and Over	—	3.6%

*   AGI levels are adjusted for inflation (U.S. Bureau of Labor Statistics 1998).
**   1992–93 data includes borrowers who received Supplemental Loans for Students.
n/a Not applicable; the Stafford Unsubsidized Loan Program did not begin until 1993–94.
—   Sample size is too low to generate a reliable estimate.

Sources: U.S. Department of Education 1998b; 1998c.

$60,000 or more increased from 9 percent of all dependent Stafford subsidized loan recipients in 1992–93 to 16 percent in 1995–96. At the same time, the proportion of borrowers from families with income of less than $40,000 fell from over 69 percent to about 59 percent. Similarly, the percentage of middle- and upper-income borrowers who received Perkins loans rose from about 6 percent to 12 percent, but the proportion of lower-income recipients dropped from around 75 percent to 65 percent.

The income levels of independent Stafford subsidized loan borrowers have changed very little. Table 5.3 shows that, in both 1992–93 and 1995–96, about half of the independent borrowers had annual income under $10,000, and the proportion of borrowers with income of $30,000 or more increased very little, from 11 percent to 14 percent.

Despite these trends, undergraduates who received need-based loans generally had lower income than those who received unsubsidized loans. This is especially true of Perkins loan borrowers. The $33,566 mean AGI of dependent Perkins loan borrowers was more than $3,000 lower than the mean AGI of dependent Stafford subsidized loan recipients, and about $28,000 lower than the mean AGI of those who were awarded unsubsidized loans (see Figure 5.2). The mean income of independent Perkins loans borrowers was $9,279, compared with $13,708 for subsidized and $17,856 for unsubsidized loan recipients.

TABLE 5.3

ADJUSTED GROSS INCOME LEVELS OF FINANCIALLY INDEPENDENT FEDERAL STUDENT
LOAN BORROWERS, 1992–93 AND 1995–96

AGI*	1992–93**	1995–96
All Federal Student Loan Borrowers		
Less Than $10,000	49.5%	48.0%
$10,000 to $19,999	27.3%	25.9%
$20,000 to $29,999	12.2%	11.8%
$30,000 and Over	11.0%	14.3%
Stafford Subsidized Loan Borrowers		
Less Than $10,000	50.0%	49.4%
$10,000 to $19,999	27.2%	27.0%
$20,000 to $29,999	11.7%	12.0%
$30,000 and Over	11.1%	11.7%
Stafford Unsubsidized Loan Borrowers		
Less Than $10,000	n/a	42.2%
$20,000 to $39,999	n/a	25.6%
$40,000 to $59,999	n/a	12.4%
$30,000 and Over	n/a	19.7%
Perkins Loan Borrowers		
Less Than $10,000	53.9%	65.9%
$10,000 to $19,999	24.8%	20.1%
$20,000 to $29,999	14.1%	7.9%
$30,000 and Over	7.2%	6.0%

*   AGI levels are adjusted for inflation (U.S. Bureau of Labor Statistics 1998).
**   1992–93 data includes borrowers who received Supplemental Loans for Students.
n/a   Not applicable; the Stafford Unsubsidized Loan Program did not begin until 1993–94.
—   Sample size is too low to generate a reliable estimate.

Sources: U.S. Department of Education 1998b; 1998c.

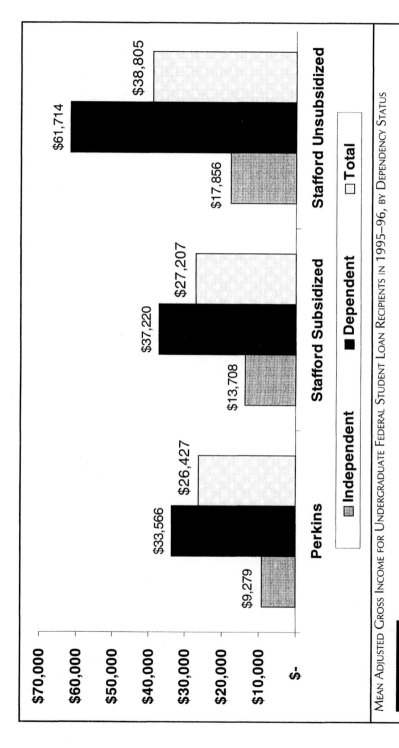

MEAN ADJUSTED GROSS INCOME FOR UNDERGRADUATE FEDERAL STUDENT LOAN RECIPIENTS IN 1995–96, BY DEPENDENCY STATUS

FIGURE 5.2

Source: U.S. Department of Education 1998c.

BORROWING COMPARED WITH FINANCIAL NEED

The changes in the 1992 Higher Education Act reauthorization clearly helped more upper-income borrowers receive need-based loans. In particular, the elimination of home equity and other assets from the need-analysis formula allowed more undergraduates from these families to qualify for need-based loans. However, the data in Table 5.4 suggest that, for some of these borrowers, the increases in their loan amounts were greater than the increases in their calculated financial need.

When adjusted for inflation, the mean amount of federal loans for dependent Stafford subsidized loan recipients from families with income of $80,000 or more increased by 18 percent, from $3,296 to $3,888, but their demonstrated financial need grew by just 5.5 percent, from $7,764 to $8,192. Borrowers from families with income between $60,000 and $79,999 also borrowed about 18 percent more; their financial need, however, increased by less than 3 percent. On the other hand, the mean amount of financial need for borrowers from low-income families rose by approximately 25 percent, but their mean amount borrowed increased by only about 17 percent.

These trends suggest that the changes in need analysis did not greatly increase upper-income borrowers' demonstrated financial need, but allowed these undergraduates to receive loans that covered a *greater share* of their estimated need. That is, the changes in need analysis, combined with the higher loan limits, likely allowed upper-income borrowers to use student loans to meet a higher percentage of their financial need.

TABLE 5.4

CHANGES IN MEAN FEDERAL STUDENT LOAN AMOUNTS AND MEAN TOTAL FINANCIAL NEED FOR FINANCIALLY DEPENDENT STAFFORD SUBSIDIZED BORROWERS, 1992–93 AND 1995–96

AGI	Mean Amount Borrowed 1992–93*	Mean Amount Borrowed 1995–96*	Percent Change	Mean Financial Need in 1992–93	Mean Financial Need in 1995–96	Percent Change
Under $20,000	$3,075	$3,609	17.4%	$9,069	$11,382	25.2%
$20,000 to $39,999	$3,157	$3,818	20.9%	$8,422	$10,285	22.1%
$40,000 to $59,999	$3,158	$3,743	18.5%	$7,762	$8,440	8.7%
$60,000 to $79,999	$3,361	$3,960	17.8%	$7,747	$7,947	2.6%
$80,000 and Over	$3,296	$3,888	18.0%	$7,764	$8,192	5.5%
All Borrowers	$3,178	$3,740	17.7%	$8,327	$9,789	17.6%

* Amounts borrowed include loans received in the Stafford Subsidized, SLS/Stafford Unsubsidized, and Perkins Loan Programs. Figures for 1992–93 are adjusted for inflation (U.S. Bureau of Labor Statistics 1998). Financial need amounts are also adjusted for students enrollment status (full-time versus part-time).

Sources: U.S. Department of Education 1998b; 1998c.

For independent students borrowing under the Stafford Subsidized Loan Program, the mean amount of federal loans grew by over 25 percent, but the mean financial need of these students increased by only about 10 percent (see Table 5.5). The inflation-adjusted need for borrowers with AGI of $30,000 or more *fell* by 3.4 percent, but the amounts they borrowed rose by more than 22 percent. The amount borrowed by all low-income independent students increased by about 27 percent, while their financial need grew by 17 percent.

TABLE 5.5

CHANGES IN MEAN FEDERAL STUDENT LOAN AMOUNTS AND MEAN TOTAL FINANCIAL NEED FOR FINANCIALLY INDEPENDENT STAFFORD SUBSIDIZED LOAN BORROWERS, 1992–93 AND 1995–96

AGI	Mean Federal Student Loan 1992–93*	Mean Federal Student Loan 1995–96*	Percent Change	Mean Financial Need in 1992–93	Mean Financial Need in 1995–96	Percent Change
Under $10,000	$3,730	$4,741	27.1%	$8,709	$10,202	17.1%
$10,000 to $19,999	$3,999	$4,759	19.0%	$7,924	$8,300	4.7%
$20,000 to $29,999	$4,059	$4,840	19.2%	$8,351	$8,569	2.6%
$30,000 and Over	$4,327	$5,283	22.1%	$7,053	$6,814	–3.4%
All Borrowers	$3,833	$4,805	25.4%	$8,356	$9,222	10.4%

* Amounts borrowed include loans received in the Stafford Subsidized, SLS/Stafford Unsubsidized, and Perkins Loan Programs. Figures for 1992–93 are adjusted for inflation (U.S. Bureau of Labor Statistics, 1998). Financial need amounts are also adjusted for students enrollment status (full-time versus part-time).

Sources: U.S. Department of Education 1998b; 1998c.

Just 7 percent of undergraduate Perkins loan borrowers in 1995–96 had financial need of less than $5,000, but 22 percent of subsidized borrowers and over 45 percent of unsubsidized loan recipients had need at this level (see Figure 5.3). Over 63 percent of Perkins loan recipients—versus 40 percent of subsidized and just 30 percent of unsubsidized borrowers—had need of $10,000 or more. The mean financial need amount for Perkins loan recipients was $12,888, versus $9,541 for subsidized and $6,814 for unsubsidized loan borrowers. This difference is accounted for, in part, by the fact that Perkins borrowers are concentrated at higher-priced four-year public and private institutions.

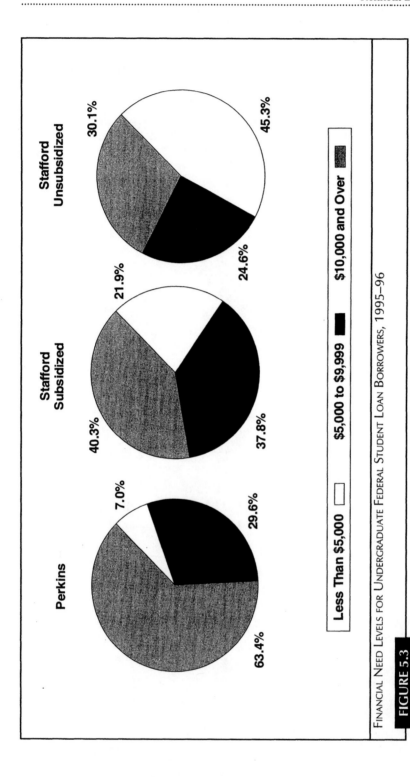

FINANCIAL NEED LEVELS FOR UNDERGRADUATE FEDERAL STUDENT LOAN BORROWERS, 1995–96

Less Than $5,000 □ $5,000 to $9,999 ■ $10,000 and Over ▨

FIGURE 5.3

Source: U.S. Department of Education, 1998c.

FINANCIAL AID PACKAGES

Student loans are generally awarded as part of a financial aid "package"; a combination of different types of aid designed to meet a student's total cost of attending a particular higher education institution. In addition to loans, the types of aid that students might receive in a financial aid package include grants, work-study,[3] and tuition waivers.[4] Financial aid packages can come in several forms, but the most typical are "grants and loans," "grants, loans, and work-study," and "loans only."

The rapid increase in borrowing, along with the decline in Pell Grant funds in the early 1990s, appears to have increased the share of undergraduate financial aid recipients who received "loans only" aid packages. The percentage of borrowers who received "loans only" packages grew from about 18 percent in 1992–93 to over 25 percent in 1995–96, while the proportion who received "grants and loans" fell from 52 percent to 48 percent (see Table 5.6). The percentage who received "grants, loans, and work-study" declined from over 13 percent to just over 11 percent.

Much of the growth in "loans only" packages was very likely due to the increasing number of financial aid applicants from upper-income families, most of whom probably were ineligible for need-based grants, but became eligible for need- and non-need-based loans. The proportion of undergraduate borrowers from families with income of $80,000 or more who received "loans only" increased from almost 33 percent to over 42 percent. The mean income of all borrowers who received loans only, when adjusted for inflation, jumped by 16 percent, from $38,643 to $44,832. The mean income of "grant, loan, and work-study" recipients rose by just 5 percent, from $29,699 to $31,112, while the mean AGI of borrowers who got "grants and loans" fell by 13 percent, from $25,354 to $22,121.

The rapid growth of borrowing also increased the share of loan recipients who were offered more than one type of loan in their aid package. Figure 5.4 shows that the proportion of undergraduate borrowers who received only a subsidized loan in their aid package fell from over 81 percent in 1992–93 to just 58 percent in 1995–96. Meanwhile, the share of borrowers who received both a subsidized and an unsubsidized loan (SLS or Stafford unsubsidized) jumped from about 14 percent to nearly 28 percent.

Perkins loan borrowers, because of their greater financial need, were even more likely to receive multiple loans in their financial aid packages. As Figure 5.5 shows, the proportion of recipients who received a Perkins loan exclusively fell from about 23 percent of the borrowers to less than 16 percent. In 1992–93, just 8 percent of the Perkins loan borrowers also received a Stafford subsidized loan and an SLS loan. In 1995–96, 7 percent received both Stafford subsidized and unsubsidized loans.

TABLE 5.6

FINANCIAL AID PACKAGES FOR FEDERAL STUDENT LOAN RECIPIENTS, 1992–93 AND 1995–96, BY ADJUSTED GROSS INCOME

AGI	Grants and Loans	Grants, Loans, and Work-Study	Loans Only	All Others
1992–93				
Less Than $20,000	64.2%	12.4%	11.2%	12.2%
$20,000 to $39,999	46.8%	16.7%	18.6%	17.9%
$40,000 to $59,999	31.3%	15.6%	31.0%	22.1%
$60,000 to $79,999	29.5%	15.0%	30.6%	24.9%
$80,000 and Over	24.2%	14.9%	32.7%	28.2%
All Borrowers	52.3%	13.2%	18.4%	16.2%
1995–96				
Less Than $20,000	64.4%	10.4%	14.3%	10.9%
$20,000 to $39,999	48.5%	13.0%	24.3%	14.3%
$40,000 to $59,999	27.3%	12.9%	39.4%	20.4%
$60,000 to $79,999	22.0%	10.3%	45.0%	22.7%
$80,000 and Over	21.7%	8.3%	42.5%	27.5%
All Borrowers	48.5%	11.1%	25.3%	15.1%

Sources: U.S. Department of Education 1998b; 1998c.

The expansion of the federal student loan programs to middle- and upper-income borrowers, and the increasing incidence of borrowers who received multiple loans, has led to higher federal student loan indebtedness. As Table 5.7 shows, the cumulative amount of federal loan debt, adjusted for inflation, increased by more than 53 percent for undergraduates who completed their degree or certificate programs in 1992–93 and 1995–96. Much of this increase was due to the rising number of upper-income borrowers. The cumulative amount borrowed by students whose families had income of $80,000 or more grew by about 50 percent, from $7,493 to $11,247. Debt for low-income borrowers rose by nearly 47 percent, while those from families with income between $40,000 and $59,999 had an increase of about 32 percent.

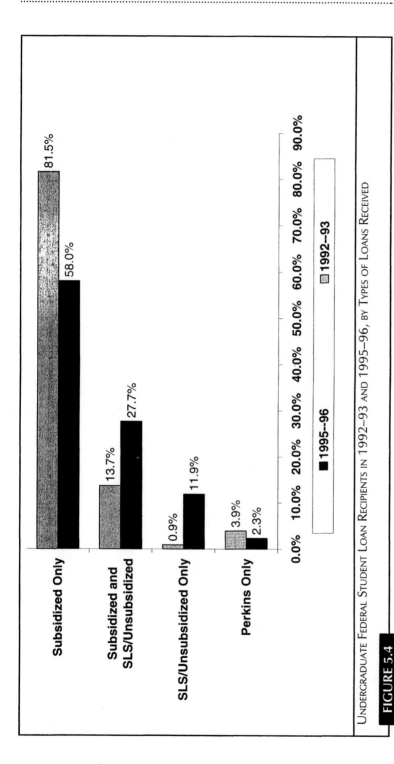

UNDERGRADUATE FEDERAL STUDENT LOAN RECIPIENTS IN 1992–93 AND 1995–96, BY TYPES OF LOANS RECEIVED

FIGURE 5.4

Sources: U.S. Department of Education 1998b; 1998c.

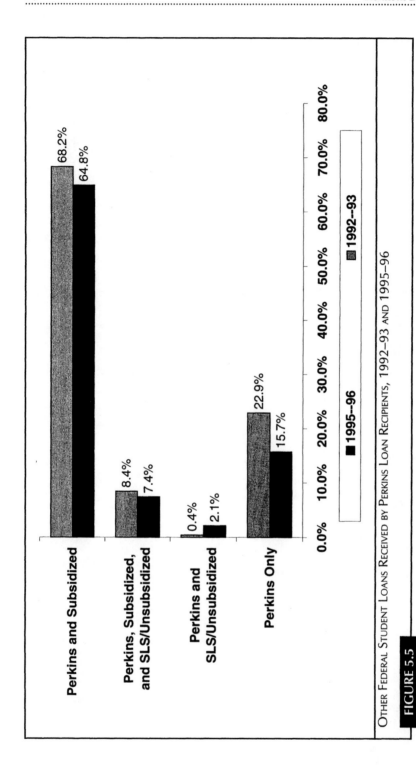

OTHER FEDERAL STUDENT LOANS RECEIVED BY PERKINS LOAN RECIPIENTS, 1992–93 AND 1995–96

FIGURE 5.5

Sources: U.S. Department of Education 1998b; 1998c.

TABLE 5.7

CUMULATIVE FEDERAL STUDENT LOAN DEBT FOR BORROWERS WHO COMPLETED
UNDERGRADUATE DEGREE OR CERTIFICATE PROGRAMS IN 1992–93 AND 1995–96

AGI	Cumulative Debt in 1992–93*	Cumulative Debt in 1995–96*	Percentage Change
Under $20,000	$8,162	$11,981	46.8%
$20,000 to $39,999	$8,958	$12,423	38.7%
$40,000 to $59,999	$8,981	$11,899	32.5%
$60,000 to $79,999	$8,367	$12,001	43.4%
$80,000 and Over	$7,493	$11,247	50.1%
All Borrowers*	$7,912	$12,120	53.2%

* Includes borrowers whose AGI was missing. Figures for 1992–93 are adjusted for inflation (U.S. Bureau of Labor Statistics 1998).

Sources: U.S. Department of Education 1998b; 1998c.

SUMMARY

Since the creation of the Stafford Subsidized Loan Program in 1965, Congress has intended for the funds to provide financial assistance to postsecondary students from low- and middle-income families. However, the changes in need analysis instituted in 1992 have allowed a greater number of upper-income borrowers to receive these need-based loans.

From 1992–93 to 1995–96, the proportion of undergraduate subsidized loan recipients from families with income of $60,000 and above increased from about 9 percent of all financially dependent borrowers to 16 percent, while the proportion from families with income below $40,000 fell from 69 percent to 59 percent. These changes occurred because the new need-analysis system made many more upper-income borrowers qualify as "financially needy." The elimination of home equity and other assets from the need-analysis formula, combined with the increases in postsecondary education costs, made more upper-income borrowers eligible for need-based federal loans. As a result, many borrowers from families with income of $80,000 or more who would not have qualified for Perkins or Stafford subsidized loans in 1992–93 were eligible in 1995–96.

While Congress intended for the need-based loan programs to meet students' financial need, the rate of increase in the average amounts awarded to upper-income borrowers was far *greater* than the rate of increase in their demonstrated financial need. Upper-income dependent students received, on average, 18 percent more in subsidized federal student loans, but their calculated financial need increased by just 5 percent. This does not mean that upper-income borrowers received loans that were greater than their financial need. However, the results indicate that the changes in the need-analysis formula allowed more middle- and upper-income borrowers to meet a greater proportion of their need with loans.

The expansion of eligibility for subsidized loans and the introduction of non-need-based unsubsidized loans has also led to a rise in the proportion of undergraduate borrowers with financial aid packages that contained loans exclusively. In 1992–93, about 18 percent of all undergraduate borrowers received a "loans only" aid package. In 1995–96, approximately 25 percent received "loans only." Much of this increase was due to the large rise in upper-income borrowers, many of whom may not have qualified for need-based grants but were eligible for subsidized or unsubsidized loans.

The changes in the need-analysis calculation and in the loan programs themselves have contributed to a large increase in cumulative federal student loan debt. Borrowers from families with income of $80,000 or more graduated from their postsecondary education institutions in 1995–96 with, on average, 50 percent more debt than undergraduates in the same income category had in 1992–93. Many of these borrowers probably owed even more than these figures show, since a number of them probably received unsubsidized loans, and they likely capitalized the accrued interest.

Borrowers from low-income families graduated with nearly 47 percent more in student loan debt. Stagnant appropriations for Pell Grants during the early 1990s, combined with the increases in Stafford loan limits, may have caused these low-income students to borrow more. Low-income borrowers probably were even more likely to receive multiple loans in their aid packages.

Thus, the changes in need analysis have led to large increases in borrowing for undergraduates at all income levels, but these increases have occurred for two different reasons. More upper-income borrowers became eligible for need-based and non-need-based loans, and many of these borrowers apparently received larger loan amounts even though their demonstrated financial need did not increase significantly. At the same time, low-income borrowers received larger subsidized and unsubsidized loans to make up for the loss of federal grants. Because college costs continue to rise while Pell Grants, when adjusted for inflation, remain flat, it is likely that these trends will continue for the foreseeable future.

NOTES

1. The cumulative amount of Stafford subsidized and unsubsidized loans that a borrower may receive for undergraduate study is $46,000.

2. Adjusted gross income (AGI) is the amount of income reported to the Internal Revenue Service when the aid applicants file their federal income tax returns. The AGI amounts reported for academic year 1992–93 are from calendar year 1991, and income amounts reported for 1995–96 are from calendar year 1994.

3. Work-study programs provide part-time jobs to postsecondary education students. The major work-study program, the federal work-study program, provided $764 million in employment earnings to undergraduate and graduate/first-professional students in 1995–96.
4. Other types of aid include tuition reimbursement from employers and research assistantships.

REFERENCES

Clohan, W. C. 1985. *The Guaranteed Student Loan Program: Overview, History, Policy Issues, and Recommendation for Reauthorization.* Arlington, VA: Consumer Bankers Association.

College Board. 1997. *Trends in Student Aid, 1987 to 1997.* Washington, DC: College Board.

National Commission on the Cost of Higher Education. 1998. *Straight Talk about College Costs and Prices.* Phoenix, AZ: The Oryx Press.

Redd, K. E. 1994. *The Effects of Higher Education Loan Limits and Need Analysis Changes on FFELP Borrowing in Pennsylvania, July to December 1992 to 1993.* Harrisburg, PA: Pennsylvania Higher Education Assistance Agency.

Sallie Mae. 1996. *1996 Factbook for Investors and Analysts.* Washington, DC: Sallie Mae, Inc.

Santiago, D. A. 1997. *Higher Education: Campus-Based Programs.* Washington, DC: Congressional Research Service Report Number 96-831 EPW.

U.S. Bureau of the Census. 1998. *Measuring 50 Years of Economic Change Using the March Current Population Survey.* Washington, DC: U.S. Department of Commerce, Bureau of the Census, Current Population Report Number P60–203.

U.S. Bureau of Labor Statistics. 1998. *Consumer Price Index—All Urban Consumers.* U.S. Bureau of Labor Statistics Web site <http://www.bls.gov/>.

U.S. Congress. 1992. *Congressional Record, House.* Statements by Congressman Louis Stokes (D-OH) and Congressman Timothy J. Penny (D-PA), 8 July 1992, 2138, 2142.

U.S. Department of Education. 1990. *1990 Campus-Based Programs Data Book.* Washington, DC: U.S. Department of Education.

U.S. Department of Education, National Center for Education Statistics. 1997a. *Digest of Education Statistics, 1997.* Washington, DC: U.S. Department of Education.

U.S. Department of Education. 1997b. *Federal Student Loan Programs Data Book, FY94–FY96.* Washington, DC: U.S. Department of Education.

———. 1997c. *1996–97 Title IV Federal Pell Grant Program End of Year Report.* Washington, DC: U.S. Department of Education.

———. 1998a. *FY 1997 Loan Volume Update.* U.S. Department of Education Web site <http://www.ed.gov/offices/OPE/PPI/>.

———. 1998b. *1993 National Postsecondary Student Aid Study, Undergraduate Data Analysis System Dataset.* Washington, DC: National Center for Education Statistics.

———. 1998c. *1996 National Postsecondary Student Aid Study, Undergraduate Data Analysis System Dataset.* Washington, DC: National Center for Education Statistics.

———. 1998d. *1998 Campus-Based Programs Data Book.* Washington, DC: U.S. Department of Education.

PART TWO

• • • • • • • • • • •

How Financing
A College Education
Is Changing

CHAPTER 6

The New Politics of Higher Education

A. Clayton Spencer

INTRODUCTION

I n the 1997 State of the Union Address, President Bill Clinton named as his "number one priority," the "greatest step of all," the "high threshold of the future we now must cross," "to ensure that all Americans have the best education in the world" (U.S. Congress 1997b). The year before, education had surfaced for the first time in national polls as the number-one issue of concern to voters—slightly ahead of crime and the economy, solidly ahead of health care and good jobs, and well ahead of foreign policy (Benedetto 1996). In the summer of 1997, Congress passed, and the president signed into law, the Taxpayer Relief Act of 1997, which contained a smorgasbord of tax benefits aimed at higher education and estimated to cost $41 billion over five years. At the same time, Congress began the process of reauthorizing the Higher Education Act—the legislation that governs the yearly flow of over $40 billion in federal grants and loans to an estimated five million students at the nation's 7,000 colleges, universities, community colleges, and vocational and trade schools.

In political terms, these would seem to be "boom times" for higher education. But a closer look reveals that education's newfound political popularity may well come at a price. Federal higher education policy—and policymaking—are in the midst of subtle but profound changes that go to the essence of the federal government's relationship to American higher education. Charles Schulz's Snoopy captured it about as well as anyone: "I love humanity, it's people I can't stand." Today, the public and political leaders love "education"—it's colleges and universities they can't stand.

To borrow a term from political scientist Hugh Heclo, higher education finds itself in the grip of a "legitimacy paradox," in which education is receiving unprecedented public and political attention, but the institutions that provide it are subject to widespread mistrust (Heclo forthcoming).[1] Polls show that a solid majority of Americans believe that a college education is so important that they would send their children regardless of price. An even larger majority, however, believe that colleges do not charge a fair price, do not do all they can to control price, and could cut tuition without lowering academic quality. Eighty percent of Americans believe that colleges make a profit (Ikenberry and Hartle 1998). Public confidence in the people running universities and colleges has declined by half in the last 30 years—from 61 percent in 1966 to 30 percent in 1996 (Nye, Zelikow, and King 1997, 212). Just as most of our recent presidents and many members of Congress run "against Washington," thus capitalizing on the widespread mistrust of government, so many in Congress today, while embracing education as an issue, in effect "run against" colleges and universities as institutions.

This chapter argues that higher education's legitimacy paradox is a reflection of forces—the rise of technology and media, the expense of campaigns and political advocacy, and the decline of party politics—that are transforming American politics at large. The discussion is intentionally schematic in order to highlight the structural implications of political and policy developments that otherwise may be viewed as simply evolutionary.

In a recent essay, "The Politics of Mistrust," political scientist Richard Neustadt catalogs the characteristic features of contemporary politics as

> the pervasiveness of polls, the commercialism of television, the lobbyists and staffs in swarms, the constituents on jets, the readiness of those who vote to split their ballots (or stay home), along with court decisions that promote the sovereignty of money. All these, I do not doubt, are heightened by the swagger of consultants and the righteousness of journalists, wrapped in their First Amendment. (Nye, Zelikow, and King 1997, 200–201)

These forces combine to erode capacity for the serious work of legislating, for building consensus and maintaining the durable coalitions necessary to sustain coherent policymaking over time.

Although these phenomena have been converging for some time, in the realm of higher education policy and politics they have remained masked to a great extent. The 1998 reauthorization of the Higher Education Act was largely "status quo," and the economic boom and resulting positive budget and revenue picture have permitted continued funding of the traditional array of popular higher education programs. Beneath the apparent continuity, however, higher education policymaking in Washington is being transformed at the structural level.

The congressional authorizing committees that have historically driven the development of higher education legislation primarily—even exclusively—are finding themselves marginalized in the face of political agendas that find their legislative homes in budget and tax-writing committees. Certain of the core substantive values that have animated federal higher education policy from its earliest days are progressively being emptied of content, replaced, or simply discarded. And the interaction of these changes in process and substance threaten to erode long-held commitments about the limited role of the federal government in higher education.

OLD POLICY

Government Role: Limited and Instrumental

The basic architecture of federal higher education policy has been relatively consistent—and exhaustively documented—for the three decades since passage of the Higher Education Act of 1965. It proceeds from the premise that the federal government will play a limited and enabling, rather than a direct and operational, role in the higher education enterprise. It is an article of faith that we have a vibrant and diverse "system" of universities, colleges, and vocational training programs, public and private, existing in the 50 states; that that system is a crucial engine of individual opportunity and national strength; and that it is the distinctive role of the federal government to remove barriers to the opportunities the system provides.

Content: Access, Choice, and Portability

Federal higher education policy aims to promote educational opportunity, defined in terms of access and choice, through the instrumentality of portable, need-based student aid. *Access* describes the goal of ensuring that no American is denied the opportunity to attend some kind of college, university, or vocational training program by reason of inability to pay. *Choice* describes the goal of giving students reasonable alternatives from which they can choose the setting that best meets their needs, talents, and aspirations (McPherson and Schapiro 1997, 2). *Portability* refers to the means by which we have chosen to pursue those goals—namely, through need-based grants and loans provided to individual students who carry that aid with them to the institutions they choose to attend. In conceptual terms, need-based student aid is the opposite of direct operational support to institutions provided by state legislatures or private giving, although in practice it functions alongside such support as one component in the higher education financing system.

A central feature of federal student aid is the partnership between the government and colleges and universities in administering the system. A student becomes eligible for federal student aid upon enrollment in a college or university certified to participate in the federal student aid program. The amount of aid that student receives is determined through a process called *need analysis*, in which the financial resources of the student and his or her family are measured against the price of attending the specific institution the student has chosen. Federal student aid dollars, in the form of grants and loans, are then "packaged" with other sources of financing—the family's own funds; grants from the institution itself; loans from private lenders, if necessary—to meet the full price of attendance. Throughout this process, the college's financial aid staff guide and advise students, and ultimately decide on the amount and composition of a given student's "package" of student aid.

This tidy recitation, of course, conceals considerable complexity and inconsistency in federal student aid programs, and it suggests a deliberateness and ideological clarity hardly characteristic of the "creakily Madisonian" (Nye, Zelikow, and King 1997, 187) legislative process that has actually delivered our higher education policy since World War II. In fact, the federal student aid system owes more to the American Legion—and the GI Bill it conceived and fought for after World War II—than to the designs of higher education experts (Skocpol 1997).

The GI Bill achieved by accident what generations of education policymakers might never have accomplished on purpose—an approach to federal student aid that, by lodging educational choice squarely with the individual, reinforced the highly differentiated, market-driven system that is the hallmark of American higher education. Although the Servicemen's Readjustment Act of 1944 was designed as a better way to structure veterans benefits (and to keep returning GIs temporarily out of the labor market)—not as a better way to get Americans to college—the GI Bill shaped American higher education in a profound and enduring way. Armed with the means to pay for college, individual veterans not only could go to college, they could go far afield and choose the best institution to which they could gain admission. Because GI Bill stipends were a veterans benefit—an alternative to the cash bonuses of earlier eras—they were naturally directed to *individuals*; namely, those who had earned them through service in World War II. In short, GI benefits were necessarily portable, and they provided their recipients with unprecedented access and choice in higher education.

The Higher Education Act of 1965 codified these principles—this time not as a reward for meritorious service, but as a weapon in the War on Poverty. When he signed the Higher Education Act into law on November 8, 1965, President Lyndon Johnson explained that the act was designed to "swing open a new door for the young people of America—the most important door that will ever open—the door to education." With the benefit of the legislation, Johnson avowed, "a high school senior anywhere in this great land of ours can apply to any college or any university in any of the 50 states and not be turned away because his family is poor" (Johnson 1965). The Higher Education Act defined in a remarkably durable way both the purpose and the instrumentalities of federal higher education policy: to remove economic barriers to educational opportunity through student aid, which from the beginning took the form of grants, loans, and work-study.[2]

Process: Insider Policymaking

The substantive consistency of federal higher education policy—in terms of purposes, instrumentalities, and the role of government—has been matched by a continuity of process, extending over two decades, from the beginning of the 1970s to the beginning of the 1990s. That process has been determined largely by the national political calendar—"the rhythm of congressional and presidential elections, the yearly budgetary cycle, the sessions of Congress and the expiration dates of statutes" (Gladieux and Wolanin 1976, 258). In particular, the development of higher education policy has been punctuated by periodic reauthorizations of the Higher Education Act, which have occurred at intervals over the last 30 years—in 1968, 1972, 1976, 1980, 1986, 1992, and 1998.

Typically, higher education reauthorization has been an insiders' game—the province of the congressional authorizing committees of jurisdiction and their staffs, relevant executive branch officials, the One Dupont Circle lobbying organizations, student loan industry advocates, policy experts, and a selection of influential college presidents. In their detailed case study of the reauthorization of 1972, Gladieux and Wolanin explained, for example, that the question of how to channel federal support for higher education that dominated reauthorization was simply not a "salient public issue," though to the interested parties "it was an issue of considerable significance" (Wolanin and Gladieux 1976, 36). Polling numbers tend to confirm this assessment. In three Gallup Polls in 1971, education ranked 10th and 12th among the problems identified, mentioned by only 1 to 2 percent of the public (Wolanin and Gladieux 1976, 256).

NEW POLITICS

Process: The Permanent Campaign

That was then. Now, arguably, the situation is reversed. Education currently seems to have more salience as a public issue than as a policy or legislative priority. With the booming economy, the end of the Cold War, and the demise of a comprehensive legislative strategy for health care, education has emerged as the top issue of voter concern, attracting, not surprisingly, a phalanx of wannabe "education" governors, senators, representatives, and presidential candidates. Meanwhile, reauthorization of the Higher Education Act, which previously defined education policymaking, was almost an afterthought in the 105th Congress. Forced to queue up behind education tax benefits and the National Commission on the Cost of Higher Education in the sequence of legislative priorities, the 1998 reauthorization was dominated by housekeeping and minor tinkering—purging the act of programs that have never been funded and reordering remaining titles and sections; making small modifications in need analysis, Pell Grants, and campus-based programs; and adjusting operational aspects of the student loan program.

The process that now seems to be driving higher education policymaking is in no small part the work of a—some would say *the*—master of "new politics," President Bill Clinton. Clinton learned as governor of Arkansas that education is a winning issue, and he honed his techniques for pursuing it. Journalist and biographer David Maraniss (1995) documents how Clinton used education as his "comeback issue" to regain the governorship of Arkansas in 1983. His new modus operandi was the "permanent campaign."

According to Maraniss, Clinton's permanent campaign comprised three basic tenets. First, means and ends—pragmatism and idealism—had to be completely interwoven. Substantive policy was never to be pursued independent of political calculations. Second, the free media would not be relied on to get Clinton's message out—they tended to report the negatives. Instead, paid media, commercials, and grassroots mailings were to be used, even during the midterm legislative session. Third, voters were to be surveyed in a perpetual fashion. According to Maraniss:

> The goal was to discover more than whether voters supported or opposed an initiative. Word by word, line by line, phrase by phrase, paragraph by paragraph, rhetorical options would be tested to see which ones were most effective in moving the public in a certain direction. (Maraniss 1995, 408)

Relying on these techniques to, among other things, play the public off against the teacher unions, Governor Clinton won passage of a comprehensive education reform package in November 1983, which included a competency test for teachers that was despised by the unions. A decade later, President Clinton would arrive in Washington armed with an education agenda extending from cradle to grave—the expansion of Head Start for preschoolers, Goals 2000 School Reform, Revision of the Elementary and Secondary Education Act, School to Work, Student Loan Reform, and National Service. With a Democratic Congress and the momentum of a new presidency, Clinton won enactment of all of these programs by the close of the 104th Congress in 1994.[3]

Of course, importing an education strategy from the state to the national level is not necessarily a straightforward proposition. States have direct operational responsibility for, and control over, elementary, secondary, and public higher education. As noted, the federal role has traditionally been more limited. After all, the federal government foots only 7 percent of the bill for public elementary and secondary education, and only 10 percent for higher education.

In the era of "new politics," however, such practical constraints do not count for much. In a 1995 paper, "Fundamental Assumptions Underlying the Principles and Policies of Federal Financial Aid to Students," Bruce Johnstone laments the absence of discipline in policy discussions concerning higher education. Having named as the first principle of federal higher education policy that "higher education is the province of the states, not the federal government," he goes on to explain that

> This point, like most that follow, might seem glaringly obvious. And yet, far too much of the time at this and dozens of other national conferences and congressional hearings will be taken up fussing about the proper workings of institutions that are simply not the federal government's to run—or even, other than the very important provision of financial aid to students and the support of basic research, the business of the federal government. (Johnstone 1995, 77)

What Johnstone ascribes to the conceptual sloppiness of policy types gathered around a conference table may instead reflect one of the symptoms of "new politics" as described by political scientist Hugh Heclo. According to Heclo, one aspect of the permanent campaign approach to governance is the "national perception of a universal realm for public policy," and the ascription to some government intent, or failure, any social result in sight. Thus:

> Abortion, crime, drugs, education, employment, health care, homelessness, and so on down a long list . . . are all considered subjects for the national government to do (or stop doing) something about, as a matter of course. . . . Since everything on such a list relates to everything else, the realm of policy knows no conceptual bounds. (Heclo forthcoming)

When political agendas are set by perpetual polling and the national media, rather than by the systematic consensus-building required for legislation, politics tends to tap into the undifferentiated fears, aspirations, or anxieties of the public without regard to whether there is an appropriate role for government, in particular the federal government, on a given issue. Thus, Clinton's education agenda, while encompassing some traditional legislative imperatives such as student loan reform and reauthorizations of expiring acts, has also concerned itself with issues that have not in the past been the subject of

federal attention—school uniforms, parent involvement, character education, early brain development, and setting curricular standards. Likewise,
politicians from both parties offered amendments to the 1998 reauthorization
of the Higher Education Act that, had they been enacted, would have reached
into central curricular and cocurricular concerns of colleges and universities.
These amendments would have regulated the number of "contact hours"
between freshmen and full professors at research institutions, the right of
students to join sororities or fraternities, and the menu of athletics offered by
colleges and universities.

The tendency of the permanent campaign to put politically popular priorities ahead of legislating has been exacerbated in the last four years by the
arrival of new members of Congress and new staff who lack experience in
education policymaking. When the Republicans gained control of the House
in 1994 for the first time in 40 years, they (quite appropriately) restructured
and renamed the House committee and subcommittees responsible for education and replaced almost all the veteran education staffers, some of whom had
served on the education subcommittees for more than 20 years. In the Senate,
the change was significant, though less dramatic, because the staffing ratios
are less skewed toward the majority and control of the Senate had shifted back
and forth more often.

Although a shake-up in House leadership and staffing was doubtless long
overdue, overnight, the transition wiped out Congress's institutional memory
and expertise in the domain of higher education. Paradoxically, this "institutional lobotomy" has not, so far, radicalized education policymaking in Congress. On the contrary, it may have been the single most important factor in
ensuring a minimalist reauthorization in 1998. With only two years and one
Congress between the assumption of House leadership and the beginning of
the reauthorization process, the learning curve for new members and staff was
far too steep to permit a strategic or innovative approach to higher education
legislation. The vacuum was not filled by the Department of Education, which
despite an unprecedented continuity of leadership and the luxury of a second
term, failed in the 105th Congress to push for any comprehensive revisions in
the Higher Education Act. Finally, having lived through the budget-cutting
threats of the 104th Congress, colleges and universities and their Washington
lobbyists encouraged the status quo approach, fearing that change might
result in a direct assault on the equity principle, fewer student aid programs,
and diminished funding.

Content: The Rise of Symbolic Politics

In their detailed analysis of the 1972 Higher Education Act reauthorization,
Gladieux and Wolanin (1976) describe the counterintuitive approach of the
Nixon administration. Although the act was a product of Great Society

liberalism, designed first and foremost to aid the poor, it won both support and increased funding from the White House. A former Nixon staffer, Senator Daniel Patrick Moynihan, explained the paradox as follows:

> In a steady succession of legislative messages he [President Nixon] proposed to spend more money for the direct provision of the needs of low-income groups than any president in history. Early on an almost schizophrenic style took hold of his Administration. Symbolic rewards were devised for "middle America," while legislative proposals were drafted for the "other America." (Moynihan 1973, 155)

The dichotomy between symbolic rhetoric designed for the middle class, who vote, and actual legislation designed to aid poor people, who don't vote, is a familiar theme in American politics. Certainly, it has been a constant in the politics of higher education since the passage of the original Higher Education Act in 1965.

Until now. In the world of new politics, symbolic rewards, seamlessly conveyed though the symbolizing medium of television, predominate over the hard work of legislating, which depends on building durable coalitions and forging consensus around long-term goals. In short, the schizophrenia described by Moynihan is increasingly being replaced by monomania, in which symbolic politics drives, and ultimately becomes one with, the legislative agenda.

MIDDLE-CLASS DRIFT

The "fake right, move left" tactic described by Moynihan and the present tendency for symbolic politics to supplant policy are different in kind. That difference, however, has been obscured over the last two decades by the gradual but relentless drift of federal student aid policy toward middle-class concerns.

The great achievement of the Higher Education Act of 1965 was the creation of the first federal scholarship program for undergraduates, which was awarded based on "exceptional financial need" and designed to promote broad access to higher education. The loan insurance program, also contained in the act, was a sop to the middle class, designed to counter mounting support in Congress for a tuition tax credit for parents with children in college (Gladieux and Hauptman 1995, 14). In 1978, an off year in the reauthorization cycle, President Jimmy Carter and congressional Democrats again faced rising anxiety about the burden of college costs on middle-class families and a resulting resurgence of congressional support for a tuition tax credit. They responded by introducing the Middle Income Student Assistance Act (MISAA), which expanded eligibility for Pell Grants and opened subsidized guaranteed loans to all students, regardless of need (a move that was reversed under President Ronald Reagan in 1981).[4]

Having expanded student aid eligibility to address middle-class—i.e., voter—concerns, Congress refused to retrench when, under President Reagan, student aid funding was slashed in the early 1980s. In fact, Congress continued to expand middle-class eligibility for student aid programs through the 1992 reauthorization, with no commensurate expansion of funding. The purchasing power of the Pell Grants thus declined dramatically: they lost 40 percent of their value between 1976 and 1996 after accounting for inflation, and they paid a diminishing share of the cost of attendance at both public and private institutions. Furthermore, the balance in federal student aid programs shifted increasingly from a reliance on grants to a reliance on loans. In the mid-1970s, approximately three-quarters of federal student aid took the form of grants, and one-quarter was in loans. Twenty years later, the reverse is true.

As college costs outpaced inflation and increases in family income throughout the 1980s and into the 1990s, the student loan program provided a convenient means for Congress to assuage middle-class concerns about affordability. While lamenting the shift in student aid from grants to loans, Congress in fact raised loan limits and made it easier for middle-income families to qualify for student aid. In 1992, Congress eliminated farm and home equity from the formula used to determine the parental contribution to college costs, raised loan limits to increase the amount that some students could borrow, and created the unsubsidized loan program (the government does not pay interest on the loan while the student is in school), for which students are not required to demonstrate need. The cumulative effect of these changes has been to diminish greatly the effectiveness of federal student aid as a targeted program directed to the neediest students.

THE SHIFT TO AFFORDABILITY

If 1980–92 was a period of "middle-class drift" in higher education policy, the years since then have seen a purposeful embrace of middle-class concerns. In three successive high-profile initiatives, the president and Congress have increasingly promoted "affordability" of college for middle-class families—as distinct from access for low-income students—as the number-one concern of federal higher education policy. This priority reflects public sentiments. While polls show that in elementary and secondary education, the overwhelming concern is the quality of public schools, in higher education quality seems to be assumed, and cost is the concern (Benedetto 1996).

One problem with an agenda directed at affordability is expense. Even if federal support is modest on a per-student or per-family basis, the costs of spreading benefits across the vast middle class are significant—as demonstrated by the education tax benefits, which cost $41 billion over five years. Compounding this problem, President Clinton entered office determined to eliminate the deficit and balance the budget, goals shared by Republicans when they assumed leadership of Congress in 1994. The challenge for President Clinton and congressional Democrats, joined ultimately by the Republican Congress, was to find ways to address the issue of college affordability without spending scarce discretionary funds.

Direct Lending

The first solution came in the form of President Clinton's direct lending proposal—a piece of legislation that actually saved money under the arcane rules of the federal budget. Direct loans are an alternative to bank-based student loans in which the federal government provides funds directly to students through their colleges and universities. Under this program, the federal government replaces banks as the providers of capital, guaranty agencies as guarantors of the loan, and secondary markets as loan purchasers and servicers. Although President Clinton proposed the program as a wholesale replacement for the bank-based guaranteed student loan program, Congress, in the Student Loan Reform Act of 1993, adopted a more conservative approach, proposing a gradual phase-in of direct lending over five years and the maintenance of the guaranteed student loan program. In 1998, with the phase-in period complete, direct lending accounted for approximately one-third of student loan volume.

Student loan reform had been a central legislative and policy concern in federal student aid for some time. Not surprisingly, however, it was billed by the Clinton administration chiefly as a means of promoting college affordability. In remarks before Illinois high school students the spring before direct lending was enacted, President Clinton (1993a) explained that "my generation owes it to you to give you the chance to be able at afford to get a good college education." To a Cleveland civic group, Clinton (1993c) claimed that the direct student loan program would "open the doors of college education to *all* Americans." To a New Hampshire college graduating class, he cited direct lending as one of several education proposals that "would restore the sense of optimism to middle-class America" (Clinton 1993b).

The introduction of direct lending brought much-needed competition to the student loan industry, resulting in lower fees and better service for students in both programs. The legislation also lowered up-front loan fees for students and offered various repayment options designed to benefit students who do not enter high-paying jobs. These included permitting students to spread payments over a longer period or elect a payment schedule tied to income. While these were important benefits, they hardly addressed in any fundamental way the issue of college affordability. Further, these changes came in the loan programs, not the grant programs, meaning that they did not materially reduce the net cost to students of attending college. In short, the Student Loan Reform Act of 1993 introduced critically important operational changes in the student loan programs that without question benefit students directly, but it is a stretch to suggest that it "opened the doors of college" to students who otherwise would not enroll.

The Student Aid Battles of the 104th Congress

Upon assuming leadership in 1994, the Republican Congress handed President Clinton and congressional Democrats their next opportunity to highlight the issue of college affordability without expending new funds. When Republicans took over Congress, their number-one priority was to achieve a balanced budget. When they introduced their budget proposal in the spring of 1994, it contained significant cuts in the mandatory side of the budget that funds entitlements, including student loans, as well as across-the-board cuts in discretionary spending that funds all other student aid programs. These cuts, extending over seven years, were designed to eliminate the deficit, achieve a balanced budget on a yearly basis, and fund a huge tax cut, estimated to cost over $280 billion over seven years. Nothing was spared—including education.

The initial Republican budget proposed an $18 billion cut in the student loan program, through the elimination of the in-school interest subsidy targeted on the neediest students. It likewise proposed a one-third cut in discretionary programs that would have reduced funding in all student grant programs unless they were specifically exempted. The White House and congressional Democrats immediately attacked this plan as picking the pockets of students to fund tax cuts for the wealthiest Americans. Joining with several student groups, higher education lobbying groups formed the Alliance to Save Student Aid, a "grassroots" campaign whose rallying cry was, "Stop the raid on student aid." In a departure from its typical, conservative lobbying style, the higher education community embraced the techniques of "new politics." It hired a Republican public relations firm to conduct polling and focus groups to calibrate public understanding of, and support for, student aid (Cook 1998).[5] It then devised a media strategy, complete with press kits and press conferences, targeted particularly on Republican House members. The alliance paid for newspaper ads, radio spots, and a toll-free telephone number that students could use to contact their congressional representatives. The campaign also encouraged student activism, which culminated in several hundred students packing the hearing room of the Senate Labor and Human Resources Committee when it met to vote on the higher education portion of the Republican budget.[6]

Facing continued pressure from students, colleges, and their lobbying associations, Republicans ultimately realized that they had miscalculated the force of public support for student aid. By the end of the 104th Congress, Republicans and Democrats were engaged in a bidding war for education funding that resulted in a 1996 budget with no significant cuts in the student loan program, a $130 increase in the maximum Pell Grant award, and modest increases in total funding for other higher education programs. The result was a major political victory for the president and congressional Democrats on education—on the cheap. They simply forced Congress to put back money the programs had in the first place.

The Taxpayer Relief Act of 1997

In the final triumph of symbolic politics over traditional student aid, President Clinton took advantage of Republican tax-cut proposals to highlight the issue of college affordability in a much more mainstream way. Between the Republican electoral victory in November 1994 and their assumption of the reins of Congress in January 1995, President Clinton delivered a televised address to lay out his plan for a "Middle Class Bill of Rights," comprising a series of tax benefits to help families paying, among other things, for child care and college. The Republicans had put close to $300 billion "on the table" with their tax-cutting proposals aimed at lowering the tax rate on capital gains and other income enjoyed by affluent Americans.

Departing from precedents set by both President Nixon and President Carter, instead of opposing the tax cut, President Clinton hijacked it. Claiming that the Republican tax cut was both too large and misdirected, Clinton proposed an alternative tax cut, including a $10,000 tuition tax deduction for families with students in college, that was both smaller and more targeted. His plan was estimated to cost $110 billion over six years, and it was directed at specific purposes, including paying for college. To fend off criticism that the proposal benefited middle- and upper-middle-class Americans at the expense of the poor, Clinton was careful to couple with his tax proposals a call for an increase in the maximum Pell Grant to $3,000. It is worth noting that the Pell Grant was worth $3,800 in 1976 if inflation is factored in.

The tax proposals died with the budget of 1995 but were revived and enhanced in the presidential election year of 1996. President Clinton added the Hope tax credit of $1,500 for the first two years of postsecondary education, and the Republicans, having learned their lesson on student aid, added additional benefits, such as a deduction for student loan interest during the repayment period, and various measures, such as education IRAs and other incentives, directed at stimulating saving for college. In a reprise of the student aid bidding war of 1996, all of these provisions, and more, found their way into the Taxpayer Relief Act, passed with overwhelming bipartisan support and signed into law in August 1997.

Tax purists condemned the education benefits as too targeted. In their view, these tax breaks are thinly disguised grant programs that will add further complexity to the tax code. Student aid purists condemned them as too diffuse, because they will go disproportionately to families in the upper-income brackets who would send their children to college anyway, thus doing little to promote access. Furthermore, they feared that tax benefits will erode support for traditional forms of student aid, thus weakening the only remaining, if attenuated, programs that do promote access. But neither could prevail against the political popularity of a large-scale measure that seemed to address a major concern of middle-class voters.

With the Taxpayer Relief Act, federal higher education policy came full circle. Moynihan's "schizophrenia" described symbolic rewards to "middle America," while legislative proposals were directed at the "other America." With the Tax Relief Act of 1997, the politically popular award for "middle America" *was* the legislative proposal, and the symbolic reward was the Pell Grant increase designed as a sop to student aid traditionalists.[7]

THE ROLE OF GOVERNMENT: FROM PARTNER TO ADVERSARY

One could, of course, chalk up the tax bill of 1997 to the politics of inevitability. With a Republican Congress determined to pass a tax cut, President Clinton and congressional Democrats were arguably well advised to capture the money for education. There was certainly not $41 billion available from any other source. But the potential implications of the dynamic introduced by the move to the tax code are worth pondering. For if the embrace of tax benefits for education is, as the evidence suggests, not simply a passing fad, but rather a reflection of deeper forces in American politics, the impact of the legislation may be both deep seated and long term.

Role Reversal

Return for a moment to the classic student aid model. Federal funds flow when a student aid officer working with a student at the college in which that student has enrolled evaluates the student's financial need and "packages" monies from a variety of sources to cover the cost of attending the institution. Often, no money is given in hand to the student—it is applied to the college's bill to cover education expenses.

Now consider the tax benefits. Federal funds flow—in the form of a tax refund or reduced tax liability—directly to taxpayers, when they, with or without the help of an accountant, calculate their tax liability and submit tax forms to the government. If a taxpayer is entitled to an education tax credit, deduction, or exclusion under the Taxpayer Relief Act of 1997, he or she receives a refund and pockets the money. The taxpayer receives this benefit in

April, not in September or January when tuition bills are due, and may or may not choose to spend that benefit on education. The college or university and its financial aid officers are not part of this picture—except that they must, for purposes of tax verification and enforcement, report to the IRS, and to the taxpayer, monies paid by students and families. Gone is the financial aid officer. Gone is the partnership.

And that is not the worst of it. Once the tax benefits were enacted, politicians, policy analysts, and editorial page columnists immediately began to worry that colleges and universities, seeing that their families had more money in hand, might "take away" the benefit through increased prices or reduced financial aid. Not only were colleges and universities no longer the partner of the government in conferring an education benefit, they were, if anything, the enemy, to be watched and monitored lest their pricing or aid policies take the benefit away. Thus Congress in the fall of 1997 passed a provision stating that colleges and universities could not consider the extra income resulting from the tax benefits when calculating financial need. It also established, in August 1997, the National Commission on the Cost of Higher Education, to examine the cost and price structure at institutions of higher education and to develop "a clearer picture of what is really happening to the cost of postsecondary education in this country, and what can be done to keep college affordable for middle-income Americans" (McKeon 1997).

The Politics of Cost

Enacting education tax benefits clearly put into sharper focus congressional concern with college affordability. But at a deeper level, government scrutiny of costs is an inevitable corollary to the political concern with affordability. As long as the goal of federal policy was access, the government could be more or less agnostic about how much students paid to go to the college of their choice. Grants were limited, loans are comparatively inexpensive for the government, and the costliest institutions supplied a great deal of their own aid to make sure that talented but financially needy students could attend.[8]

When "affordability" is the issue, however, politicians and public policymakers inevitably become concerned not simply with financial aid, but with the overall pricing policies of colleges and universities. Because the major costs of running an institution of higher education are lodged in the labor-intensive enterprise of teaching and learning, concern with cost leads the government into the core operations of colleges and universities. Thus the National Commission on the Cost of Higher Education was charged with examining 11 specific areas, including the heart of the educational enterprise—"trends in faculty work load and remuneration, faculty-to-student ratios, the number of hours spent in the classroom, and tenure practices" (U.S. Congress 1997a). It is ironic that a Republican Congress opposed to "big government" is unselfconscious about such dramatic expansion of the government's scope of concern.

The transformation of colleges and universities from partners to adversaries is not only an inevitable by-product of the shift to affordability, it is also good politics. It permits politicians to highlight, and keep highlighting, a question of major concern to voters—the price of college—without spending money. By condemning the rise in college tuition, demanding better reporting of costs, or threatening to impose penalties on colleges that do not constrain tuition increases, politicians carve out a field of action, or apparent action, that requires neither government expenditures nor legislative heavy-lifting.

IMPLICATIONS

Because tax benefits, once enacted, function as "automatic" expenditures, or entitlements, they enjoy a natural budgetary advantage over discretionary student aid programs that must be appropriated for each year from available funds. That advantage will become more pronounced as entitlements continue to squeeze the federal budget—particularly in the event of an economic down-turn. Beyond the mechanical edge enjoyed by tax expenditures, the political forces that combined to produce them point to an erosion of the coalition that supported traditional student aid for the last 30 years. Although student aid programs have survived so far, they may well be living on borrowed time.

Plainly, the federal commitment to "access" for low-income students can no longer be taken for granted. Nor can colleges and universities assume that the public and political leaders regard them as good-faith actors performing a vital function. Although the public knows that higher education is an increasingly important engine of both individual and social success, and politicians recognize its value as a political issue, they do not necessarily appreciate the institutions that actually deliver it.

The erosion of a functional commitment to promoting access, backed by programs and funds actually designed to achieve that goal, threatens the role of education as an engine of opportunity in this country. Research over the last two decades of federal student aid funding shows that although the country has made tremendous gains in the percentage of high school students who go to college, participation and graduation rates vary greatly depending on race, ethnicity, and income—and the divergence has increased, rather than decreased, since 1980 (McPherson and Schapiro 1997). A recent study by the Commission on National Investment in Higher Education and the Rand Corporation (1997) called this growing disparity a "time bomb" ticking under the nation's social and economic foundations. In testimony before Congress in 1995, one of the study's authors and former governor of New Jersey, Thomas

Kean, warned, "Ever since the GI Bill half a century ago, higher education has served as the great leveler in our country. But more and more it is becoming the great stratifier" (Kean 1995).

It seems clear that, consciously or not, we are already making our way down a new path in the politics and policy of higher education. In a world increasingly dominated by images, the techniques of "new politics" will doubtless continue to drive the political agenda. The challenge for higher education is to harness some of those techniques in service not of short-term political goals, but rather for the long-term project of rekindling the commitment of the public and policymakers to preserving our system of higher education as an engine of quality and opportunity.

NOTES

1. Hugh Heclo uses the term "legitimacy paradox" to describe the fact that although public mistrust of government has never been higher than it is now, the public has never been more closely watched and courted than it is now by Washington. I do not use the term exactly as defined and applied by Heclo, but to describe an analogous situation of apparent paradox in the field of higher education.

2. In the original Higher Education Act, the grants and work-study funds were "campus-based," meaning that funds were given to colleges and universities to be allocated to the most needy students. The loan program consisted of federal advances to establish or strengthen state or private nonprofit student loan insurance programs and the provision of loan insurance for students without reasonable access to such plans. The reauthorization of 1972 rounded out the student aid system and gave federal student aid policy its modern shape. In 1972, at President Richard Nixon's urging, Basic Educational Opportunity (now Pell) Grants, administered at the federal level directly to students, were added to the act, and campus-based programs were retained. The 1972 amendments also established the Student Loan Marketing Association (Sallie Mae), which gave the student loan program the liquidity and capital availability necessary for growth. Finally, also in 1972, Congress created the State Student Incentive Grant program, a matching program designed to encourage states to increase funding for need-based grants (Gladieux and Hauptman 1995). With these additions, federal student aid achieved the basic contours it has today.

3. Significantly, Clinton completed his entire first-term education agenda, while the health care strategy foundered in Congress and welfare legislation never got introduced.

4. The Basic Educational Opportunity Grants added to the Higher Education Act in 1972 were not changed to Pell Grants until the reauthorization of 1980. For purposes of clarity, this chapter refers to "Pell Grants" throughout.

5. In fact, polling conducted for the Alliance to Save Student Aid revealed that public support for student aid was second only to public support for Social Security.

6. The Labor and Human Resources Committee, chaired in the 104th Congress by Senator Nancy Kassebaum from Kansas, with Senator Ted Kennedy as the ranking Democrat, is the Senate committee responsible for education legislation.

7. Of course, the tax expenditure is very real. The education tax benefits are "symbolic," however, because it is not obvious that they promote educational goals.
8. Indeed, as the value of federal grants declined progressively from 1980 onward, independent colleges and universities dramatically increased their institutional aid budgets to maintain the commitment to access. Now, independent colleges and universities spend more money on grants out of their own funds than the federal government spends on financial aid grants for all of higher education.

REFERENCES

Benedetto, R. 1996. "Keys to '96 Campaign." *USA Today* January 10: A1.

Clinton, W. J. 1993a. "Remarks and a Question-and-Answer Session with High School Students in Bensonville, Illinois." *Administration of William J. Clinton* May 10: 616.

———. 1993b. "Remarks at the New Hampshire Technical College Commencement Ceremony in Stratham, New Hampshire." *Administration of William J. Clinton* May 22: 723.

———. 1993c. "Remarks to the Cleveland City Club." *Administration of William J. Clinton* May 10: 607.

Commision on National Investment in Higher Education and Rand Corporation. 1997. *Breaking the Social Contract: The Fiscal Crisis in Higher Education*. Santa Monica: Rand Corporation.

Cook, C. E. 1998. *Lobbying for Higher Education*. Nashville: Vanderbilt University Press.

Gladieux, L. E., and A. M. Hauptman. 1995. *The College Aid Quandary: Access, Quality, and the Federal Role*. Washington, DC: Brookings Institution/College Board.

Gladieux, L. E., and T. R. Wolanin. 1976. *Congress and the Colleges: The National Politics of Higher Education*. Lexington, MA: Lexington Books.

Heclo, H. Forthcoming. "Presidential Power and Public Prestige." In *Presidential Power Revisited*, edited by R. Porter.

Ikenberry, S. O., and T. W. Hartle. 1998. *Too Little Knowledge Is a Dangerous Thing: What the Public Thinks and Knows about Paying for College*. Washington, DC: American Council on Education.

Johnson, L. B. 1965. "Remarks at Southwest Texas State College upon Signing the Higher Education Act of 1965, November 8, 1965." *Public Papers of the Presidents* 602: 1102.

Johnstone, D. B. 1995. "Starting Points: Fundamental Assumptions Underlying the Principles and Policies of Federal Student Aid to Students." Washington, DC: U.S. Department of Education.

Kean, T. H. 1995. "Prepared Statement of Governor Thomas H. Kean." Hearing before the Subcommittee on Education, Arts, and Humanities of the Committee on Labor and Human Resources, United States Senate, 104th Cong., 1st sess., S. Hrg. 104-23 (February 2): 37–39.

Maraniss, D. 1995. *First in His Class, the Biography of Bill Clinton*. New York: Simon and Schuster.

McKeon, H. 1997. "Statement of the Honorable Howard P. 'Buck' McKeon, Chairman, Subcommittee on Postsecondary Education, Training, and Lifelong Learning." Meeting of the National Commission on the Cost of Higher Education, August 11, Washington, DC.

McPherson, M. S., and M. O. Schapiro. 1997. *The Student Aid Game: Meeting Need and Rewarding Talent in American Higher Education*. Princeton, NJ: Princeton University Press.

Moynihan, Daniel P. 1973. *The Politics of a Guaranteed Income: The Nixon Administration and the Family Assistance Plan.* New York: Random House.

Nye, J. S., P. D. Zelikow, and D. C. King, eds. 1997. *Why People Don't Trust Government.* Cambridge, MA: Harvard University Press.

Skocpol, T. 1997. "The G.I. Bill and U.S. Social Policy, Past and Future." *Social Philosophy and Policy* 14(2) Summer: 95–101.

U.S. Congress. House. 1997a. Emergency Supplemental Appropriations Act. 105th Cong., 1st sess., H.R. 1871. *Congressional Record* 143(82), Daily ed. (June 12): H3770–H3771.

————. 1997b. State of the Union Address. 105th Congress, 1st sess. *Congressional Record* 143(12) Daily ed. (February 4): H273-278.

CHAPTER 7

Merit-Based versus Need-Based Aid

The Continual Issues for Policymakers

Joseph D. Creech and Jerry Sheehan Davis

INTRODUCTION

For as long as financial aid has been available to college students, aid programs have had to establish eligibility criteria for their awards or assistance. Different criteria have been employed over the years, but the eligibility criteria used by current programs generally fall into two broad categories: merit-based criteria and need-based criteria. In deciding whether to create and fund a merit-based program, a need-based program, or a program that combines merit- and need-based criteria, policymakers must consider many questions. For example: What are the goals of their aid program? What kinds of students do they want to assist? For what purposes do they want to assist them? How much and what kinds of aid do they want to provide?

This chapter provides a brief history of merit-based and need-based aid programs, describes recent trends in the creation of merit-based grant programs by states, and offers some guidelines intended to help policymakers decide which kinds of programs are most likely to meet policy goals. We focus our discussion on state grant program activities because there are far more state-funded than federally funded grant programs, and because many states currently are devoting a great deal of attention to how they might revise their current programs or create new ones.

FINANCIAL AID PROGRAM ELIGIBILITY CRITERIA

Eligibility criteria in *merit-based programs* are used to determine whether potential recipients merit assistance. For example, recipients may be considered meritorious if they exhibit records of outstanding academic, artistic, or athletic achievement. Or, recipients might merit assistance if they have performed some valuable service to society, such as having served in the military. Other programs might consider applicants meritorious if they intend to perform a valuable service after they finish college, such as teaching math or science in elementary and secondary schools or practicing medicine in an underserved region.

Need-based programs emphasize eligibility criteria that measure their recipients' financial need and/or their ability to pay for college. "Ability to pay" is the assessment of the income, savings, and assets of the student and the student's family to ascertain how much they can reasonably afford to pay for a year of postsecondary education. The determination from such an assessment is called the expected family contribution (EFC). "Financial need" generally refers to the difference between a student's costs of education for a year of study and EFC, or ability to pay (for more information on need analysis, see Chapter 3). Financial need is expressed by the formula:

College Costs – Expected Family Contribution = Financial Need

Despite the standardized definition of need, need-based programs take many forms. One of the most important distinctions among programs is the criteria used to rank applicants. Whether a need-based program emphasizes ability-to-pay criteria or financial-need criteria can greatly affect which kinds of applicants receive its assistance. If a program ranks applicants by ability to pay and gives award priority to students with the least ability to pay, then less-affluent applicants are more likely to get awards, because they are least likely to be able to pay for college. On the other hand, if a program ranks applicants according to their financial need and gives award priority to students with the highest need, more recipients will be students from middle- and upper-income families who attend higher-cost colleges.

The data displayed in Table 7.1 illustrate these points with examples of EFC (ability to pay) and financial need for three students from different financial circumstances who plan to attend three colleges with widely different prices. Each of the three students has one sibling and two parents, is the first and only family member in college, has earned $1,000 from part-time jobs in the last year, and has saved $1,000 to help meet college costs. For financial aid purposes, the major differences in these three students are in the price of the college they plan to attend and in how much their parents earn. John's parents earned $25,000 last year, and their expected contribution is only $350. Since he intends to enroll at a community college where the total college costs are about $6,000, John's financial need is $5,650. Mary's parents earned $50,000 and the family contribution is $4,880. She wants to attend a four-year public college where the college price is about $10,000; her financial need is $5,120. Hector's parents earned $75,000 and his family contribution is about $10,000. He plans to attend a private university that costs $21,000. His financial need will be $11,000.

TABLE 7.1			
ILLUSTRATION OF ABILITY TO PAY AND FINANCIAL NEED			
	John	Mary	Hector
Family Income	$25,000	$50,000	$75,000
College Price	$6,000	$10,000	$21,000
Ability to Pay (Expected Family Contribution)	$350	$4,880	$10,000
Financial Need	$5,650	$5,120	$11,000

In a financial aid program that ranked them according to the least *ability to pay* for college, John would rank first, Mary would rank second, and Hector third. The two students with lower family incomes would be more likely than Hector to get awards. In a program that ranked applicants according to their *financial need*, Hector would rank first and John would rank second, even though Hector's family income is three times greater than John's, and his family's ability to pay is almost 30 times greater. Mary, whose family income is between those of John and Hector, would rank second in ability to pay but third in financial need.

Students who receive awards from need-based student aid programs can come from quite different family financial circumstances, depending on whether the programs emphasize ability to pay or financial need (and depending on the applicants' college costs). If John, Mary, and Hector attend the same college and are awarded financial aid on the basis of need, their awards will reflect ability to pay. It is when they attend different institutions, especially institutions with widely different costs, that ranking by ability to pay results in a different ordering than ranking by financial need.

THE PAST AS PROLOGUE TO TODAY'S DISCUSSIONS OF MERIT-BASED AND NEED-BASED AID

Prior to the late 1940s, virtually all student financial aid programs were funded by private donors or by the colleges themselves. College-funded aid programs sought the "best and brightest" from among their potential applicants, and they looked for evidence of merit among the applicants. The emphasis on merit did not mean that colleges disregarded ability to pay or financial need. Many colleges used eligibility criteria to identify the most "worthy and deserving" among their applicants, with "worthy" students having the best academic records or most potential and "deserving" students needing financial support. Scholarship recipients frequently were considered "worthy" because they had demonstrated outstanding achievement or potential *and* "deserving" because they had done well in spite of their disadvantaged financial or socioeconomic circumstances.

It is quite likely that a substantial share of the early college-funded student aid dollars were awarded to students who were financially needy; that is, the amount they could afford to pay for college was less than the price of attendance (Wick 1997). But the college programs generally emphasized the merit criteria, in that the students had to "merit" an award prior to consideration of their financial need. Providing assistance to students *only* because they were financially needy was not a widespread practice.

After World War II, the federal government created the single largest merit-based student aid program in United States history, in the form of veterans education benefits from the GI Bill. Recipients of veterans benefits were considered meritorious by virtue of having served their country in the military. The nation wanted to reward the veterans for their service; also, paying for their postsecondary education and training enhanced the national labor force. Although need-based criteria were not applied in veterans benefits programs, the majority of veterans likely would have qualified for need-based awards had there been such criteria.

Before the 1960s, most institutional, state, and federal aid programs emphasized merit criteria in determining eligibility for assistance. Award recipients may have demonstrated financial need, or may have had limited ability to pay for college, but those characteristics generally were not crucial to receiving assistance. Students did not have to be "needy" to get awards. Aid programs generally focused awards on recipients who displayed outstanding academic promise, had performed some valuable service to society (such as having served in the military), or who planned careers in areas deemed important to the nation. A good example of the latter type of program is the National Defense Education Loan Program established in 1958. Aid recipients had to be committed to careers in mathematics and science, or to teaching those subjects.

Things changed during the 1960s. The civil rights movement drew attention to the importance of postsecondary education in helping minority group members overcome the effects of segregation, thereby helping publicize the value of such education to all citizens and increase interest in attending. America's political leaders placed growing emphasis on postsecondary education's role in developing the economy and winning the Cold War. Political leaders also began to address social unrest by expanding economic opportunities via postsecondary education. The federal student financial aid programs of the Johnson administration's Great Society grew from the idea that extending educational opportunities to all who would benefit from them, not just to the "best and brightest," would make our nation stronger. Additionally, the demand for postsecondary education was growing because rising numbers of students who qualified for additional study were graduating from high school.

The federal financial aid programs created in the 1960s and 1970s emphasized financial need and ability to pay as primary eligibility criteria. Merit-based eligibility criteria became secondary to need-based criteria. Between the passage of the Higher Education Act of 1965 and 1980, annual federal financial aid program awards grew from under $200 million to over $14.4 billion (Gillespie and Carlson 1983). In 1980, in constant dollars, the federal government awarded almost 30 times as much money, and 16 times more money per student, than in 1965. The vast majority of these dollars were from need-based programs.

During this same period, the number of states with need-based grant programs nearly quadrupled, rising from 13 to 51 (including the District of Columbia). In 1969, the earliest year for which comprehensive data are available, states collectively awarded $200 million in need-based grant aid to their residents (Fenske and Boyd 1981). By 1980, the annual amount had grown to over $870 million (NASSGP 1981).

During the 1965–80 period, student financial aid policy discussions at the state level focused primarily on issues of student access to, and choice among, postsecondary institutions (Boyd 1975; Marmaduke 1983). Those who were concerned about "access" generally favored programs and policies that made it possible for lower-income students to receive some form of postsecondary education, usually a public two- or four-year college. Those who were concerned more about "choice" generally favored programs and policies that made it possible for students of low and modest financial means to attend higher-cost private colleges or, put another way, they favored programs that emphasized financial need over ability to pay.

Policymakers who considered access to be of highest priority argued that it was more important to use limited student aid resources to help the most financially disadvantaged students enroll somewhere—even if the institutions students could afford to attend were not ideal for all of them—because any postsecondary education would improve their socioeconomic status and benefit society.

Policymakers who regarded choice as vital argued that student aid must help recipients afford to attend institutions of their choice—those they most wanted to attend—because they would be much more likely to succeed at such institutions. They also contended that the opportunity to attend premier institutions should not be restricted to the children of the affluent, that the education available at such institutions is valuable to all, and that having a more economically diverse student body adds to the educational experience for all students at all types of institutions.

Some state leaders believe choice is vital because aid recipients can attend private colleges and thereby save the taxpayers' money. The logic of this argument is as follows. If the state gives students financial aid awards to attend private colleges *and their award amounts are less than the amount of direct per-student subsidies the state pays to public colleges*, then both the students and the taxpayers will benefit. The students will enroll at institutions they want to attend but could not otherwise have afforded without the assistance, and the state will have helped produce college-educated citizens at lower per-student costs to taxpayers.

Many educators believe that there are not enough resources to support financial aid programs that will ensure both access and choice. Those who want program efforts and funds targeted on providing access for the most economically disadvantaged students are concerned that many such students will be unable to take advantage of programs that give aid recipients options among colleges, because they will not be eligible for admission to higher-cost selective private colleges. This is not to say that no low-income students attend high-cost colleges. Many do. But the correlation between students' socioeconomic status and college admissions test scores and high school grades are such that low-income students are much less likely than high-income students to be admitted to higher-cost selective colleges.

During the 1960s and most of the 1970s, students with the least ability to pay for any postsecondary education were the primary target populations for the vast majority of federal and state student financial aid programs and dollars. Eligibility criteria and formulas that assessed need for assistance placed large shares of all aid dollars in the hands of the lowest-income students and families, with the intent to help as many as possible gain access to some form of postsecondary education. However, in some states, the eligibility criteria and award formulas directed some funds toward middle-income students with higher ability to pay, to support their attendance at higher-cost private colleges. This happened, in part, because those programs were intended to strengthen private-sector colleges by helping students afford them.

Aid recipients during this period were not without merit. Many were quite capable and all had to meet the admissions standards of their institutions. They also had to maintain the standards of satisfactory academic progress required of their peers in order to remain eligible for aid. But eligibility for financial aid generally did not depend on students meeting merit criteria. Need-based eligibility criteria were foremost in student aid policymaking.

During the 1970s, new expectations of student aid programs arose. Their purpose was no longer merely to help make it possible for recipients to attend college but also to provide students with incentives to enroll. Prior to World War II, when colleges and private foundations provided the vast majority of student aid funds, it was believed that potential recipients who wanted to attend college had only to receive financial help to do so. But when the federal government began to furnish the majority of aid funds, and when the access goal began to dominate financial aid policy discussions, these beliefs changed.

Policymakers, analysts, and researchers identified four major barriers to access to postsecondary education: (1) financial barriers, meaning that students and their families could not afford the costs of education; (2) academic barriers, meaning that students were not adequately prepared for college; (3) attitudinal barriers, meaning that students (and sometimes their families) did not believe that college was worth the effort and sacrifices needed to attend, or else they doubted that they could be successful in college; and (4) geographic barriers, meaning that no affordable colleges were within reasonable distances of where students lived (Ferrin 1970). Many persons expected student financial aid programs to alleviate the financial barrier and also provide incentives to students and families to help them overcome the academic, attitudinal, and geographic barriers. In other words, it was not sufficient for financial aid programs to merely help students pay college costs. Many policymakers believed that aid programs should encourage students to prepare for and attend college. These beliefs are still extant, and likely somewhat stronger, today.

Things changed again in student aid during the 1980s. Between the mid-1970s and the mid-1980s, the annual number of students graduating from high school decreased by about 16 percent, from 3.1 million to 2.6 million (U.S. Department of Education 1997b). Thus, the potential applicant pool from which colleges could draw students decreased. Colleges reacted in many ways to the reduction in the traditional college-going population, but two responses had great effects on student aid programs and policies. First, colleges began to actively recruit and enroll older, nontraditional students. This increased the demand for student financial aid because many of these new recruits were "independent" of parental financial support—the students and their colleges could not expect any financial contributions toward tuition and fees from parents. Additional student aid would be needed to compensate for the absence of parental contributions if many nontraditional students were to afford enrollment.

Second, colleges began to develop retention programs or expand existing services. They gave more attention to how many students left without completing a degree and why they dropped out. The colleges concentrated on policies and practices that encouraged students to remain in college and persist to graduation. Because some students drop out of college for financial reasons, student aid policies were expected to support the goal of increasing graduation rates. Financial aid programs were expected to increase student access to some form of postsecondary education, to enhance student choice among institutions of widely different costs, *and* to improve student ability to remain enrolled and to complete a degree. From the institutional viewpoint, another important goal of student financial aid programs was to assist in recruitment of students.

In addition to efforts by colleges to expand and maintain enrollments, other phenomena affected student aid programs and policies. More students and families became eligible for need-based student aid because higher college prices meant they could demonstrate financial need. Thus, more middle-income students and parents began to compete for student aid funds with lower-income students and parents, as well as with "independent" students. Since middle-income parents are more likely than lower-income parents to vote and otherwise participate in political processes, it is understandable that many politicians favored providing more aid to middle-income students. Aid program eligibility criteria and need-analysis formulas were modified to help more middle-income students receive awards from publicly funded aid programs. In addition, college prices rose faster than the ability of the majority of students and parents to pay them which, in turn, increased the demand for student aid dollars.

During the 1980s, the growth in federal funding of student aid programs slowed dramatically from the rates for the two preceding decades. Table 7.2 summarizes the amounts of federal aid awards *per full-time student*, in current and constant dollars, between 1965 and 1990.

TABLE 7.2

FEDERAL AID PER FULL-TIME STUDENT, 1965–90

Year	Current Dollars	Percent Change	Constant Dollars	Percent Change
1965	$48	—	$232	—
1970	$566	+1,089%	$2,218	+856%
1980	$2,025	+258%	$3,736	+68%
1990	$2,711	+34%	$3,153	−16%

Sources: U.S. Department of Education 1997b; Gillespie and Carlson 1983.

In the 1980s, most states steadily increased funding for their need-based grant programs, in part to compensate for the slowed growth in federal assistance. Annual aggregate awards from state need-based grant programs grew by over 90 percent between 1980 and 1990, from $879 million to $1,675 billion (NASSGP 1992). But many states also created non-need-based and merit-based aid programs during this period. For example, 19 states created merit scholarship programs designed to reward top high school graduates and provide them with incentives to attend in-state schools (NASSGP 1992). These merit-based programs typically awarded far fewer aid dollars than did their state's need-based ones, but they represented a response to the public demand for recognition of achievement.

The scholarship programs also represented a response to middle-income families' demands for financial assistance. Children from middle-class homes would not be disqualified from receiving aid from a merit-based program because they could not demonstrate financial need. Some policymakers favor merit scholarships on the basis of their economic efficiency. Since the scholarship recipients are academically better prepared than many need-based aid recipients, they are more likely to complete their degree programs. Therefore, the states are less likely to have "wasted" scholarship money on students who drop out. Another efficiency argument is that scholarship recipients, who may only use their awards at in-state schools, will be more likely to attend colleges in their own states.

THE 1990s AND NEW DISCUSSIONS ON FINANCIAL AID POLICY

By the 1990s, the goals of student financial aid programs had evolved from the initially simple intent to help a relatively few worthy and deserving students to attend specific colleges to the much more complex purposes of enhancing access, choice, and retention for many students at many types of postsecondary institutions; helping students overcome the financial barrier and encouraging them to overcome attitudinal, academic, and geographic barriers to postsecondary education; rewarding talented students and providing incentives to others to achieve excellence; equalizing tuition charges so private colleges could compete for students with public colleges; and encouraging students to pursue careers that are considered valuable to society and to the nation's economic development (Davis 1995).

Rising college prices during the 1980s and early 1990s drove the demand for student financial aid upward so that the competition for funds became keen, and it remains so today. An ever-growing proportion of students receives financial aid. In 1969–70, fewer than 25 percent of all full-time undergraduates got financial aid (Haven and Horch 1972). By 1989–90, 57 percent of all full-time undergraduates got financial aid from some source (U.S. Department of Education 1993). Only six years later, in 1995–96, about

68 percent of all full-time undergraduate students received some kind of financial assistance from some source (U.S. Department of Education 1997b).

Because so many more students began to receive financial aid in the 1990s, and because aid programs were expected to achieve so many objectives, it is not surprising that student aid policy discussions became more complex and often more contentious. The discussions and debates on financial aid policy were energized in 1993 with the creation of the Georgia HOPE Scholarship program. This program differed from other and earlier state scholarship programs in significant ways. First, it is broad based, in that it is potentially available to thousands of Georgia students, regardless of their family incomes and the types of colleges they attend. Second, HOPE Scholarship recipients do not have to be the top students in their classes; they need only achieve a B average in a college-prep curriculum to qualify for assistance. Third, the program is not funded by appropriations but instead uses profits from the state lottery for its awards. The Georgia HOPE Scholarship has grown from making $21.5 million in awards to 19,000 students in 1993–94 to awarding $153 million to 128,000 students in 1996–97.

Further evidence of the popularity of the Georgia HOPE Scholarship program is found in the fact that other states are establishing similar programs. In 1997 and 1998, Florida, Kentucky, Louisiana, Maryland, and South Carolina passed legislation for HOPE-type programs.

These merit-based programs have several goals or purposes in common. They are intended to help reduce the effects of rising college prices—especially tuition at public four-year colleges—on middle-income families. They are expected to promote better preparation for college while students are in high school and better academic achievement after they reach college. Policymakers also expect these programs to save money because better-prepared students are less likely to need remedial courses and are more likely to complete their degree programs in a timely fashion. Finally, these programs aim to encourage their states' talented students to attend in-state colleges and remain residents after graduation.

These new programs share several important characteristics. First, they respond to the public's expectation that states should encourage students to prepare for college and help families to afford the costs. Second, they promote important state objectives such as developing an educated citizenry and producing a more skilled labor force. Third, they are easy to understand and they have clear eligibility and renewal requirements. If students achieve specific, well-publicized grades and/or test scores, they will be eligible for an award.

Fourth, the programs have a well-defined application process and award structure. In the traditional need-based programs, students have to complete

Salient Characteristics of
Selected Recent State Scholarship Initiatives

• **Arkansas Academic Challenge Scholarships**
Established
1991
Academic Requirements
C average on core courses and ACT score of 19 or higher, but eligibility based partially on family income and size
Maximum Award
$1,500, with a $500 incentive for a cumulative 3.0 GPA

• **Florida Bright Futures**
Established
1997 (First awards to be made in the 1998–99 academic year)
Academic Requirements
Academic: 3.5 GPA in college-preparatory curricula
Merit: 3.0 GPA in college-preparatory curricula
Gold Seal Vocational: 3.0 and 3.5 GPAs in vocational courses
Maximum Award
Academic: Full tuition, fees, and book allowance
Merit: 75 percent of tuition and fees
Gold Seal Vocational: 75 percent of tuition and fees

• **Georgia HOPE Scholarship**
Established
1993 (First awards in 1994)
Academic Requirements
B average in high school (3.0 GPA in college preparatory curricula, 3.2 GPA in other curricula); maintain B average to renew awards
Maximum Award
$3,000 per year, minus any Pell Grant awards; awards are based on tuition, fees, and book allowances

• **Louisiana Tuition Opportunity Program for Students**
Established
1997 (First awards to be made in the 1998–99 academic year)
Academic Requirements
Honors: 3.5 GPA and ACT score of 27 or higher
Performance: Top 5 percent of high school class, 3.5 GPA, and ACT score of 23 or higher
Opportunity: 2.5 GPA and ACT score at or above the state average
Maximum Award
Honors: Tuition plus $800
Performance: Tuition plus $400
Opportunity: Tuition at a public institution, or an amount equal to the average public college tuition to attend an independent college

continued

• **South Carolina Palmetto Scholars**
Established
1996
Academic Requirements
Top 5 percent of high school class and 3.5 GPA, 1200 SAT scores or ACT
equivalent; must maintain a B average to renew awards
Maximum Award
$5,000 not to exceed costs of attendance, less grant aid

Source: Southern Regional Education Board 1997.

applications that describe in detail their family financial circumstances. Applicants sometimes have difficulty understanding why they need to supply these data, and data sometimes are hard to obtain and assemble for the application. Furthermore, it is difficult for applicants to understand the formulas for assessing ability to pay or financial need, so some students and families are unable to effectively plan to meet college expenses. If families do not know whether they will be eligible for assistance, or how much assistance they might get, it is difficult to develop a plan to pay for college costs with personal and family financial resources and student financial aid. In these scholarships programs, students and families know what is required and why, and they know the amount of the award that will be available to them.

Fifth, because these programs' eligibility criteria are clear for the applicants, and because the terms and conditions of the awards are clear for the programs, the result of the process is clearer for citizens and taxpayers.

The new merit-based state scholarship programs have strengths and weaknesses. They reward student achievement, which is a traditional financial aid program goal. Because the award amounts are significant, and certain, the programs are presumed to motivate students to pursue specific high school curricula and achieve above-average grades. The programs also help middle-income families, whose children frequently have difficulty qualifying for grant aid from need-based programs. The programs promote higher performance levels, in that students must achieve a higher standard of "satisfactory academic progress" to continue to receive their awards.

However, an important weakness of the programs is that they are not need based, so some students who get the scholarships could afford to attend college without them. This means that some recipients would have gone to college without the awards, so the states will spend some money unnecessarily. Some policy analysts say it is better to use the government's limited student aid resources to make larger need-based grant awards to more low-income students who cannot afford the costs of attendance. On the other hand, while affluent scholarship recipients might be able to afford college costs without the scholarships, they might not choose to attend an in-state college without the awards. Moreover, the scholarships provide all students with incentives to get better grades than they are likely to get if the programs were not available.

Another serious weakness of the programs is that they generally do not (or will not) help the students who are most in need of assistance. Students who come from poor families and have made only average grades in high school generally will not receive the merit-based state scholarships. It can be (and is) argued that such students need society's help much more than do students from affluent families whose advantaged circumstances likely helped them earn good grades and prepare for college (Mortenson 1997).

The programs also are criticized because they apparently shift some public resources from poor families to middle- and upper-income ones. This is because the correlation between family socioeconomic status and academic performance is such that lower-income students are less likely than wealthy students to have good high school grades and to qualify for awards.

In Georgia, a shift of public dollars from poorer citizens to richer citizens is said to occur in part because disproportionate numbers of lower-income Georgians play the state lottery that supports HOPE Scholarships, while disproportionate numbers of middle- and upper-income students receive awards. This criticism would be more powerful if the program were funded by a compulsory state tax instead of lottery proceeds. Playing the lottery is an entirely voluntary decision.

Some critics believe that widespread use of scholarship programs with modest (B level) grade requirements will lead to grade inflation at the secondary and postsecondary levels as students plead with teachers and professors for grades that will make (or keep) them eligible for scholarship awards. But, so far, there is no conclusive evidence of grade inflation in Georgia, where these programs began.

FUTURE CONSIDERATIONS
FOR FINANCIAL AID POLICYMAKERS

The debates between persons favoring merit-based eligibility criteria and those favoring need-based eligibility criteria will probably continue for as long as governments fund student financial aid programs. We have shown how the emphases on various eligibility criteria have changed over time with changes in financial aid program goals and increased demand for financial assistance. Where will the discussions lead from here? And what factors should guide policymakers' decisions?

Future discussions might be enhanced by considering what is already known and agreed upon and placing that knowledge within a new framework. There are, after all, some things on which agreement is nearly universal. First, all those with a stake in higher education can readily agree that there are deep concerns throughout our nation about the price of college, and the average American's ability to afford it, at a time when education and training beyond high school are crucial to personal and societal prosperity (National Commission on the Cost of Higher Education 1998). The public recognizes that now, more than ever before, postsecondary education represents the gateway to better jobs and financial success.

Second, it is readily apparent that combined student financial aid funds from all sources (state, federal, institutional, and private) are insufficient to meet all students' needs, let alone their demands, for assistance. Statewide and regional studies of "unmet need," since the first ones in the late 1960s, always have shown that at least some students and families need more financial aid funds than are available to them. It is very unlikely that student aid funds will become sufficient in the foreseeable future.

Third, because college tuition and net college price (the cost to a student for attendance, after financial aid), as a proportion of family financial resources, differs widely among states and by the types of colleges available to different students (Davis 1997), it seems self-evident that what is needed in some states will not be needed, or will not work, in other states. Program policies must differ because there are different needs among the states.

Fourth, it is apparent that, especially for low-income students, lack of funds is just one of several barriers to college attendance. Indeed, the financial barrier may be one of the least difficult problems to overcome. A recent national study shows that, when students successfully prepare for postsecondary education *and apply for admittance*, their probabilities of enrolling are no longer affected by their socioeconomic status or racial-ethnic group membership (U.S. Department of Education 1997a). The gap in attendance rates between low- and middle-income students exists because low-income students are less likely than their middle-income peers to be adequately prepared for college and, if prepared, are less likely to apply for admission. These findings suggest that financial barriers to postsecondary education are surmountable—if students can overcome the academic, attitudinal, and geographic barriers to attendance.

Finally, those in higher education know that many parents make financial sacrifices that are disproportionate to their means, and disproportionate to the sacrifices of other families, to pay college costs. Parental and family willingness to make such sacrifices has a great influence on whether students successfully plan for, attend, and complete postsecondary education (Davis 1989; PACU 1984). The absence of willingness and/or the ability to make such sacrifices can and does prohibit attendance.

PARTICIPATION AS A NEW FRAMEWORK FOR STUDENT AID POLICY

This knowledge must be considered within a student financial aid policy framework that goes beyond concern for achieving the traditional access-choice-retention goals of the past decades. Since more education for more persons is better, let us consider a new goal for postsecondary education and the financial aid programs that support it. That goal should be producing the greatest increases in participation in postsecondary education.

Increasing participation in postsecondary education goes beyond making institutions financially accessible (Adelman 1996). It means making sure that students who graduate from high school are ready to begin postsecondary education; providing programs and services that help students complete programs of study after they enroll; and establishing policies and practices that make the process of transferring credits between institutions clearer and simpler. For example, although tuition and fees are lower at public two-year colleges, the savings can be lost if the credits earned are not transferable and do not apply to degree programs at four-year colleges.

Student financial aid programs play a major role in who participates in postsecondary education. No one advocates denying financial assistance to students who do not have the financial ability to pay college tuition. Nor does anyone advocate giving a "free ride" to students who can readily afford college. But few states, if any, have sufficient funds available to provide access *and* choice to all who want to attend college or some other form of postsecondary education. Thus, state leaders have to implement student aid programs and policies that most effectively and efficiently enhance participation in postsecondary education for as many citizens as possible.

In a growing number of states, many policymakers have come to believe that financial aid programs, especially those providing grant assistance, should feature eligibility criteria that provide incentives for taking more challenging courses in high school and performing at more than minimal levels in secondary and postsecondary education. They believe such programs are the optimum way to enhance participation.

If these programs' award recipients are better prepared academically for postsecondary education, they will be more likely to successfully enroll and complete their programs in a timely fashion. The students won't have to take remedial courses (which are costly to the colleges and states), and they will be less likely to fail other courses. Thus the programs will enhance postsecondary education participation.

As was mentioned above, one of the arguments against merit-based programs is that students from families of lower socioeconomic status (who are presumed to be most in need of financial assistance to afford college) are less likely than others to get high school grades that are good enough to qualify for an award. But award criteria could be set at a slightly-above-average level so that most lower-income students, if they are admissible to any college, can qualify for an award.

Possibly the greatest argument for employing merit criteria in the ways they are used by the HOPE-type programs is that the criteria are specific and knowable. Consequently, students understand that—if they achieve a certain level of performance—they will receive a certain award amount. The availability of need-based student financial aid is widely publicized, but, because of the complexities of need analysis, it is impossible, in advance of filing an application, for students to predict with any precision whether they will qualify for assistance and how much they might get. Thus, most financial aid programs are limited in their ability to provide incentives to students to plan financially and prepare academically for postsecondary education.

Regardless of their socioeconomic status, when parents are confident that their children can qualify for financial assistance and afford college, they are more likely to encourage them to prepare and enroll, thereby helping them to overcome the academic, attitudinal, and geographic barriers to postsecondary education. The HOPE-type programs provide parents with assurance of financial assistance in ways that need-based programs do not. So, it is possible that the HOPE-type programs may, in the long run, do more to enhance access to postsecondary education for more lower-income students than the traditional need-based programs have done.

Giving affluent students non-need-based grants is often criticized as an inefficient use of public funds because those recipients would have gone to college without the awards. But if, in attempting to qualify for a grant, the recipients work harder to get better grades and better prepare themselves for college, and that effort helps them get through college more quickly, then the inefficiency argument loses some of its importance. The non-need-based grants may not enhance access or choice for affluent recipients, but they will increase overall participation, the goal we are advocating here.

This chapter has presented the pros and cons of using merit-based and need-based eligibility criteria, discussed how trends in their use have changed over time, and has offered a different framework for considering financial aid programs and policies. We hope it proves useful to financial aid policymakers and campus leaders who must address and answer the basic question: How can limited student aid resources best be utilized to increase participation in postsecondary education?

REFERENCES

Adelman, C. 1996. "The Truth about Remedial Work." *Chronicle of Higher Education* October 4.

Boyd, J. D. 1975. "History of State Involvement in Financial Aid." In *Perspectives on Financial Aid.* New York: College Entrance Examination Board.

College Board. 1990. *Trends in Student Aid: 1980 to 1990.* Washington, DC: The Washington Office of the College Board.

———. 1996. *Trends in Student Aid: 1986 to 1996.* Washington, DC: The Washington Office of the College Board.

Creech, J. D. 1997. Unpublished analysis. Southern Regional Education Board, Atlanta, GA.

Davis, J. S. 1989. *The Role of Parents and Their Preferences in Junior High School Students' Postsecondary Plans*. Harrisburg, PA: Pennsylvania Higher Education Assistance Agency.
———. 1995. "Designing a State Grant Program: The Basic Question for Policy Makers." *Journal of Student Financial Aid* 24(3): 33–39.
———. 1997. *College Affordability: A Closer Look at the Crisis*. Washington, DC: Sallie Mae Education Institute.
Fenske, R. H., and J. D. Boyd. 1981. *State Need-Based College Scholarship and Grant Programs: A Study of Their Development, 1969–1980*. College Board Report No. 81–7. New York: College Entrance Examination Board.
Ferrin, R. I. 1970. *Barriers to Universal Higher Education*. Palo Alto, CA: Access Research Office, College Entrance Examination Board.
Gillespie, D. A., and N. Carlson. 1983. *Trends in Student Aid: 1963 to 1983*. Washington, DC: College Board.
Haven, E. W., and D. H. Horch. 1972. *How College Students Finance Their Education: A National Survey of the Educational Interests, Aspirations, and Finances of College Sophomores in 1969–70*. New York: College Scholarship Service of the College Entrance Examination Board.
Marmaduke, A. S. 1983. "State Student Aid Programs." In *Handbook of Student Financial Aid*, edited by R. H. Fenske and R. P. Huff. San Francisco: Jossey-Bass Publishers.
Mortenson, T. G. 1997. "Georgia's HOPE Scholarship Program: Good Intentions, Strong Funding, Bad Design." *Postsecondary Education Opportunity* (February).
National Association of State Scholarship and Grant Programs (NASSGP). 1981. *National Association of State Scholarship & Grant Programs 13th Annual Survey, 1981–82 Academic Year*. Harrisburg, PA: Pennsylvania Higher Education Assistance Agency.
———. 1992. *National Association of State Scholarship & Grant Programs 23rd Annual Survey, 1991–92 Academic Year*. Harrisburg, PA: Pennsylvania Higher Education Assistance Agency.
———. 1998. *National Association of State Student Grant and Aid Programs 28th Annual Survey Report, 1996–97 Academic Year*. Albany, NY: New York State Higher Education Services Corporation.
National Commission on the Cost of Higher Education. 1998. *Straight Talk about College Costs and Prices*. Phoenix, AZ: Oryx Press.
Pennsylvania Association of Colleges and Universities (PACU). 1984. *Parents, Programs and Pennsylvania Students' Plans for Postsecondary Education*. Harrisburg, PA: Pennsylvania Association of Colleges and Universities.
U.S. Department of Education, National Center for Education Statistics. 1993. *Financing Undergraduate Education: 1990*. Washington, DC: Government Printing Office.
———. 1997a. *Access to Postsecondary Education for the 1992 High School Graduates*. Washington, DC: Government Printing Office.
———. 1997b. *Digest of Education Statistics, 1997*. NCES 98–105. Washington, DC: Government Printing Office.
Wick, P. G. 1997. *No-Need/Merit Scholarships: Practices and Trends, 1643–Present*. New York: College Board.

CHAPTER 8

Student Aid after Tax Reform
Risks and Opportunities

Thomas J. Kane

INTRODUCTION

During the summer of 1997, Congress and President Bill Clinton reached agreement on a series of new tax provisions for higher education. The provisions of the Taxpayer Relief Act of 1997, estimated to cost $41 billion over the next five years, represent the largest single increase in federal funding for higher education since the GI Bill. The purpose of this chapter is not to weigh the merits and deficiencies of these changes in tax policy—that water has long passed under the proverbial bridge—but to consider the ramifications for college pricing decisions and the design of other federal financial aid policies.

In the discussion that follows, I first provide a brief description of the tax policy changes contained in the 1997 legislation. In the remainder of the chapter, I discuss the risks and opportunities created by the interaction of the new tax law with existing student aid policies.

RECENT TAX LAW CHANGES

The new tax law contains seven primary components relating to higher education. First, families with students in their first two years of college receive a tax credit of up to $1,500 per student for out-of-pocket tuition expenses. This tax credit, referred to in the legislation as the "Hope Scholarship" credit, is provided on 100 percent of tuition expenses (less any federal, state, or private grant aid) up to $1,000, and 50 percent of any remaining expenses up to $2,000. Payments for room and board cannot be counted toward the credit. Eligibility for the credit is phased out for joint filers with income between $80,000 and $100,000 and for single filers with income between $40,000 and $50,000. The credit is nonrefundable—meaning that those eligible for a credit larger than their tax liability will not receive a refund for the difference. Students who are part of a taxpaying unit with no tax liability—either because their parents have very low income or because they are independent students with little income in the current year—are not eligible for any credit for postsecondary expenses.

Second, while the Hope tax credit is limited to those in their first two years of college, those taking classes beyond their first two years of college will be eligible to receive a 20 percent "Lifetime Learning" tax credit on the first $5,000 of net tuition expenses (after subtracting any grants received). The maximum that a family can claim for this credit will be raised to $10,000 in 2003.[1] The income limits for eligibility are the same as for the Hope tax credit, and like the Hope credit, the Lifetime Learning credit is nonrefundable.

Third, parents will be able to withdraw funds from existing IRA accounts to pay tuition or room and board. Such withdrawals to pay higher education expenses will not be subject to a 10 percent penalty, as they otherwise would have been.

Fourth, a child under the age of 18 can have $500 per year deposited on his or her behalf into a new "Education IRA" to help pay future tuition and room and board expenses. Any single-filing taxpayer with income less than $110,000 or joint-filing taxpayer with income less than $160,000 can establish Education IRAs. However, unlike "regular" IRAs, the capital gains on Education IRAs will not be taxable, up to the cost of tuition and room and board.

Fifth, parents or students will be able to deduct up to $1,000 of the interest paid on loans used to meet education expenses. This limit will be raised in $500 increments to $2,500 in the year 2001. Eligibility for the deduction will be limited to individual filers with income less than $40,000, or $60,000 for joint filers.

Sixth, student loans provided by tax-exempt organizations—such as universities or state governments—can now be forgiven with no tax liability for the beneficiary, as long as the person is working for a tax-exempt organization or governmental unit in an "underserved" occupation or geographic area. In the past, graduates had to pay federal income tax on any nonfederal loans that were forgiven.

Seventh, participants in state-run prepaid tuition plans receive a relatively small incremental benefit. Previously, funds could be withdrawn only to pay the cost of tuition. Such funds now can be used to pay room and board, as well as tuition. The primary tax advantage offered by such plans—that no tax is paid on the income of the plans until withdrawal—will remain in place.[2]

IMPLICATIONS OF THE TAX LAW CHANGES

The final legislation improved upon the initial proposal from the Clinton administration in a number of ways. Indeed, the administration itself supported many of the improvements. For instance, Congress wisely dropped a requirement that students maintain a B grade-point average in order to qualify for the tax credit. When added to the cost of verifying which students are in their first two years of college, the administrative costs of verifying students' grade-point averages would have proved overwhelming. Moreover, given the likelihood of grade inflation at some colleges and of grade-cautious coursework choices by risk-averse students, it was not at all clear that the proposed change would have generated a positive change in students' dedication to their academic work (and may even have had perverse effects).

Another improvement was the decision to treat federal Pell Grants the same as other grants in determining an eligible student's expenditures. In the administration's original proposal, the first dollar of any Pell Grant was to be subtracted from the tax credit one could receive, thus eliminating the credit for Pell Grant recipients, even if they were attending expensive institutions and had significant out-of-pocket expenses. In the final legislation, Pell Grants are treated like any other education grants: they are subtracted from tuition charges to establish eligible educational expenses.

Even with these improvements, a number of problems remain with the new provisions. For instance, during the debate leading up to the passage of the tax law changes, the primary complaint of many in the financial aid community was that the new tax benefits were primarily targeted at students from middle- and upper-income families even though youth from these families already enroll in college at high rates (Kane 1997). Youth from low-income families, on the other hand, are the one group that has not responded to the changes in the labor market during the 1980s that have made some type of postsecondary education a virtual necessity. Despite this, the new tax law changes offer low-income families very little. First, because neither of the tax credits are refundable, families must have federal income tax liability to receive the benefit. Moreover, because only out-of-pocket expenses are counted—tuition minus any grants received—the new tax law offers less to those who receive grants, thereby effectively reducing the progressivity of existing means-tested student aid programs. Similarly, the allowance of early withdrawals from existing IRAs to pay for education expenses is a windfall for those with already-substantial IRA assets, but low-income students are less likely to be in families with IRA savings.

Below, I describe other risks and opportunities presented by the new tax law and suggest solutions to avert some of these risks.

Potential Abuse of the
Credit for Leisure-Oriented Course Work

By providing a full tax credit for the first $1,000 in out-of-pocket expenses, the Hope Scholarship credit is a tempting source of funding for leisure-oriented courses. As long as such courses can be argued—however superficially—to qualify for degree credits, income-eligible students will be fully reimbursed for expenses up to $1,000. For instance, colleges could offer $1,000 whale-watching tours to taxpayers, as long as they granted participants half-time credit toward a marine biology degree. The requirements that the student be enrolled at least half-time and that the courses be creditable toward a degree are the sole regulatory mechanisms available to the IRS for curtailing such abuse. The IRS cannot be expected to monitor course content.

The Hope tax credit is essentially a grant, requiring no copayment from qualifying taxpayers for the first $1,000 of tuition expenses. However, the risk of abuse is even larger than for the Pell Grant program, since the number of eligible persons is likely to be much larger than the number qualifying for a means-tested aid program. Only those with sufficiently low income (roughly $30,000 or less) are eligible for Pell Grants. The market for Hope Scholarship subsidies encompasses the majority of American families—from those with incomes just high enough to benefit from a nonrefundable tax credit all the way up to those with $100,000 in income. Therefore, an opportunistic higher education institution that finds a way to grant half-time degree credit to middle-income taxpayers stands to reap enormous rewards. The temptation may prove too great for many institutions to resist.

The Prospects for Tuition Inflation at Private Institutions

The new tax legislation is unlikely to lead to dramatic increases in student charges at those institutions with tuition already above $5,000. The reason is simple: there is little effect on the marginal cost to families when such institutions raise tuition. The few institutions with tuition below $1,000 will have a clear incentive to raise their tuition, since students in families with sufficient taxable income would be paying nothing on the margin for any tuition increase. Likewise, those with tuition between $1,000 and $2,000 will be receiving 50 percent tax subsidies to cover the cost. However, those with out-of-pocket tuition costs above $2,000 will be receiving, at most, 20 percent on the margin for tuition increases up to $5,000. (Indeed, first- and second-year students at such institutions will be paying 100 percent of any tuition increase, since they would be expected to be taking the Hope Scholarship credit rather than the other type of tax credit.) Above $5,000, families would be paying 100 percent of any tuition increase.

For those already paying more than $5,000 per year to attend college, the primary impact of the tax law changes will be an income effect rather than a price effect—as if the federal government were sending families a tax refund unrelated to how much more they spend on college. These families may spend some of their tax savings on higher education, but they are just as likely to spend it on other consumption—such as a summer vacation or new furniture. High-tuition colleges may capture a portion of the benefit if families choose to consume more education with their tax windfall, particularly those colleges with considerable market power. However, outside of the most selective private institutions, relatively little of the tax relief is likely to make it to such education-related needs as faculty salaries, dormitories, and libraries.

Tuition Inflation and State-Federal Cost Shifting at Public Institutions

In contrast to the likely small impact on private institutions, the new tax credits may encourage state policymakers to raise tuition and/or cut aid at low-cost public institutions.[3] Both the new tax credits and the subsidized student loan programs absorb a share of the cost when a low-tuition institution raises its tuition or cuts its aid to middle-income students.[4] For instance, the subsidized Stafford loan program pays the interest while a student is enrolled in school. When the interest rate is 8 percent and a student borrows to pay the full amount of tuition, the in-school interest subsidy alone is equivalent to a 26 percent subsidy on the cost of one year's tuition for a freshman. However, the subsidy only applies at lower tuition levels since, under the subsidized loan program, a student is allowed to borrow only $2,625 during the freshman year, $3,500 during the sophomore year, and $5,000 per year after the sophomore year.

In combination, the new tax credits and the in-school interest subsidy can function essentially as a federal cost-sharing scheme, absorbing a large share of the cost when state legislatures raise tuition. Since the average tuition at a public two-year and four-year college is below the combined limit for student loans and the new tax credits, many state legislatures—moreso than the private institutions that already have tuition far above the limits—are likely to be tempted by the tax credits to raise tuition.

The tax credits probably are more likely to appeal to legislators in this way, because families and students are reimbursed directly. Of course, even subsidized loans must be repaid and the in-school interest subsidy is simply a discount on the total interest bill that a borrower must eventually pay on a student loan. Students often choose not to take advantage of subsidized student loans—especially at low-cost institutions—because they may be credit-averse, don't want to be saddled with loan payments after they leave school, and can come up with the funds they need through other means, such as working. Still, at the theoretical level at least, it is important to look at all the possible subsidies that students and parents might claim, and the in-school interest subsidy is an important part of this picture.

Consider a numerical example. Suppose that a state legislature cut its appropriation and raised tuition from $1,500 per year to $1,600 per year. How much would this actually cost families? Because of the additional $100 tuition, middle-income families would qualify for $50 more per year in tax credits during the first two years of college and $20 more per year during the junior and senior years, assuming no additional tuition increases over that time. If the family deposited these tax credits in an account earning 8 percent interest, they would be worth $176 at the end of four years. In addition, if the student had not yet borrowed the maximum amount allowable under the student loan programs, he or she might qualify for an additional $86 in in-school interest subsidies while enrolled in school. At the end of four years of college, the $400 increase in tuition ($100 each year) would cost the family only $224 ($400 – $176). However, in the meantime, the federal government will have lost $176 in revenue due to the tax credits and may have paid $86 in interest through the subsidized student loan program (for a total of $262). Therefore, at the end of four years, families who are eligible for both the federal subsidized student loan program and the tax credits will have paid only 46 percent of the cost of a $100 hike in annual tuition— $224 ÷ ($224 + $262). Federal taxpayers will have paid the remainder.

Table 8.1 reports the share of any tuition increase paid for by the families of students, and by federal taxpayers, for institutions with different starting tuition levels. When an institution with tuition below $1,000 raises its tuition, the subsidy rate is even higher: 81 percent of the cost will be borne by the federal government for some families. However, by the time tuition has been raised to above $2,625 (which exceeds the Hope Scholarship limit and the student loan limit for the student's freshman year), students and their families are paying at least 80 percent on the margin over a four-year college career when their institution raises tuition. Therefore, although the extent of implicit federal cost-sharing declines at higher tuition levels, the combination of federal programs provides a very strong incentive for low-tuition institutions to raise tuition.

As emphasized in the recent report by the federal cost commission (National Commission 1998), much of the increase in tuition during the 1980s and early 1990s was due to state and local decisions to reduce appropriations to public institutions, not to an extraordinary rise in cost at those institutions. The structure of federal subsidies may have played some role in encouraging states to raise tuition, by absorbing a large share of the cost when low-tuition institutions raised their charges. The recent tax expenditures will simply add to that temptation.

TABLE 8.1

SHARE OF RISE IN TUITION PAID BY FAMILIES OF STUDENTS AND BY FEDERAL TAXPAYERS OVER A FOUR-YEAR COLLEGE CAREER, BY THE INITIAL TUITION LEVEL OF THE INSTITUTION

Initial Tuition Range	Federal Cost Sharing			Share Paid by Students and Their Families
	Hope Scholarship Tax Credit	Lifetime Learning Tax Credit	In-School Interest Subsidy	
0–$1,000	54%	9%	18%	19%
$1,000–$2,000	27%	9%	18%	46%
$2,000–$2,625	0%	9%	18%	73%
$2,625–$3,500	0%	9%	10%	80%
$3500–$5000	0%	9%	5%	86%
$5,000+	0%	0%	0%	100%

Note: For simplicity, students are assumed to be eligible for the subsidized Stafford loan program and are assumed to be borrowing to pay for tuition expenses only. In addition, the interest rate on student loans is assumed to be the same as the return available from other investments, 8 percent.

Relabeling Room and Board Charges as Tuition Charges

The tax credits also provide incentives for institutions with large residential student populations to find ways to relabel "room and board" charges as "tuition" charges. The federal financial aid system has historically treated tuition charges and room and board charges equivalently. Both are used to calculate the cost of attendance used in the allocation of such aid. However, only tuition charges qualify for the new tuition tax credit. In other words, students at an institution with tuition charges of $5,000 and room and board charges of $1,000 would qualify for a $1,500 Hope Scholarship tax credit during each of their first two years, and a $1,000 in Lifetime Learning tax credit in each of their remaining years. In contrast, students at an institution with tuition of $1,000 and room and board charges of $5,000 would qualify for much less—only a $1,000 Hope Scholarship tax credit for each of the first two years and a $200 Lifetime Learning tax credit for each of the last two years. Some dormitory costs may qualify as education expenses; for instance, the costs associated with resident advisers who do academic counseling or dormitory tutoring programs might legitimately be transferred to tuition. To the extent institutions find ways to shift these costs into tuition charges, the new tax provisions may prove to be more expensive than expected.

Interaction between Need Analysis and IRA Savings

As part of the 1992 reauthorization of the Higher Education Act, home equity was excluded from the federal need-analysis formula. As mentioned above, the new tax law also allows families to use their IRA savings to pay for their children's education and creates a new savings vehicle, the Education IRA, to encourage parents to save for a child's education. IRA balances are excluded from the federal need-analysis formula. Therefore, the only parents whose savings will now be taxed by the federal need-analysis system are those who did not have the foresight or tax savvy to shift their savings into one of these excluded savings vehicles. As such, the continued consideration of savings account balances, mutual funds, and securities in the federal need-analysis system—while IRA balances and home equity are excluded—is no longer an indirect tax on family wealth, but a tax on nonstrategic behavior.

A remedy would be to exclude all savings from the federal need-analysis formula and simply to increase the benefit reduction rate on income. Such a change would not only avoid punishing nonstrategic behavior, it would also help simplify the Free Application for Federal Student Aid (FAFSA) form, which families find so perplexing, since asset information would no longer be required. In the past, changes in the treatment of parental assets were made without an offsetting increase in the benefit reduction rate applied to family income. However, simplification need not provide a windfall to high-income families. The need-analysis system could simply be readjusted to preserve the same average expected family contribution at each income level.

To experiment with how closely a simplified formula could be constructed to replicate the need-analysis formula, I used the data from the 1992 National Postsecondary Student Aid Survey to calculate expected parental contributions based on just two characteristics: family income and family size. My results suggest that a simple 10 by 10 table, reporting the mean expected parental contribution by family income decile and family size (with family size ranging from 2 to 11), would capture nearly two-thirds of the variance in the Congressional Methodology formula for expected parental contribution for dependent students.[5] In other words, we could come fairly close to the complicated need-analysis formula simply by distributing to high school students a 10 by 10 table reporting expected family contribution by family size. Although some would lose under such an approach (those with more than one youth in college) and others would gain (those with more than average assets for a given level of family income), one would have to weigh the loss of target efficiency against the gain in terms of transparency. It is not obvious that the value of transparency would lose in that trade-off.

Retargeting the Pell Grant Program
to the Lowest-Income Students

In 1997, the president and Congress also agreed to raise the Pell Grant maximum to $3,000 from $2,700. This came after the federal need-analysis formula had been made increasingly less progressive over time by the exclusion of state taxes paid and home equity. Without additional change in the need-analysis formula, raising the Pell Grant maximum makes more families higher up the income scale eligible for Pell Grant benefits. For example, a family of four with an adjusted gross income of $45,000[6] would have an expected family contribution of roughly $3,000. Notably, in 1993, $45,000 was the median income of a married-couple family with children under the age of 18 (U.S. Department of Commerce 1996, 735). Therefore, with no change in the need-analysis formula, raising the Pell Grant maximum to $3,000 essentially opens up Pell Grant eligibility to families with incomes at roughly the median for two-parent families with children. The lowest-income youth also receive larger grants, but not as much as would be true if the need-analysis formula were better targeted. One might argue that Pell Grant resources would be better targeted by raising the benefit reduction rate on family income and using the savings to raise the Pell Grant maximum further.[7]

Although a change in the need-analysis system has always been a possibility, the availability of the Hope Scholarship tax credit has changed the trade-offs. For instance, if those families in the $35,000 to $45,000 income range were to lose eligibility for Pell Grants, part of the gap would be filled with Hope Scholarship credits, since these families would be expected to have sufficient tax liability to benefit from the tax credits.

TAX POLICY: AN ALTERNATIVE ROUTE
THROUGH AN INCOME-CONTINGENT LOAN PROGRAM

Since the passage of the Budget Enforcement Act of 1990 (BEA), federal policy toward higher education has been driven largely by the details of federal budget rules, as opposed to the political interests of traditional higher education constituencies or the technical merits of alternative policies. Although little noticed even at the time of its passage, the BEA has quietly stacked the cards in favor of entitlement programs and tax policy, as opposed to discretionary programs such as the Pell Grant program.

Many higher education policy analysts argued in 1997 that the large sums devoted to the tax law changes would be better spent elsewhere, such as in raising the Pell Grant maximum and supporting other discretionary spending programs better targeted at low-income families. However, such a large increase in discretionary spending was politically impossible—not only because of political resistance in Congress to funneling more funds through the federal bureaucracy but, as is not often understood, because of federal budget rules. Before passing a $41 billion increase in any discretionary spending program, current budget rules would have required Congress to cut some other discretionary spending programs by an equal amount. The budget rules simply do not allow Congress to trade spending increases on the discretionary side of the budget for cuts in entitlement programs or increases in tax revenue. While the Clinton administration could propose to pay for the new tax expenditures with revenue increases elsewhere in the tax law, the same revenue increases could not have been used to pay for an increase in discretionary programs. According to the strictures of the BEA, increases in discretionary programs can only be paid for with discretionary cuts, while increases in tax expenditures can be offset either by cuts in other entitlement spending or by increases in tax revenue. For this reason, rather than any more profound concern about policy design, tax policy has become the primary outlet for changes in student aid policy.

Although there are certainly costs to complicating the tax code further, it is worth considering some alternative ways in which the tax code might have been used to provide more equitable access to higher education. For instance, at least since Milton Friedman discussed the idea in *Capitalism and Freedom* in 1962, income-contingent loans have been offered as a vehicle for financing higher education. The basic idea is to offer entering college students a loan—unrelated to their own resources or their parents' circumstances—and to base repayment on lifetime earnings, forgiving a portion of the loan for those with low lifetime earnings.

Some variants of the idea require borrowers with higher lifetime earnings to subsidize the payments of low-income borrowers. However, such measures risk scaring off the potential borrowers who are most confident about their employment prospects after college, leaving only those borrowers with less-certain prospects in the borrowing pool. An alternative approach would be to subsidize with taxpayer support those with low postgraduation earnings and to require those with high postgraduation earnings to pay no more than the principal and accumulated interest on their loans.

The income-contingent repayment option currently offered to students under the direct lending program is intended to work this way. Graduates with high earnings are expected to choose one of the standard repayment plans. However, those with lower earnings or with highly variable earnings would be expected to choose the income-contingent option, in which payments are based upon a borrower and his or her spouse's adjusted gross income reported for the previous year. Those with remaining balances at the end of 25 years of repayment would have their balances forgiven. Thus, there is a mechanism in place for providing income-contingent loan forgiveness through the existing student loan programs. However, the current repayment schedules have been defined with relatively little subsidy built into the repayment scheme. Graduates with low earnings may pay over a longer period than they would if they were on the standard repayment plan, but the repayment schedule has been specified such that relatively few students can expect to have their loans forgiven at the end of 25 years. A larger subsidy could be provided by establishing a more generous repayment scheme.

However, any expansion of income contingency would require a rise in discretionary spending and, as such, is probably not an option. An alternative strategy would be to use tax policy to create a de facto income-contingent loan program. Borrowers could be asked to report annual payments on federal student loans. Those whose payments exceeded some percentage of their income could be provided a tax credit for the difference. Since student loan payments are readily verifiable, the administrative difficulties for the IRS would be less burdensome than the current Hope Scholarship tax credit, which requires establishing some mechanism for verifying current enrollment status for students attending one of the more than 3,000 Title IV–eligible institutions in the United States. Moreover, private lenders, who often have opposed income-contingent plans, may be more supportive of a plan that does not require them to administer their loans on an income-contingent basis.

In contrast to the traditional form of means-testing in student aid, the means-testing implicit in such income-contingent loan forgiveness would be based on a forward-looking assessment of a student borrower's ability to pay. Forward-looking means-testing has several advantages. First, it offers assurance to both high- and low-income families concerned about whether their children will be able to shoulder their student debt. Parents and students may value the additional peace of mind even if they never actually receive subsidies through the income-contingent option.

Second, forward-looking means-testing does not involve the same difficulty in distinguishing dependent students—those whose parents' resources are considered in the determination of need—from independent students. The distinction between dependent and independent students becomes moot if subsidies are dispensed on the basis of future incomes, rather than on the basis of the current income and assests of a student and his or her parents.

Third, the most onerous administrative burden imposed by our financial aid system—that parents and students spend long hours each year filing complicated financial aid forms—could be lightened if a larger share of available subsidies were provided on a forward-looking basis. Indeed, transferring other loan subsidies—such as in-school interest subsidies and preferential rates on Perkins loans—into income-contingent loan forgiveness would relieve millions of parents of the need to file financial aid forms every year to establish their eligibility. Only those requesting institutional aid (primarily the quarter of students who attend private four-year institutions) and those seeking federal grant or work-study aid would have to file a financial aid application.

Fourth, forward-looking means-testing can greatly diminish the marginal tax rates on income and savings implicit in the financial aid formula, since available subsidies would be distributed over an entire career of income rather than "taxing" a single year of parental income or repeatedly assessing a family's stock of accumulated assets.

CONCLUSION

Driven by the political concerns of the middle class, as well as by federal budget rules that favor tax expenditures over discretionary spending programs, Congress and the Clinton administration have dramatically shifted the terms of federal higher education policymaking. After years of debate over incremental changes to the Pell Grant and student loan programs, in 1997, $41 billion was found on the tax side of the budget for new spending in higher education.

The world of higher education is likely to become quite different as a result of the recent tax law changes. First, institutions will probably find creative ways to offer leisure-oriented courses for college credit to millions of middle-income taxpayers eligible for as much as $1,500 in tax credits for up to two years of college course work. The temptation will be stronger than that provided by past federal student aid programs, since the sum of the potential subsidies across the eligible population exceeds any previously available. Pell Grant aid has traditionally been limited to low-income families; the new subsidies are available to the vast middle class. Second, state legislatures in low-tuition states are likely to raise tuition to take advantage of the federal tax and student loan subsidies now available to those with low tuition levels. To not do so would mean forgoing rather generous new federal subsidies for state taxpayers. Third, only those private institutions with considerable market power will succeed in capturing much of the tuition tax credit by changing their distribution of grant aid; because of competitive pressures, most private institutions will be unable to take advantage of the credit. Fourth, high-income parents will take advantage of the new savings vehicles to save for their children's education. However, less of these savings will be taken into consideration in federal need-analysis calculations.

In response, I propose three changes to the federal need-analysis system and future tax policy. First, given that home equity has been excluded from federal need analysis and that parents are now allowed to withdraw their retirement savings to help pay for college, only those without the requisite tax savvy or knowledge of federal need-analysis rules will have their savings assessed by the federal need-analysis system. Therefore, it may be more equitable—and it would simplify the federal FAFSA form—to simply drop the asset test from the federal need analysis and to adjust the need-assessment formula to maintain the same average expected family contribution, based on family income. No asset test may be preferable to an arbitrary asset test.

Second, increases in the Pell Grant maximum and a gradual decline in progressivity of the federal need-analysis system over the past two decades have combined to open up eligibility for Pell Grant receipt to those even at the median family income level. Better targeting of federal aid through an increase in the progressivity of the federal need-analysis formula would enable an increase in Pell Grant spending to benefit those with the lowest income. Both goals might be achieved by dramatically simplifying the need-analysis formula to consider only parental adjusted gross income, family size, and student income and savings. The availability of the Hope Scholarship tax credit makes this option more attractive than in the past, since the tax credit would partially reimburse many of the moderate-income families who, if these changes were implemented, would be excluded from Pell Grant eligibility.

Third, to the extent that federal budget rules continue to favor tax expenditures over discretionary programs, we should think more creatively about the potential uses of federal tax expenditures in higher education. For instance, federal tax expenditures could be used as a means for providing income-contingent loan forgiveness by providing tax credits to those with student loan payments exceeding some percentage of their income.

All over Washington, higher education policy analysts are brushing up on their knowledge of tax law. If the 30-year war over student aid spending is to be fought on this new front, it may be worthwhile to take a fresh look at the traditional sources of student aid spending. The shift in the battlefields may offer opportunities for improved policymaking.

NOTES

1. The limit applies to each taxpaying unit, not to each student.
2. Participants will still pay a tax on any capital gains at withdrawal.
3. In fact, the legislative analyst's office in California has already recognized the opportunity and has recommended that the legislature raise tuition to take advantage of the new federal subsidies (Basinger 1998).
4. The Pell Grant program does not have the same impact on marginal cost for families because the grant amount is based on student characteristics and, since 1992, has been largely unrelated to actual tuition charges.
5. In statistical terms, the R^2 for a regression of expected parental contribution on the full set of interactions between family income decile and family size was .62. Such a method would probably explain more of the variation today, since housing assets were excluded after 1992.

6. One must assume that the family has no countable assets above the asset limit ($40,900 for two-parent families in the 45–49 age group) and that both parents are working. I also assume that the family is paying U.S. income tax of $4,950 (11 percent), Social Security tax of $3,442 (7.65 percent) and state income tax of $3,600 (8 percent).

7. Hauptman and Rice (1997) make a similar argument.

REFERENCES

Basinger, J. 1998. "California Legislature Urged to Raise Tuition to Offset Federal Tax Credits." *Chronicle of Higher Education* February 16.

Friedman, M. 1962. *Capitalism and Freedom.* Chicago: University of Chicago Press.

Hauptman, A., and L. Rice. 1997. "Coordinating Financial Aid with Tuition Tax Benefits." Brookings Policy Brief No. 28 (December).

Kane, T. J. 1997. "Beyond Tax Relief: Long-Term Challenges in Financing Higher Education." *National Tax Journal* 50 (June): 335–49.

National Commission on the Cost of Higher Education. 1998. *Straight Talk about College Costs and Prices.* The Report of the National Commission on the Cost of Higher Education. Phoenix, AZ: Oryx Press.

U.S. Department of Commerce, Bureau of the Census. 1996. *Statistical Abstract of the United States, 1995.* Washington, DC: Government Printing Office.

CHAPTER 9

State Policy Response to the Taxpayer Relief Act of 1997

Kristin D. Conklin and Joni E. Finney

The Taxpayer Relief Act of 1997 (TRA 1997) is the largest single increase in federal funding for higher education since the GI Bill. This chapter explores the impact of this new federal law on state higher education policy and offers options and recommendations for state response. These recommendations are based on the belief that programs which support both *access* and *affordability* are necessary to advance the larger national policy of *college opportunity*, but that affordability should not be allowed to supersede access as a policy goal.

The definitions of access and affordability used in this chapter differ somewhat from those used elsewhere in this volume. At the federal level, the general assumption is that programs to support access are targeted and need-based, such as the Pell Grant program. In contrast, programs to support affordability, such as Stafford unsubsidized loans, are those made available to all students regardless of income. With these definitions, it usually is an easy matter to distinguish programs and policies that support access from those that promote affordability.

At the state level, however, these distinctions do not apply—there, affordability and access typically are linked. For example, low tuition policies have been implemented by many states to address these paired goals. Similarly, many state need-based financial aid programs address both access and affordability; for example, California, New York, and Illinois use broad income parameters for student aid eligibility and provide aid dollars for students to attend private institutions. Thus, because we are concerned with state policy in this chapter, we make the basic assumption that access and affordability are inextricably linked.

Despite states' traditional coupling of access and affordability, over the past two decades, affordability has become an increasingly important policy goal. Tuition increases outpacing growth in family incomes, along with the public's growing perception of higher education as essential, have led to political pressure for state policies that explicitly address the affordability concerns of the middle class—a focus that usually does not consider the needs of low-income students. State college savings and prepaid tuition plans are examples of this new priority. At the federal level, the shift from grants to loans as the centerpiece of student aid is the most striking example of a long-term change in priorities, from supporting college access for the needy to promoting college affordability for the middle class. TRA 1997 is only the most recent evidence of this shift in policy focus. Whether TRA 1997 will trigger further movement by the states in the direction of emphasizing affordability remains to be seen.

This chapter hopes to influence state policy decision making by describing the arguments for and against various policy options. It begins with a description of the provisions of TRA 1997 and a discussion of which students and families will benefit from them. We then discuss interactions between TRA 1997 and state policy and outline options for state policy response, along with our own recommendations. The chapter closes by describing a scenario under which states might use TRA 1997 as an opportunity to build a new consensus about how responsibility for paying for higher education ought to be shared among students and their families, colleges and universities, and government.

THE TAXPAYER RELIEF ACT OF 1997

In 1997, the federal government paid attention to college access and affordability—but not in balanced measure. Combining the one-year costs of the tuition tax credits with the Stafford unsubsidized loan program, federal financial aid policies directed solely at affordability now make up 50 percent of all federal aid. Just six years ago, in the 1992–93 academic year, federal financial aid was almost entirely focused on access—non-need-based aid provided by the federal government comprised just 1 percent of all federal aid.[1] TRA 1997 is a noteworthy new direction for federal higher education policy, both in terms of the magnitude of the investment and its design; Table 9.1 summarizes its seven major provisions.[2]

In magnitude of new resources, the federal government shifted its emphasis from providing access to making college more affordable. Just months after passing TRA 1997, Congress and President Bill Clinton also expanded eligibility for the federal government's largest need-based program designed to provide college access, the Pell Grant. Specifically, the maximum award and

TABLE 9.1

MAJOR PROVISIONS OF THE TAXPAYER RELIEF ACT OF 1997

Provision	General Description	Income Too Low for Any Benefits	Income Too Low for Full Benefits	Income Too High for Full Benefits	Income Too High for Any Benefits
Hope Tax Credit	Worth up to $1,500 for the first two years of college, at least part-time	$17,500 dependent $6,800 independent	$27,500 dependent $16,800 independent	$80-$100,000 file joint $40-$50,000 file single	$100,000+ file joint $50,000+ file single
Lifetime Learning Tax Credit	Worth up to $1,000 a year for college past first two years, or less than part-time until 2002	$17,500 dependent $6,800 independent	$24,100 dependent $13,450 independent	$80-$100,000 file joint $40-$50,000 file single	$100,000+ file joint $50,000+ file single
Education IRA	Deposit up to $500 a year; interest earned tax-free; deductions excluded from beneficiary's income			$150-$160,000 file joint $95-$110,000 file single	$160,000+ file joint $110,000+ file single
Traditional IRA	Early withdrawal penalty waived if funds used for college				
Prepaid College Tuition Plan	Extends savings in state plans to room and board costs				
Student Loan Interest Deduction	Interest paid deductible for first 60 months of repayment ($1,000 in 1998)			$80-$100,000 file joint $40-50,000 file single	$100,000+ file joint $50,000+ file single
Student Loan Forgiveness	Loans forgiven for work in high-need areas are excluded from taxable income				

Note: Figures for dependent students assumes a family of four with married parents filing jointly.

Sources: U.S. Department of the Treasury 1997; 1998.

the number of students who can receive Pell Grants were increased. The Pell Grant maximum was increased by $300 to a new maximum award of $3,000. The income protection allowance was increased for both independent students and dependent students who work, allowing more students to qualify for grants. Combined, these new changes to the Pell Grant Program cost approximately $650 million for FY 1998, or 7 percent of the expected cost in 1998 for the tuition tax credits ($9 billion).

In design, TRA 1997 moves away from the historical role the federal government has played in providing access to college for students from low-income families. It contains a set of nonrefundable tax credits designed to reduce the cost of college attendance—measures that will not stimulate new college enrollment to any great extent. Research on student enrollment responses to price changes resulting from financial aid has consistently shown sizable increases for low-income students when prices decline and either small or nonexistent changes for middle- and high-income students (Manski and Wise 1983; Schwartz 1986; and McPherson and Schapiro 1991).[3] With the low-income population benefiting least from the price reductions that result from the new tuition tax credits, it is unlikely that enrollment response will be great.

Three aspects of TRA 1997 are of particular importance.

- There is no cap on the possible "cost" of the tax credits in foregone tax revenue. The Hope and Lifetime Learning tax credits are projected to cost approximately $40 billion over five years, but changes in state and institutional policy can quickly increase these costs. Already, the tax credits are projected to equal the cost of all other federal financial aid combined, including Pell Grants, State Student Incentive grants, and student loan interest subsidies.

- Income tax benefits accrue in the current year for tax-related activities of the prior year. Under TRA 1997, the tax credit benefits are realized only after the student is enrolled in a postsecondary institution. The delay between tuition payment and receipt of the tax credit can be up to 15 months, assuming tuition is paid in January of one tax year and taxes are filed in April of the next year. Traditional price incentives, such as outright grants, scholarships, or loans, are, for practical purposes, realized directly at the time of enrollment. This new, deferred, and less-direct delivery method will cloud assessment of the credits' impact. That is, it will be difficult to evaluate the extent to which a particular benefit has accomplished its primary objective of helping taxpayers pay for college, as opposed to helping pay for other, noneducational items.

- The tax credit benefits of TRA 1997 are tax expenditures and, as such, will not be subjected to review in the annual appropriations process as are most other federal student aid programs, or in the periodic reauthorization that all federal aid programs undergo. As a result, the regular examination of college access and affordability policies will exclude one of the federal government's largest financial aid programs.

Student and Family Beneficiaries of the New Federal Affordability Policy

Middle- and upper-middle income students and their families benefit most from the federal Hope and Lifetime Learning tax credits. The new tax credits reduce federal taxes for eligible students (or for the families of dependent eligible students). Table 9.2 shows how families and students at different income levels can use federal student aid programs to help pay for college. In general, families who qualify for a Pell Grant cannot receive the maximum tax credit from the Hope Scholarship.[4] For instance, a family with a student in a four-year public college and with a taxable income of $30,000 or less will not receive the maximum Hope tax credit.

TABLE 9.2

ESTIMATED BENEFITS OF FEDERAL STUDENT AID, FOR UNDERGRADUATES AT FOUR-YEAR PUBLIC COLLEGES AND UNIVERSITIES, BY TAXABLE INCOME

Taxable Income	Pell Grant	Loan Subsidy	Hope Tax Credit	Total Aid
$10,000	$3,000	$875	$0	$3,87
$20,000	$3,000	$875	$0	$3,875
$30,000	$2,450	$875	$550	$3,875
$40,000	$950	$875	$1,500	$3,325
$50,000	$0	$875	$1,500	$2,375
$60,000	$0	$0	$1,500	$1,500
$70,000	$0	$0	$1,500	$1,500
$80,000	$0	$0	$1,500	$1,500
$90,000	$0	$0	$750	$750
$100,000	$0	$0	$0	$0
Average Tuition = $3,000			Average Total Price = $10,000	

Notes: Calculations are for full-time freshmen, and income is defined as adjusted gross income for joint filers with two dependents. Pell Grants are for families of four with one child in college. Loan subsidy is based on maximum subsidized loan for freshmen, $2,625. Eligibility for tax credit is determined by calculating tuition less all grants, scholarships, and other tax-free educational assistance. Tax credit is $0 if family income is less than $30,000 or net tuition is negative. Maximum allowable tax credit is $1,250 for 2-year colleges and $1,500 for 4-year colleges.

Source: Hauptman and Rice 1997.

As shown in Table 9.3, families with taxable income between $40,000 and $90,000 a year will find that the Hope tax credit can reduce the percent of income needed to pay for a four-year public university by between one and three percentage points. In contrast, families earning $30,000 a year or less will not benefit from the tuition tax credits.

TABLE 9.3

ESTIMATED TOTAL PRICE OF ATTENDANCE BEFORE AND AFTER ENACTMENT OF THE HOPE TAX CREDIT, BY TAXABLE FAMILY INCOME, FOR UNDERGRADUATES AT FOUR-YEAR PUBLIC COLLEGES AND UNIVERSITIES

Taxable Income	Total Price before Tax Credit	Total Price as % of Income	Total Price after Tax Credit	Total Price as % of Income
$10,000	$6,125	61%	$6,125	61%
$20,000	$6,125	31%	$6,125	31%
$30,000	$6,125	20%	$6,125	20%
$40,000	$8,175	20%	$6,675	17%
$50,000	$9,125	18%	$7,625	15%
$60,000	$10,000	17%	$8,500	14%
$70,000	$10,000	14%	$8,500	12%
$80,000	$10,000	13%	$8,500	11%
$90,000	$10,000	11%	$9,250	10%
$100,000	$10,000	10%	$10,000	10%

Average Tuition = $3,000	Average Total Price = $10,000

Notes: Calculations are for full-time freshmen. Taxable family income is defined as adjusted gross income for taxpayer filing jointly with two dependents. Pell grants are for families of four with one child in college. Loan subsidy is based on the maximum subsidized loan for freshmen, $2,625. Eligibility for tax credit is determined by tuition less all grants, scholarships, and other tax-free educational assistance. Tax credit is $0 if family income is less than $30,000 or net tuition is negative. Maximum allowable tax credit is $1,250 for two-year colleges and $1,500 for four-year colleges. Total price equals tuition, required fees, and room and board—minus scholarships, grants, and other tax-free educational assistance received by the student.

Source: Hauptman and Rice 1997.

Students at higher-priced institutions benefit more than students at lower-priced institutions, particularly community colleges. Students at public community colleges who are from low-income familes can get some or all of their tuition and fees paid by federal need-based Pell Grants. Community college students are eligible for the maximum Hope tax credit only if their family income is between $50,000 and $80,000; students with family income of $40,000 receive a partial credit. This occurs because Pell Grants, and other grant assistance, cover most or all of tuition for community college students with income below $40,000. In contrast, students attending more expensive private four-year colleges can receive the maximum Hope tax credit when their family income falls between $30,000 and $80,000 because Pell Grants pay only a fraction of the higher tuition and fees.

In addition, community colleges are at a disadvantage because they enroll a large proportion of the students whose income is too low to qualify for the tax credit. In 1994, between one-third and one-half of all college students whose families made $30,000 or less attended a public community college (Horn and Berkhold 1998). Under TRA 1997, community college students who receive Pell Grants and whose families make $30,000 or less are not eligible to receive any tax credit.

Many of the students eligible for the Hope and Lifetime Learning tax credits are also most likely to participate in the new savings programs. Findings from an August 1995 U.S. General Accounting Office study of state prepaid tuition programs showed that these plans most benefit middle- and upper-income families (U.S. General Accounting Office 1995). In Kentucky, 61 percent of the participating families had income over $50,000, while only 10 percent of participants were from families with income under $25,000. In Florida, 51 percent of the participating families had income above $100,000, and another third had income between $50,000 and $100,000; only 5 percent of participants were from families with income less than $25,000.

Nearly all students and families who borrow money to pay for college will benefit to some extent from the student loan interest deduction. The U.S. General Accounting Office (1998) reports that students whose family income is below $45,000 are 2.5 times more likely to borrow than students whose family income falls between $60,000 and $100,000. However, it also found that students with higher income tend to borrow more when they do borrow; their large interest payments would qualify them to file for larger income tax deductions. Income caps will disqualify some students, and loan volume and tax rates will determine variation in the absolute dollar value of the benefit. Nonetheless, this provision benefits students from across the income spectrum.

Traditional college-age students (ages 18 to 24) and their families are the primary beneficiaries of the Hope Scholarship and Lifetime Learning tax credits. Younger students are classified as dependent for purposes of financial aid and are expected to rely on their family income to help pay for college. In 1995–96, the average dependent student was 20 years old. In comparison, independent students, who are on average 33 years old, tend to pay for college with their own income and, as result, have lower income on average. Even though independent students who are single filers qualify for the Hope tax credit at lower income levels than dependent students whose parents file jointly, they are still less likely to be eligible for some or all of the tax credits. Based on income data from 1995–96, 47 percent of independent undergraduates would be ineligible for any tax credit, compared with 26 percent of dependent undergraduates (TERI 1997).

The Interaction of New Federal Policy and Existing State Policies

Although the federal income tax credits flow directly to taxpayers, they have significant implications for state policy. Specifically, TRA 1997 creates incentives for states to capture federal tax credit dollars by implementing measures that also have the effect of weakening access. States could, by reducing need-based aid or by increasing tuition, gain a larger share of the tax credit dollars. In general, the total dollar amount of the benefit for each state from TRA 1997 will vary based on the income levels of college students and their families in that state, distribution of students among lower-priced and higher priced institutions, amount of state-sponsored financial aid, and the number of college students or their families who file in a state.

In the prior section, we examined the impact of student and family income levels on the benefits to be expected from the 1997 act. Here, we evaluate how these benefits vary because of differences in state policies.

States with large financial aid programs of their own will find that residents at some income levels will not qualify for the full federal tax credit if they receive state support. This is because tax credit eligibility is based on tuition and required fees *minus all grants and scholarships*, whether they are awarded on a need or merit basis. New York, for instance, provides its residents with need-based financial aid through its Tuition Assistance Program. Under this entitlement program, which costs about $630 million annually, New York families with a student in a four-year public college would not be eligible for the maximum Hope tax credit unless their taxable income is $45,000 or higher. Based on national averages, most families would be eligible for the full Hope tax credit if their annual taxable income is $40,000. This aspect of TRA 1997 has caused the New York State Higher Education Services Corporation to recommend studying whether federal funds can be substituted for state funds (New York State 1998). Similarly, Pennsylvania has a significant need-based scholarship program, $240.5 million in 1996–97, which will offset eligibility for a federal tax credit dollar-for-dollar, and will lower the average tax credit per student.

In contrast, Montana, which has one of the smallest state-sponsored scholarship programs in the country with total expenditures of just $316,000 a year, will see larger than average tax credits. The average tax credit per student projected for Montana is one of the largest among the states—$712, compared with the national average of $698.[5]

Some states have historically supported access through low tuition and fees. These states will be tempted to increase tuition. In California, for example, 60 percent of the college population attend community colleges, where fees are less than $400 per year; thus, none of these students are eligible for the maximum credit. The California's Legislative Analyst's Office has recommended that community college fees be raised to capture the full value of the tuition tax credit, while, at the same time, increasing financial aid for those students ineligible for the tax credits (California Legislative Analyst 1998). The latter component is critical. California and other states with similar policies should not raise fees simply to capture the federal tax credits of eligible taxpayers without ensuring access for those who are ineligible.

POLICY OPTIONS AND RECOMMENDATIONS FOR THE STATES

We believe that governors and state legislatures should explicitly establish, in advance, that any measures they adopt because of TRA 1997 will not diminish the overall level of state support for higher education. Further, we urge that they make sure that the affordability problems of middle-income students and families are not addressed at the expense of access to college for low-income students. Indeed, TRA 1997 creates an opportunity for many states to assist middle-income families *and* address the financial needs of low-income families.

Options are available to the states because TRA 1997 adds a major new revenue stream to the public financing of higher education. In 1998–99, the first year of the new tax provisions, California's students and families are expected to receive $1.2 billion in Hope and Lifetime Learning tax credits— the highest state total. In comparison, they received $785 million in 1995–96 for *all other federal financial aid combined*. Alaska will receive the lowest state total, and its students and families are projected to receive $19 million annually in federal tax credits, in comparison with $4.6 million in 1995–96 for all other federal financial aid.

If budget numbers were the only consideration, the federal program creates a golden "opportunity" for a state to reduce its financial commitment to higher education. By substituting federal dollars, a state could shift costs to the federal government by increasing tuition or by reducing need-based financial aid, or both. But money is not the only consideration; meeting the access and affordability needs of all citizens should remain the fundamental state policy objective.

Because of the sheer size of this new federal investment, most states should examine and review their financing of higher education. Specifically, they should evaluate the impact of state and federal policies on existing and prospective student populations using current, state-level data. This examination should enable states to determine the impact of the new federal tax policies on existing state policy, not only in terms of dollars, but also in terms of the access and affordability needs of all state citizens. State policymakers should then ask how any proposed response to TRA 1997 will reinforce the state's particular policy goals.

After such examination, a state may take action—or it may choose not to do anything. The latter alternative—no action—deserves consideration. TRA 1997 does not require that states change existing policies or enact new policies and, as we write, most states are waiting to see how the new federal program is implemented.[6] By taking no action, policymakers can endorse the federal objective of making college more affordable for middle-income families; however, since this option may have adverse implications for the state's access policies, states should explore these implications before a final decision is made.

If a state government chooses to take action, many policy options are available. We have already noted the opportunity to change tuition policies to capture revenue from the new federal tax credits. Because low-income students do not benefit from the new federal tax provisions, and would be harmed disproportionately by a tuition increase, the primacy of access as a state policy objective dictates that a state should *never* increase tuition and fees for the *sole* purpose of capturing federal revenue. Tuition should be increased if—and only if—the needs of low-income students are met by sufficient increases in need-based aid.

The particular circumstances in each state will determine how, if at all, a state responds to the new federal law. Depending on the circumstances, the major options and recommended actions are as follows:

- States could consider treating the federal tax credits as income when calculating state student aid eligibility. Some middle-income students who would have previously qualified for state financial aid programs will no longer qualify because of their participation in the federal tax credit program. Savings gained in the state financial aid programs would then be available to target state resources toward lower-income students not eligible for any or all of the federal tax credits. Or, savings gained could be used to enhance or initiate college preparation programs in the public schools.

- State policymakers could react to TRA 1997 by restraining the growth of new state grant programs aimed at addressing the affordability concerns of middle- and upper-income parents. Such programs convey benefits on the same students and families eligible to receive federal tax credits and, because the tax credits are based on tuition less all grants and scholarships, would substitute state funds for the federal tuition tax credits.

- States should conform their state tax codes to incorporate the new provision for making interest on student loans deductible for state income tax purposes. Conformation will maintain simplicity for both the state and the taxpayer and will facilitate auditing of state tax returns by keeping the definition of adjusted gross income comparable.
- States should not conform state tax codes to accommodate the federal tuition tax credits. Conformation would duplicate the benefits already afforded to middle-income students and their families by the federal tax credits. Conforming the state tax code to the new federal tax credit provisions would further complicate state income tax returns because filing for a duplicate state tuition tax credit would add an additional line to the tax form.
- States without a state-sponsored prepaid tuition plan should consider establishing one. TRA 1997 expanded eligible expenses for which withdrawals can be made to include reasonable costs of room and board. This increased exclusion of interest earnings is a new incentive for states to develop prepaid plans.
- States could encourage use of the federal tax credits by making "bridge" loans available at the beginning of the academic year, to be repaid when the tax credit is received.

As states examine the impact of TRA 1997 on their own student financial aid programs, other options undoubtedly will emerge. Although states may defer changes in their policies, all states should encourage maximum knowledge and use of the new, federal tax benefits by making information about them widely available—at a minimum through public service announcements, high schools, and guidance counselors.

POLITICS, ACCESS, AND AFFORDABILITY

Historically, higher education has been less subject to federal and state political intervention—partisan or otherwise—than have other state services. Nevertheless, colleges and universities—both public and private—have been greatly influenced by federal policy initiatives and state policy responses; the land-grant act and the GI Bill are prime examples of such influence. The Taxpayer Relief Act of 1997 is the latest and one of the most significant federal policies supporting higher education. Its emphasis on tax benefits for middle-class families is based on a political reality: middle-class families pay taxes and are a critical class of voters whom politicians must attract to be elected.

While TRA 1997 provides an opportunity for states to address both access and affordability, it also provides an opportunity—and incentives—for states to reduce their overall financial commitment to higher education. The true test of this grim scenario likely will come within the next 10 years when states experience a normal cyclical recession and turn to students and families to fill any "budget gap" created by decreases in state appropriations. The federal tax credits provide an opportunity to compensate for lost state dollars. We strongly urge that states not reduce their overall financial commitment to higher education but, instead, redirect resources to other areas of need within higher education.

With no intent to disparage the needs of the middle class, we urge that this new federal initiative be used by governors and state legislators as a catalyst for reaffirming and expanding college access policies for all citizens. Polls and surveys show that middle-class voters are not narrowly focused on their own children. Rather, they are equally concerned with educational opportunity for all qualified students, regardless of their financial circumstances. Neither the middle class nor most Americans have forgotten that college opportunity must comprise both access *and* affordability. The findings of a 1998 national survey are relevant: roughly twice as many respondents believed that students from low-income families had less opportunity for college than did those either from minority racial or ethnic backgrounds or from middle-class families. Perhaps the major finding of the survey was:

> Because higher education has become so important, Americans are convinced that no qualified and motivated student should be denied an opportunity to go to a college or university merely because of the price. (Immerwahr 1998)

Most urgently needed by states is the development of a new consensus on how the costs of higher education ought to be shared among government, students and their families, and institutions. While it was not the original intention of TRA 1997 to further such a policy agenda, if it provides such an occasion in the states—and we hope it will do so—state policies supporting accessible *and* affordable higher education need not be separated, but joined to ensure the traditional commitment to educational opportunity for the next generation.

NOTES

1. Figures are projected costs for generally available federal aid for 1997–98, including Pell Grants, SSIG, work-study, Perkins loans, Ford direct loans, and Family Education

    loans. Excludes $2.3 billion in specially directed financial aid, such as aid to veterans and the military.

2. The provisions of the 1997 act are described in detail by Thomas J. Kane in "Student Aid after Tax Reform: Risks and Opportunities" in this volume.

3. These studies focused on receipt of traditional grants and scholarships; the expected enrollment response to financial aid delivered through the income tax system may be lower.

4. Grants and scholarships reduce eligibility for either of the tuition tax credits, but loan subsidies do not affect eligibility.

5. All projections of foregone federal tax revenue and estimated number of beneficiaries by state were produced by the U.S. Department of Education and are based on enrollment, income, and tuition data from the 1995–96 academic year. A full account of projected tuition tax credit revenue by state and average credit per recipient is provided in Tables 1 and 2 of the National Center for Public Policy and Higher Education's Report 98-6 "Federal Tuition Tax Credits and State Higher Education Policy."

6. A full accounting of state activity as of June 1998 is provided in Table 6 of the National Center for Public Policy and Higher Education's Report 98-6 "Federal Tuition Tax Credits and State Higher Education Policy."

REFERENCES

California Legislative Analyst. 1998. *Taking Advantage of New Federal Higher Education Tax Credits*. Sacramento, CA: California Legislative Analyst.

Hauptman, A., and L. Rice. 1997. *Coordinating Financial Aid with Tuition Tax Benefits*. Brookings Policy Brief No. 28 (December). Washington, DC: The Brookings Institution.

Horn, L., and J. Berkhold. 1998. *Profile of Undergraduates in United States Postsecondary Institutions, 1995–96*. Washington, DC: National Center for Education Statistics.

Immerwahr, J. 1998. *The Price of Admission: The Growing Importance of Higher Education*. San Jose, CA: The National Center for Public Policy and Higher Education.

Manski, C. F., and D. A. Wise. 1983. *College Choice in America*. Cambridge, MA: Harvard University Press.

McPherson, M., and M. Schapiro. 1991. "Does Student Aid Affect College Enrollment? New Evidence on a Persistent Controversy." *American Economic Review* 81 (March): 309–18.

New York State Higher Education Services Corporation. 1998. "Preliminary Report on the Restructuring of New York's Grant and Scholarship Programs, including the Tuition Assistance Program." Albany, NY.

Schwartz, J. B. 1986. "Wealth Neutrality in Higher Education: The Effects of Student Grants." *Economics of Education Review* 5(2): 107–17.

TERI (The Education Resources Institute) and the Institute for Higher Education Policy. 1997. *Missed Opportunities: A New Look at Disadvantaged College Aspirants*. Washington, DC: The Institute for Higher Education Policy.

U.S. Department of Treasury, Internal Revenue Service. 1997. Form 1040 U.S. Individual Income Tax Return. Washington, DC: Internal Revenue Service.

———. 1998. *Tax Benefits for Higher Education.* Publication 970. Washington, DC: Internal Revenue Service.

U.S. General Accounting Office. 1995. *College Savings Information on State Tuition Prepayment Programs.* Washington, DC: Government Printing Office.

———. 1998. *Report on Student Debt Burdens.* Washington, DC: Government Printing Office.

CHAPTER 10

Crisis or Convenience
Why Are Students Borrowing More?

Jacqueline E. King

Since 1994, when it became clear that student borrowing had jumped by over 40 percent in one year, many policy analysts—including this author—have taken educated guesses as to how the distribution of loan dollars has changed and which students and institutions are responsible for the increase in borrowing. Data from the 1995–96 National Postsecondary Student Aid Study (NPSAS:96) shed new light on these matters, confirming some of the preliminary interpretations, refuting others, and providing additional insights on how college affordability and student borrowing have—and have not—changed (U.S. Department of Education 1998a).

Why did student borrowing increase so rapidly? In 1992, as part of the reauthorization of the Higher Education Act, Congress broadened access to the Stafford loan program. Traditional-aged single undergraduates who did not qualify for subsidized Stafford loans were made eligible for unsubsidized Stafford loans.[1] Congress also raised the annual limits on student borrowing and liberalized the system for determining federal aid eligibility, which enabled more students to qualify for Stafford subsidized loans. As a result, between academic years 1992–93 and 1995–96, undergraduate borrowing through the main federal student loan programs increased more than 100 percent.[2]

CRISIS OR CONVENIENCE?

Some have decried this increase in loan volume as evidence of a general crisis of student indebtedness and college affordability (TERI 1995). The popular press has interpreted such statements to mean that loan volume is more closely related to tuition prices than to statutory changes in eligibility or borrowing limits. If this were the case, one would expect to see loan volume increases paralleling increases in tuition prices. Instead, loan volume spikes after every reauthorization because increases in annual and cumulative loan limits and changes in eligibility are made at that time.

Thus, most analysts reject the notion that increased borrowing is a direct result of tuition increases. Rather, the common wisdom has been that the increase in undergraduate borrowing is due to two phenomena: (1) newly eligible dependent students borrowing largely for convenience, and (2) other students reacting to the stimuli of new borrowing limits, even when there may have been no changes in their financial need.

The term "convenience" is not meant pejoratively. Borrowing has not almost doubled so that students could take lavish spring break trips to Mexico or the Caribbean. Convenience borrowing simply means that students are using loans to substitute for, or to augment, other sources of funding. Dependent middle-income students who took out unsubsidized loans after the 1992 reauthorization were able—somehow—to afford college before this form of credit became available. It may have been difficult for them to scrape together the necessary funds, but they were able to do so. The availability of unsubsidized loans did not lead to an increase in the enrollment of middle- and upper-income students; they were no less likely to attend college before 1992. The only change was that now they could substitute unsubsidized student loans for some other less convenient form of financing.

The second phenomenon has sometimes been referred to as the "goldfish rule": all else being equal, the more a goldfish is fed, the more it will eat. When eligibility was broadened and loan limits raised, students were offered larger loans in their financial aid packages. Many simply checked "accept" next to those amounts on their financial aid award letters, not considering either whether they *really* needed the money or how the increased debt would affect them after graduation. This explanation of increased borrowing is confirmed by research. In Pennsylvania, the state student loan guaranty agency compared individual students who borrowed before and after the reauthorization and found that students whose financial circumstances were unchanged borrowed more money when their eligibility was increased (Redd 1994). To some extent, this is another form of convenience borrowing, although many middle-income borrowers might argue vociferously that they "need" the additional funds. In many cases, this may be true. Still, whether or not students and parents ever recognize it, student loan funds frequently either augment or replace other sources of funding.

While the NPSAS:96 data largely confirm these hypotheses, they also make clear that low-income students are borrowing more to meet basic education and living expenses, and that low-income independent undergraduates, in particular, are borrowing considerably more than they did prior to the last reauthorization.[3] The increase in borrowing by this latter group was not predicted and may very well constitute a true crisis. As so often is the case, the situation is far more complex than anyone had predicted.

WHO IS BORROWING MORE, AND WHY?

Understanding the financial circumstances of students responsible for most of the growth in loan volume should allow policymakers to craft more tailored financial aid policies. In 1992–93, undergraduates borrowed $8 billion through the Stafford loan program; three years later, borrowing had jumped to almost $18 billion. What types of students were primarily responsible for this dramatic change, and why did their borrowing increase?

To answer these questions, data on the personal characteristics of Stafford borrowers, on the college costs they faced, and the resources available to meet those costs are presented. Two variables will be relied on primarily: (1) the net price[4] of the institution and (2) the amount the federal government expects a family to contribute to their child's education. The student groups used throughout this chapter are defined in Table 10.1.

TABLE 10.1

STUDENT GROUP DEFINITIONS

Student Classification		Annual Income**
Dependent*	Low-Income	AGI under $30,000
	Middle-Income	AGI $30,000 to 69,999
	Upper-Income	AGI $70,000 or More
Independent*	Low-Income	AGI under $10,000
	Middle-Income	AGI $10,000 or More

AGI   Adjusted gross income.
*   Under the current definitions, *dependent* students are those undergraduates who are under 24 years of age, are unmarried, or have no dependents. Conversely, *independent* undergraduates must be at least 24 years old, or must be married or have dependents. The income and assets of independent students' parents are not considered when determining eligibility for federal student aid.
**   Annual income for dependent students includes both student and parent income.

For dependent students, the income groups were chosen to correspond roughly to the lowest quartile, middle 50 percent, and upper quartile of families with children in college nationally. The independent student categories correspond to the lowest quartile of independent students and the remaining 75 percent. There are very few independent students who report AGI over $50,000, so no attempt is made to distinguish between middle- and upper-income independent students. Figure 10.1 breaks out the growth in Stafford loan volume for these five types of students.

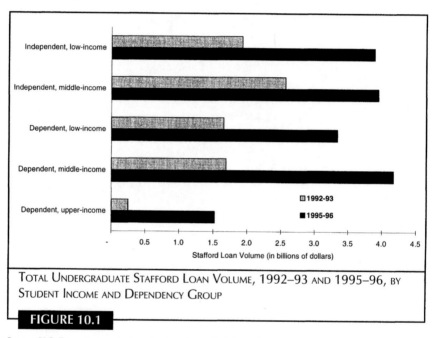

TOTAL UNDERGRADUATE STAFFORD LOAN VOLUME, 1992–93 AND 1995–96, BY
STUDENT INCOME AND DEPENDENCY GROUP

FIGURE 10.1

Source: U.S. Department of Education 1998a; analysis by author.

This chapter presents descriptions of the three groups among these five that account for the largest share of the increase in Stafford Loan volume. Figure 10.2 shows that these three groups are

- dependent middle-income students
- dependent low-income students
- independent low-income students

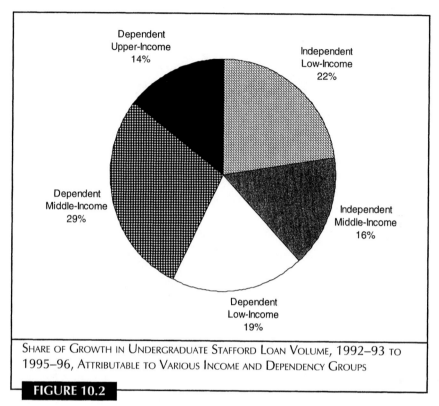

SHARE OF GROWTH IN UNDERGRADUATE STAFFORD LOAN VOLUME, 1992–93 TO
1995–96, ATTRIBUTABLE TO VARIOUS INCOME AND DEPENDENCY GROUPS

FIGURE 10.2

Source: U.S. Department of Education 1998a; analysis by author.

Dependent Middle-Income Students

Figure 10.2 shows that middle-income dependent borrowers were responsible
for the largest share of loan volume growth (29 percent of new volume). These
students represented 34 percent of the increase in the number of student
borrowers over this period (see Figure 10.3).

The "convenience" borrowing characterization outlined above generally
describes the behavior of this group of students. However, almost one-third of
middle-income dependent borrowers attend private institutions where borrowing is often necessary to meet basic education and living expenses. While
most of these students receive a large amount of grant aid from their institutions, they still face substantial expenses that must be met either by their
parents or through self-help (work and/or loans). Almost 90 percent of
middle-income borrowers at private institutions receive grant aid, and the
average amount received is a substantial $6,400. Nonetheless, when grant aid
is subtracted from the institution-set student budget, these borrowers face an
average net price of $13,000.

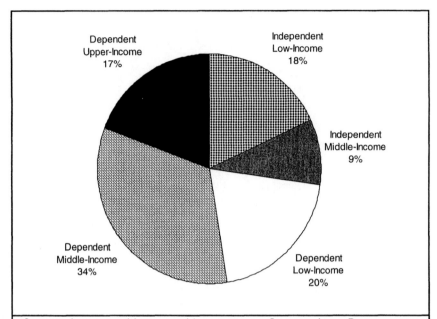

SHARE OF INCREASE IN NUMBER OF UNDERGRADUATE STAFFORD LOAN BORROWERS, 1992–93 TO 1995–96, ATTRIBUTABLE TO VARIOUS INCOME AND DEPENDENCY GROUPS

FIGURE 10.3

Source: U.S. Department of Education 1998a; analysis by author.

Half of middle-income borrowers attend public institutions where they face an average net price of $9,000. According to the federal formula designed to estimate how much a family can afford to pay from current income and savings (expected family contribution, or EFC), the average parents' contribution for this group of students should be $5,700. Presumably, after the parental contribution is made, the remaining amount could be met through earnings from a part-time job. Of course, averages inadequately portray the situation for students at the extremes of a distribution—those with little grant aid, for example, or those with extraordinary family circumstances that limit the amount their parents can actually contribute. Nonetheless, it seems clear that the average requirements of middle-income dependent students should not have necessitated such a dramatic jump in borrowing.

It is important to note that the measures used here to define "need" are largely abstractions to students. They may see an institution-set budget figure on their financial aid award letter (or some other such document), but this figure may bear little resemblance to what they believe they need to "get by" in a given semester. At best, a student and his or her family may have established a budget for the term or year based on the institution's charges and their educated guesses about living expenses. Most likely, however, students have only a vague notion of what they will need and assume that they must borrow in order to meet this uncertain level. With some thought and planning, many of these students might decide not to borrow at all or might choose to borrow less than the maximum amount for which they are eligible.

This analysis does not take into account other types of debt students might incur, including car loans and, of course, credit card debt. Financial aid administrators (Hart 1996) are growing increasingly concerned that middle-income students are saddling themselves unwisely with more debt than they may be able to comfortably handle, and that much of this debt is in the form of consumer credit that is very difficult to track. Focus groups conducted for the Sallie Mae Educational Institute and the American Council on Education suggest that middle-income students are particularly susceptible to overreliance on credit cards because they tend to have had little direct responsibility for managing their money prior to college and because they believe that, if they were to run into real financial trouble, their parents would "bail them out." One student summed up his attitude toward debt this way:

> My main concern right now is getting my assignments done, and I've never been one to worry much about money anyway. I've always just kind of had it and spent it and got some more . . . it's never been a big deal to me . . . I've lived a cushy life and got my parents to fall back on. (KRC Research and Consulting 1998)

Independent Low-Income Students

The student group with the second-largest share of new loan volume is independent students with adjusted gross incomes (AGIs) under $10,000. These students were responsible for 22 percent of additional Stafford loan volume and represented 18 percent of the increased number of borrowers (see Figures 10.2 and 10.3).

In 1992, Congress changed the definition of financial independence. Previously, students under the age of 24 had independent status if they were not claimed as dependents on their parents' income tax. The 1992 reauthorization of the Higher Education Act tightened the definition to include only students aged 24 or older, and those under 24 who are married and/or have children. Due to this change and to new loan eligibility for dependent students, independent students declined as a share of total Stafford loan borrowers from 48 percent in 1992–93 to 40 percent in 1995–96. Given that the number of independent borrowers has increased at a slower pace than dependent borrowers, it is doubly significant that this group of very-low-income independent students are responsible for almost one-quarter of new Stafford loan volume.

Who are these students? The available data suggest that independent borrowers with less than $10,000 income are more likely than other borrowers to be African American or Hispanic, to be single parents, to have received a GED instead of a high school diploma, and to be the first in their families to attend college. In terms of educational experiences, these students also are much more likely to attend proprietary institutions and are much less likely to attend private nonprofit colleges and universities. Whereas 12 percent of all undergraduate Stafford borrowers attend proprietary institutions, 22 percent of low-income independent borrowers attend these institutions. They also are more likely to attend college part-time or part-year and to be working toward an associate's degree or certificate rather than a bachelor's degree.

Previous studies have shown that many of these personal characteristics are associated with failure to complete a degree program and with student loan default (Greene 1989; Pascarella and Terenzini 1991; Volkwein and Szelest 1995). These low-income independent students are borrowing over twice as much as they did in 1992–93—almost $4 billion in 1995–96. They have garnered little attention from the media, but these students are in far greater danger of leaving postsecondary education without a degree and without adequate means to repay their loans than are middle-income dependent borrowers.

Students at public four-year colleges and universities represent just one-third of low-income independent borrowers, but they borrowed almost half of the Stafford funds loaned to this group in 1995–96.[5] These students represent an exception to the pattern of convenience borrowing. They saw a $1,500 increase in student budgets at public institutions, but only a $100 increase in average grant aid between 1992–93 and 1995–96. They faced an average net price of $8,300 at public four-year institutions—similar to the net price cited for middle-income dependent students—but their average expected family contribution was only $750. Because these students are financially independent, the family contribution does not include parental funds.

The evidence for the financial difficulty experienced by this group is plain. Low-income independent students who could meet their expenses without loans in 1992 had little choice but to borrow in 1995. This problem is addressed, in part, by a change to the system for determining federal aid eligibility enacted in 1998 that will allow more independent students to qualify for federal grants, but it is only a first step toward reversing the trend of dramatically increased reliance on loans among this group of very needy students. A long-term commitment to increased funding for grant assistance at the federal *and* state levels is needed to relieve the disproportionate debt presently being incurred by low-income independent students.

Dependent Low-Income Students

Low-income dependent students were responsible for 19 percent of the growth in loan volume since 1992–93 and represented 20 percent of the new borrowers. These students are somewhat different from their low-income independent peers. They are less likely to attend community colleges or proprietary institutions. One quarter of them attend private institutions and 44 percent attend public four-year colleges and universities.

The data on low-income dependent students at public institutions suggest that much of the increase in borrowing among this group may have been fueled by something other than declines in affordability. Average budgets for these students increased by $1,000 between 1992 and 1995, but average grants increased by almost as much ($700), and the number of borrowers who received grant aid grew by over 50 percent. Despite the increase in grant aid, the number of low-income dependent borrowers increased by 70 percent and the total amount borrowed jumped by 110 percent, suggesting that the "goldfish rule" may also apply to these students. They may have borrowed more than they absolutely needed to meet basic expenses.

Despite dramatic increases in institutional aid expenditures, low-income dependent students at private institutions doubled their borrowing. In 1992–93, on average, grants covered 40 percent of the total student budget for low-income dependent borrowers at private institutions. By 1995–96, despite a $3,000 increase in the average student budget, grants continued to cover the same share of costs. The average grant increased from $6,250 to $7,500.

Notwithstanding this stability in net price, the number of low-income dependent borrowers at private institutions grew by 50 percent. In 1992, approximately 200,000 low-income students at private institutions received Stafford loans. By 1995, that number had swelled to 300,000. Net costs are high enough at private institutions that one would expect these students to borrow; still, most of them must have been just as needy in 1992, and many found a way to meet past costs without loans.[6]

Are low-income dependent students and their families making the same poor decisions about assuming debt as their middle-income peers? Or were the relatively small additional net costs faced by these students enough to cause them to borrow when previously they had been able to manage without loans? The latter seems unlikely. These low-income students probably responded to the stimulus of increased loan limits and broadened eligibility in the same manner as their middle-income peers. They began to borrow, or borrowed more than they had previously, because the funds were available. Of course, most of these students come from families with many competing financial demands, and the additional funds provided by student loans probably made it possible for the family to meet other basic needs. Again, the term convenience borrowing should not suggest that student borrowers do not have real financial requirements or that students are borrowing for frivolous purposes.

Does the increased borrowing by this group constitute a crisis? According to a recent national study, over 75 percent of students who began their undergraduate careers at four-year institutions had either earned degrees or were still enrolled five years later (U.S. Department of Education 1996), so the increased borrowing by these students may not pose a huge long-term problem. The vast majority of students who complete a degree repay their loans on time. Given the substantial financial—and nonfinancial—returns on a college education, there is no doubt that student loans are a wise investment. But for those who do not complete a degree or who choose low-paying fields, student debt could present a substantial burden. Additional grant aid to reduce the net price for low-income dependent students, coupled with counseling and information on the wise use of credit, could prevent low-income dependent students from saddling themselves with debt unnecessarily.

BORROWING AND STUDENT WORK

An important sidebar to any discussion of student debt concerns the extent to which enrolled students substitute work for borrowing. According to NPSAS:96, 8 out of 10 undergraduates work while enrolled. As part of the survey, these students were asked to identify their primary role as either a student who works to pay college expenses or an employee who also studies. The answers are revealing. Two-thirds of those who work, or one-half of all undergraduates, said they were "students who work." Most of these students are dependent, and over half of them attend school full-time and/or are enrolled at four-year institutions. They work an average of 25 hours per week—an amount of time that has been shown to have a detrimental effect on both academic performance and persistence (U.S. Department of Education 1998b).

Only about one-third of these students borrowed in 1995–96, suggesting that, at least for some students, the problem may not be too much borrowing but, rather, too little (King 1998). Borrowing to reduce the amount one must work per week—and to thereby increase the odds that one will achieve good grades and graduate—makes good economic sense. It is possible that stories in the media about students "drowning in debt" have influenced students to substitute work for borrowing in the mistaken belief that working is safer financially. The task for campus officials is complex—to encourage students to borrow if they need more than they might make working 10 to 15 hours per week and, at the same time, to counsel them against borrowing more than necessary.

CONCLUSION

So what does all this information mean? Does increased undergraduate borrowing constitute a crisis, or is it merely a matter of convenience? The data presented here reinforce some of what analysts have suspected—that much of the increase in student borrowing since 1992–93 is a reaction to broadened eligibility rules and increased loan limits. Middle-income students were responsible for the largest share of loan volume growth and, on the whole, it appears that this group largely engaged in convenience borrowing. Similarly, low-income dependent students increased their borrowing substantially, despite very small increases in net college price; thus, it seems most likely that this, too, was convenience borrowing.

In contrast, low-income independent borrowers had little choice but to borrow to meet their basic education and living expenses. As a group, low-income independent students are more likely to have characteristics that are associated with failure to complete a degree and with student loan default. These students clearly would benefit from a renewed commitment to need-based grant assistance by the federal government and the states. Given the political attractiveness of increasing assistance to the middle-class, it will be up to institutions, students, and other interested parties to hold policymakers accountable for helping low-income students and families. I hope that the information presented here will assist in that effort.

NOTES

1. Under the Stafford *subsidized* loan program, the federal government pays the interest students accrue while enrolled and for six months after leaving postsecondary education. Students must demonstrate financial need in order to qualify for this program. The Stafford *unsubsidized* loan program is open to dependent undergraduates who do not qualify for subsidized loans, as well as to all independent students and graduate students. Prior to 1992, only graduate students and independent undergraduates were eligible for unsubsidized loans, then called Supplemental Loans for Students (SLS).

2. The main federal student loan programs, which are the subject of this paper, fall under the general title Stafford Student Loans. They include loans made under the traditional bank-based guaranteed student loan program, as well as those made through the new federal direct loan program. Stafford loans may be subsidized or unsubsidized, as described in Note 1.

3. Under the current definitions, dependent students are those undergraduates who are under 24 years of age, are unmarried, or have no dependents. Conversely, independent undergraduates must be at least 24 years old, or must be married or have dependents. The income and assets of independent students' parents are not considered when determining eligibility for federal student aid.

4. Net price is the institution-set total cost estimate for a student, including tuition and fees, books, transportation, and living expenses, less all grant aid.

5. The largest group of low-income independent borrowers attend community colleges, but they borrowed only 15 percent of the almost $4 billion borrowed by all low-income independent students.

6. About one-quarter of 1995 borrowers in this category borrowed unsubsidized Stafford loans only, suggesting that these students have additional means that are not reflected in the adjusted gross income measure, and that they borrowed for much the same reasons as middle-income students.

REFERENCES

Greene, L. 1989. "An Economic Analysis of Student Loan Default." *Educational Evaluation and Policy Analysis* 11(1), Spring: 61–68.

Hart, N. K. 1996. "Financial Aid Administration Today: Considerations for Campus Leaders." *Educational Record* 77(1), Winter: 37–41.

King, J. E. 1998. "Too Many Students Are Holding Jobs for Too Many Hours." *Chronicle of Higher Education* May 1: A72.

KRC Research and Consulting. 1998. *Students in Debt: Attitudes and Behavior of College Students toward Borrowing Money*. Washington, DC: Sallie Mae Educational Institute and American Council on Education.

Pascarella, E., and P. Terenzini. 1991. *How College Affects Students*. San Francisco: Jossey-Bass.

Redd, K. 1994. *The Effects of Higher Loan Limits and Need Analysis Changes on FFELP Borrowing in Pennsylvania, July to December 1992 to 1993*. Harrisburg, PA: Pennsylvania Higher Education Assistance Authority.

TERI (The Education Resources Institute) and the Institute for Higher Education Policy. 1995. *College Debt and the American Family*. Boston: The Education Resources Institute.

U.S. Department of Education, National Center for Education Statistics. 1996. *Descriptive Summary of 1989–90 Beginning Postsecondary Students: 5 Years Later*. NCES 96-155. Washington, DC: Government Printing Office.

———. 1998a. National Postsecondary Student Aid Study. Dataset. Washington, DC: National Center for Education Statistics.

———. 1998b. *Profile of Undergraduates in U.S. Postsecondary Institutions: 1995–96*. NCES 98-084. Washington, DC: Government Printing Office.

Volkwein, J. F., and B. P. Szelest. 1995. "Individual and Campus Characteristics Associated with Student Loan Default." *Research in Higher Education* 36(1), February: 41–72.

CHAPTER 11

Financial Aid Is Not Enough

Improving the Odds for Minority and Low-Income Students

Lawrence E. Gladieux and Watson Scott Swail

A t the close of the twentieth century, higher education appears to be more important than ever—to our nation's economy and competitive position in the world, and to an individual's chances of sharing in American prosperity. In an era of increasing income inequality, strengthening and broadening educational opportunity is key not only to economic growth but to narrowing the gap between rich and poor.

There are no guarantees in life—with or without a college diploma—but increasingly, the odds are stacked against those with the least education and training. As illustrated in Figure 11.1, the more education one has, the more, on average, one earns. This linkage has become conventional wisdom. People understand that who goes to college—and often, which college—determines more than ever who has entree to the best jobs and the best life chances.

More than 50 years ago, the original GI Bill demonstrated to skeptics in both government and academia that higher education could and should serve a much wider segment of society. More than 30 years ago, in the heyday of the civil rights movement and the War on Poverty, Congress passed the Higher Education Act and committed the federal government to the goal of opening college doors to all, regardless of family income or wealth.

Federal student aid and related efforts have helped fuel a half-century of explosive growth in college attendance and educational attainment. In 1996, American colleges and universities enrolled over 14 million students, 1.5 times the number enrolled in 1965, 6 times the enrollment in 1950, and 10 times the pre–World War II levels (Figure 11.2) Meanwhile, the proportion of

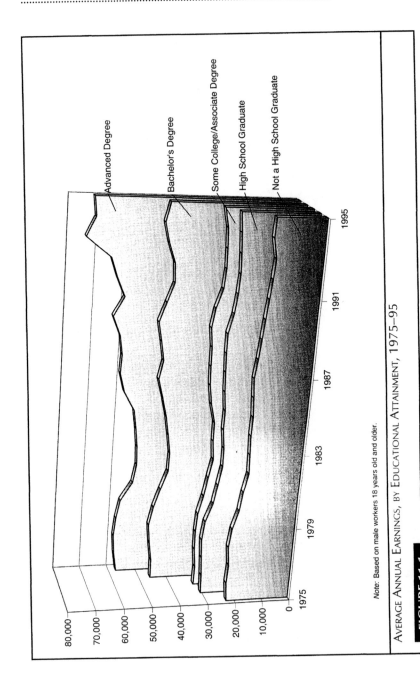

Note: Based on male workers 18 years old and older.

FIGURE 11.1

AVERAGE ANNUAL EARNINGS, BY EDUCATIONAL ATTAINMENT, 1975–95

Source: U.S. Bureau of the Census 1997.

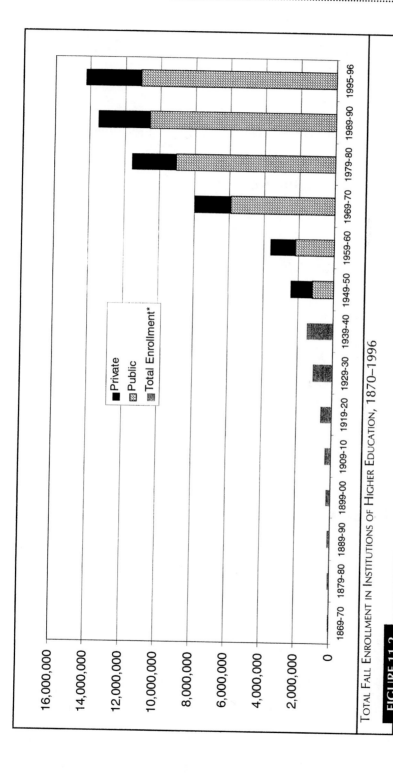

TOTAL FALL ENROLLMENT IN INSTITUTIONS OF HIGHER EDUCATION, 1870–1996

FIGURE 11.2

Source: U.S. Department of Education 1997b; data from 1869–70 to 1929–30, Table 171; data from 1939–40 to 1995–96, Table 172.

the population 25 to 29 years of age who have completed at least four years of college has quadrupled since 1940 (U.S. Department of Commerce 1993). Yet large gaps persist, by family income and by race, in who benefits from higher education in America. In virtually every country of the world, participation in higher education—as measured by rates of entry and completion, as well as by type and prestige of institution attended—is closely associated with socioeconomic status (Johnstone 1986). This association may be less pronounced in the United States, as we have surely created the most open, diverse, and accessible postsecondary system in the world. But the gaps are persistent nonetheless, and are a primary contributor to the social and economic stratification of American society.

This chapter begins by using available statistics to answer the following questions: Who goes to college? Who goes where? and Who succeeds in higher education? We then ask why the goal of equity is so elusive—why more progress has not been made in narrowing the gaps in opportunity. This book is about financing higher education—the programs, patterns, mechanisms, and issues of paying for college. But it is common sense that access to, and success in, higher education hinges on much more than finances. In this chapter, we look at the roots of unequal opportunity, and we suggest directions for public policy and institutional practice to address some of the underlying problems.

WHO GOES TO COLLEGE?

The most clear-cut advance in postsecondary opportunity over the past three to four decades has been gender parity. The rise of women's educational attainment has been a spectacular achievement. Women closed the enrollment gap in 1978 and have since constituted a majority of total graduate and undergraduate students. However, by discipline and courses taken, differential rates of participation remain. For example, women are still significantly underrepresented in "hard" sciences and engineering (U.S. Department of Education 1998).[1] Nonetheless, today women of all ages make up more than 55 percent of the postsecondary population, and women aged 25 to 29 are slightly more likely than men to have attained at least a baccalaureate degree (U.S. Department of Education 1997c, 185, 324).

When we look at trends by socioeconomic status, the picture is much less encouraging. There are many indicators, but we start with the most widely cited source—data from the U.S. Census. Figure 11.3 traces a broad index of postsecondary participation for 18- to 24-year-old high school graduates over the past 25 years. All income groups show gains. But low-income 18- to 24-year-olds attend college at much lower rates than those with high income, and participation rate gaps are about as wide today as they were in 1972.

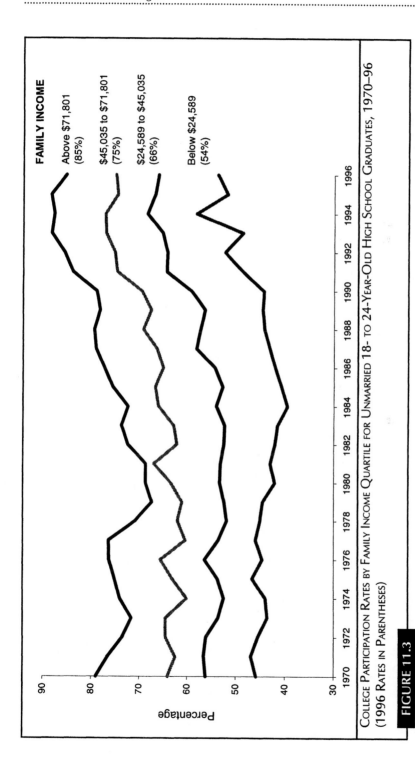

COLLEGE PARTICIPATION RATES BY FAMILY INCOME QUARTILE FOR UNMARRIED 18- TO 24-YEAR-OLD HIGH SCHOOL GRADUATES, 1970–96 (1996 RATES IN PARENTHESES)

FIGURE 11.3

Source: Mortenson 1998.

The Census Bureau figures have limitations and tend to be volatile from year to year.[2] Yet other data sources yield similar results. Longitudinal studies conducted by the National Center for Education Statistics on the high school senior classes of 1972, 1980, and 1992, for example, show a clear trend of rising postsecondary participation, especially for blacks and Hispanics (U.S. Department of Education 1996a, 25). However, as shown in Figure 11.4, significant gaps remain among socioeconomic groups.

WHO GOES WHERE?

Where students go to college can be as important as whether they go. As broadly illustrated in Figure 11.1, average economic returns from education increase with institutional level. Students attending less than four-year schools are not as likely to receive the same economic rewards as those who end up with a bachelor's degree or higher.

Figure 11.4 shows the enrollment patterns and trends by socioeconomic status using the high school senior cohorts of 1972, 1980, and 1992. In the most recent cohort, only one in five students from the lowest socioeconomic quartile enrolled in a four-year institution, compared with two in three from the highest quartile. The gaps between the lowest and highest quartiles are about as wide as they were two decades ago. Meanwhile, the most disadvantaged students who do go to college are increasingly likely to enroll in two-year colleges.

Michael McPherson and Morton Schapiro (1998, 42) suggest that institutional choice is closely linked to parental income.

> Although the issue of "choice" is often expressed in terms of public versus private alternatives, opportunity to attend a flagship public university or indeed any four-year public institution is importantly constrained by income in many states.

Basing their analysis on data from the UCLA/ACE American Freshman Survey,[3] McPherson and Schapiro (1998, 45) found that the percentages of middle- and higher-income students attending two-year colleges decreased significantly between 1980 and 1994. Conversely, the percentage of the lowest-income students attending these institutions increased slightly during the same period.

Thus, not only are students from disadvantaged backgrounds accessing higher education at lower rates than other groups, but their enrollment appears to be increasingly concentrated at two-year institutions.

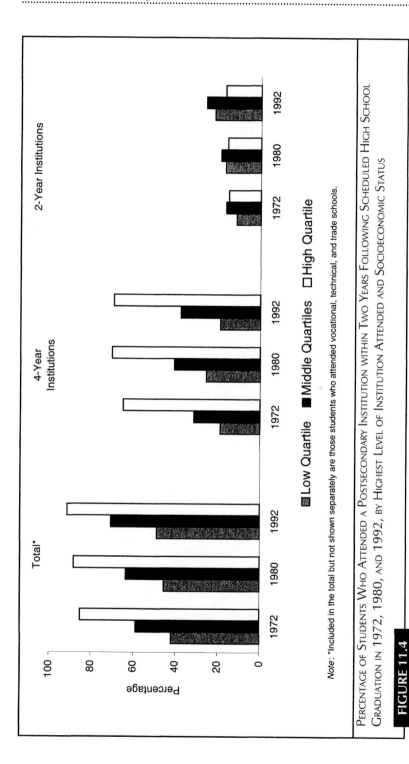

Percentage of Students Who Attended a Postsecondary Institution within Two Years Following Scheduled High School Graduation in 1972, 1980, and 1992, by Highest Level of Institution Attended and Socioeconomic Status

FIGURE 11.4

Source: U.S. Department of Education 1997b, 65, Indicator 9.

WHO COMPLETES?

We have briefly summarized the record on overall access and choice of institution. The more important question is whether students complete their programs. Some students fall short of a degree yet go on to productive careers. But our economy and labor market rely heavily on credentials. As Vince Tinto has stated, "the point of providing students access to higher education is to give them a reasonable opportunity to participate in college and attain a college degree" (Tinto 1997, 1).

Roughly three-quarters of high school seniors go on to higher studies (U.S. Department of Education 1997a). Half receive some type of degree within five years of entering postsecondary education, and about one-quarter receive a bachelor's degree or higher. As with access patterns, we see wide disparities by socioeconomic status and race, as reflected in Figure 11.5. More than 40 percent of the most advantaged students received a bachelor's degree or higher within five years, compared with only 6 percent from the least advantaged group. And white students are considerably more likely to receive a bachelor's degree than black and Hispanic students. While these degree completion rates rise for all groups in the sixth, seventh, and subsequent years, long-term attainment gaps for white in comparison with black and Hispanic students who attend four-year colleges remain in the 19 to 26 percent range (U.S. Department of Education 1996a, 25).[4]

Getting students in the door is not sufficient. In fact, some students may be left worse off if they have borrowed to finance their studies, as is increasingly the case for low-income students, and do not finish their programs. They leave college with no degree, no skills, and a debt to repay.

WHY HAVEN'T WE DONE BETTER?

Why do gaps in opportunity remain so stubbornly wide? National policy has focused for the better part of four decades on access to higher education. As we have seen, there remains a long way to go to equalize access, especially by income level. As we have also suggested, the greater challenge is to increase the likelihood that students actually *succeed* in reaching their goals, which in most cases means completing a degree.

Enrollment and success in higher education are clearly influenced by many factors: prior schooling and academic achievement, the rigor and pattern of courses taken in secondary school, family and cultural attitudes, motivation, and awareness of opportunities—not just ability to pay, which has been the primary emphasis of federal policy. For low-income students, removing financial barriers is critical, but so are many things starting much earlier both in life and in the educational pipeline.

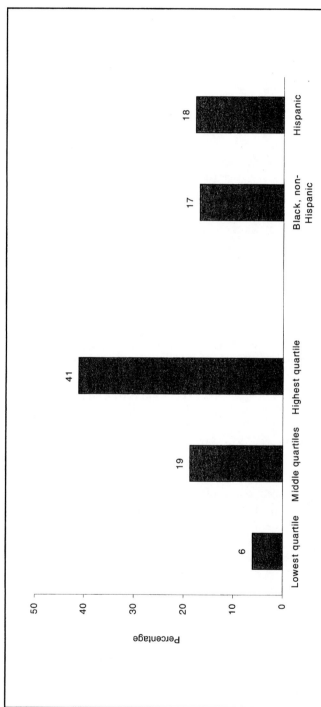

PERCENTAGE OF 1989 BEGINNING POSTSECONDARY STUDENTS WHO RECEIVED A BACHELOR'S DEGREE OR HIGHER AS OF 1994, BY SOCIOECONOMIC STATUS AND RACE/ETHNICITY

FIGURE 11.5

Source: U.S. Department of Education 1996b, 34, Table 1.3.

The problem of unequal opportunity has proved more intractable than anyone anticipated in the early years of the Higher Education Act. In the late 1960s and early 1970s, widely publicized reports showed that a college-age youth from a wealthy family was five times more likely to enroll in college than a youth from a poor family. The Carnegie Commission on Higher Education and other national groups called for federal leadership and need-based financial aid to close this gap (Carnegie Commission 1968; College Board 1973). As originally conceived, federal student aid was meant to send an early signal to young people and their families that college was a realistic goal. Sponsors of the Pell Grants, in particular, hoped that the promise of aid would have a powerful motivational effect (Kramer 1998).

The reality of today's patchwork student aid system falls short of such a vision. This is not to say that the aid programs have failed, but rather that too much may have been expected of them. In their book, *Beating the Odds: How the Poor Get to College*, Arthur Levine and Jana Nidiffer (1996) conclude that "financial aid is a necessary but insufficient condition for college attendance by the poor . . . financial aid simply does not reach young kids . . . it plays no part in their lives . . . [and] does little to place a poor student at a college's doorstep."

Of all the variables that influence who enters and who succeeds in higher education, aspirations and academic preparation are probably the most powerful. And both must start early. "By the time students reach the 12th grade, it is too late to . . . increase the numbers of students who are ready for college," according to research by Laura Rendón (1997, 7). "In fact, it could be said that students begin to drop out of college in grade school."

Expectations are important. If students expect to go to college, they are more inclined to take the necessary steps to make it happen. The most important step is taking the right courses. Research has repeatedly shown that students who take rigorous, progressively more challenging course work through high school are far more likely to plan for and enroll in college (King 1996; U.S. Department of Education 1997a). In his analysis of the Department of Education's longitudinal data on high school senior cohorts, Clifford Adelman (1997, 41) says that the answer to the question "Who finishes bachelor's degrees, and why?" is always the same: those "who were best prepared, regardless of race, regardless of financial aid."

In fact, the data suggest that the die is cast for many students by the eighth grade. Students without the appropriate math and reading skills by that grade are unlikely to acquire them by the end of high school, regardless of race or ethnicity (U.S. Department of Education 1997d).

There are many "gatekeepers" to postsecondary opportunity embedded in the secondary school curriculum. One of the most publicized is course-taking patterns in mathematics. A recent study by the U.S. Department of Education

(1997e) found that "high school students who take algebra, geometry, and other rigorous mathematics courses are more likely to go on to college." The results from a College Board project, EQUITY 2000, echo this finding. Specifically, 83 percent of students who took Algebra I and geometry went on to college within two years of their scheduled graduation, compared to only 36 percent for students who did not take those two courses. Early course-taking sets the pattern. Sixty percent of students who completed Algebra I by the end of the eighth grade took calculus in high school.[5]

Nearly all eighth-graders say they expect to go to college. Even low-income students overwhelmingly envision postsecondary education in their future. However, while almost all high-income students reach that goal, only two-thirds of low-income students do (U.S. Department of Education 1997a, 16–17).[6]

The problem is that the course-taking patterns of low-income and minority students make it difficult for them to meet their expectations. As a result, they finish high school less prepared, on average, than higher-income, non-minority students. Tracking policies, school resources and quality, and societal conditions and expectations all have a part in creating this disparity.

Whatever the roots of the problem, the stark reality is reflected in Figures 11.6 and 11.7. According to a college-qualification index developed for the National Center for Education Statistics, only half of low-income high school graduates are qualified to go to college, compared with 86 percent of high-income students. And by this index, black and Hispanic students also are far less qualified than white students (U.S. Department of Education 1997a).[7]

Among high school graduates who actually enrolled in four-year institutions, less than half of low-income students were judged to be highly or very highly qualified, compared with two-thirds of high-income students. Twenty-nine percent of black students and 44 percent of Hispanic students were similarly qualified, compared with 61 percent of white students. Starkest of all may be the fact that 30 percent of black students were considered marginally qualified or not qualified for college.

Two problems are evident in these data. Low-income and minority high school graduates are less well prepared in general, and a significant percentage of those who actually do go on to four-year higher education may not have the academic tools required for success. Unfortunately, these students may have been set up for disappointment. As Adelman (1997, 40) suggests, if high school graduates are ill-prepared, "we do them no favors by sitting them down in front of a college chemistry textbook or a web site loaded with historical documents and watching them cry in frustration."

The question is what can be done through public policy and institutional practice to address these issues.

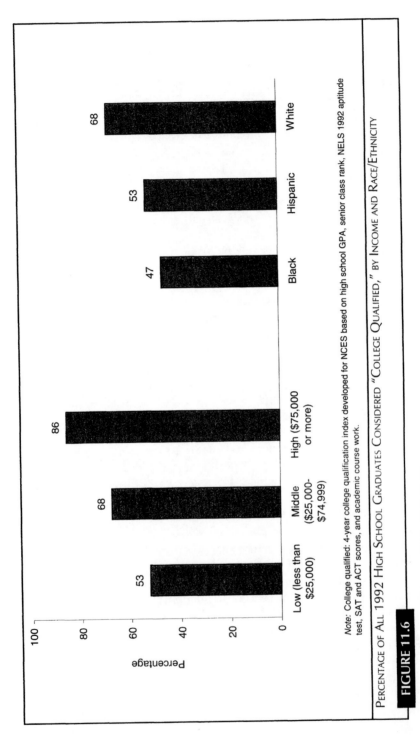

PERCENTAGE OF ALL 1992 HIGH SCHOOL GRADUATES CONSIDERED "COLLEGE QUALIFIED," BY INCOME AND RACE/ETHNICITY

FIGURE 11.6

Source: U.S. Department of Education 1997a, 29, Table 15.

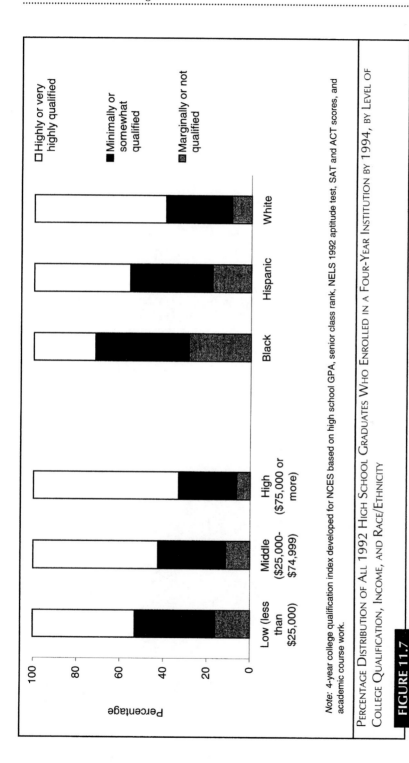

□ Highly or very highly qualified

■ Minimally or somewhat qualified

▨ Marginally or not qualified

Note: 4-year college qualification index developed for NCES based on high school GPA, senior class rank, NELS 1992 aptitude test, SAT and ACT scores, and academic course work.

PERCENTAGE DISTRIBUTION OF ALL 1992 HIGH SCHOOL GRADUATES WHO ENROLLED IN A FOUR-YEAR INSTITUTION BY 1994, BY LEVEL OF COLLEGE QUALIFICATION, INCOME, AND RACE/ETHNICITY

FIGURE 11.7

Source: U.S. Department of Education 1997a, 28, Table 14.

PUBLIC POLICY

The growing reliance on student loans, the erosion of need-based aid-allocation standards, the political emphasis on college cost relief for the middle class,
the new federal tuition tax breaks, growing state investment in merit-based
aid and prepaid tuition programs—these and related public policy developments have major implications for access to higher education. Tuition and
financial aid policies make a difference, and the whole system seems to be
shifting in ways that may reduce opportunities for students with the least
resources. Such developments are extremely important to the postsecondary
prospects of low- and moderate-income students, and other chapters of this
volume address those issues.

Our focus here, however, is the earlier, more fundamental problems of
student motivation and readiness for higher education. The easy thing to say
is that we need comprehensive reform of American K–12 education, to lift
student performance in general and to reduce the disparities in academic
preparation documented above. And we do, indeed. Some form of state and
national standards are surely needed to set clear benchmarks of what students
should know and be able to do. Current expectations often are too low. We
have noted that students who took Algebra I and geometry were much more
likely to take higher-level courses and enroll in college. The reality is that only
28 states currently require algebra and geometry for high school graduation
(Council of Chief State School Officers 1996).

Standards alone will not raise the achievement of low-income, black, and
Hispanic students. Safety nets must be in place to ensure a supportive environment for learning. Students must have opportunities to learn in secure set-
tings, with up-to-date materials and the encouragement to believe that they
can achieve at high levels.

Neither, surely, can all of the problems of educational failure be laid at the
schoolhouse door. Learning is hardly exclusive to the classroom. It has been
said that only one-tenth of a child's learning happens at school. We need to
look far beyond classroom walls—to parents, families, and community resources—to increase the motivation and academic performance of students.
What happens to kids during nonschool time is at least as important as what
happens in school.

In the long run, it is hoped, school-reform strategies and experiments will
effect change and benefit generations to come. In the short run, we need
direct outreach to more of the current generation through intervention
programs that make a difference in the lives of young, disadvantaged kids early
in their schooling, widening their horizons and encouraging them to stay in
school, study hard, take the right courses, and keep their options open. Early
and sustained guidance and support are needed to make postsecondary education a realistic possibility later on.

Research and experience tell us that when a student from disadvantaged circumstances beats the odds by enrolling and succeeding in college, the critical difference can often be traced to a particular individual who touched or changed the student's life at some point along the way; someone who served as a role model or otherwise sparked a sense of possibility for the future. That individual might have been a relative, a neighbor, a counselor, a teacher, a coach, or a tutor; anyone who cares enough to try to make a difference.

Getting poor people prepared and into college, Levine and Nidiffer (1996, 143) suggest, "is retail, not wholesale, work in the sense that it requires intensive involvement with individuals rather than passing contact with larger numbers." According to their study (1996, 65, 139):

> In simplest terms, the recipe for getting to college is mentorship—one arm around one child. . . . What mattered most is not carefully constructed educational policy but rather the intervention by one person. . . . Sometimes the mentor was a loving relative; other times it was someone paid to offer expert advice. In either case, it was the human contact that made the difference.

Scores of early intervention and mentoring programs have developed across the country (Fenske et al. 1997; Swail 1995). More than 15 years ago, Eugene Lang started a movement with his "I Have a Dream" promise to 60 East Harlem sixth-graders that he would pay their college tuition if they graduated from high school. Today, Lang and other philanthropists are investing considerable wealth and personal commitment in such programs, including not just the tuition guarantee but the critical mentoring, counseling, tutoring, and other support to keep students from falling between the cracks. Many of these programs work, but for the millions of youngsters whose life chances are slim and who might be lifted by an "I Have a Dream" or similar program, the movement is almost like a wheel of fortune. A youngster must be lucky enough to be in the right city, the right school, the right classroom.

The challenge for public policy is to leverage such programs that work to a vastly larger scale. Upward Bound, Talent Search, and other so-called TRIO programs have been a companion to federal student aid policy since the Higher Education Act was first enacted in 1965, providing information, outreach, counseling, encouragement, and academic support for students from the lowest socioeconomic levels. TRIO appropriations have grown over the years to more than a half-billion dollars, yet these programs are estimated to serve less than 10 percent of the eligible student population. Further, only a small portion of TRIO services is dedicated to intervening with kids and their families during middle school or earlier.

The 1998 reauthorization of the Higher Education Act reflects a growing recognition by policymakers of what is required to make a difference. The amended law gives a big boost to early-intervention efforts, aiming to reach a million kids in 2,500 middle or junior high schools with mentoring and related support over the next five years. Building on proposals from the Clinton administration and Congressman Chaka Fattah of Pennsylvania, a new program titled Gaining Early Awareness and Readiness for Undergraduate Programs (GEAR UP) will support school-college and school-community partnerships in this area. GEAR UP also calls for early notice to low-income sixth graders of their potential eligibility for federal aid if they graduate from high school and are accepted to college.

Just as we need to reach kids earlier, we need to do a better job helping students once they have enrolled in college to persist and complete their degrees. Again, the TRIO programs provide support here. But public policy, and federal policy in particular, has focused too narrowly on access to the system. More attention and incentives should be directed at persistence among students who are economically and academically at risk. Some analysts, for example, have suggested that students who complete their degrees should receive a financial aid bonus, perhaps in the form of loan forgiveness (Nettles, Perna, and Millett 1995, 107–16). Others have suggested that TRIO funds be allocated to institutions based on the number of Pell Grant recipients they graduate (Hauptman 1998). Both proposals have drawbacks. The first would tend to penalize those most at risk of dropping out: those who can least afford the cost of higher education. The second might encourage institutions to lower their graduation standards.

The point is, we need a new debate. Public policy has done a fairly good job facilitating initial entry into the system. How can we better promote persistence and completion?

HIGHER EDUCATION'S RESPONSIBILITY

According to a 1995 report from the National Center for Education Statistics (U.S. Department of Education 1995), only one-third of colleges and universities sponsor precollegiate outreach programs for disadvantaged students, most such programs rely on federal funds, and faculty involvement is minimal. Yet postsecondary institutions have a direct stake in such efforts, especially given the coming generation of students.

Looking toward the year 2010, Sam Kipp (1998, 109) projects:

> While the potential pool of high school graduates and college students will increase substantially, the only thing that will be traditional about this growing cohort will be its age. The nation's college-age population will be even more ethnically diverse than the general population because of differential birthrates and migration patterns. Furthermore, the most rapid growth will occur among groups traditionally more

likely to drop out of school, less likely to enroll in college-preparatory course work, less likely to graduate from high school, less likely to enroll in college, and least likely to persist to earn a baccalaureate degree.

America is an ongoing experiment in diversity, and American higher education's part of the social contract has been to help extend the possibility of a better life to disadvantaged groups in society. It will be in the enlightened self-interest of institutions to invest more heavily in partnerships with school systems to expand the potential college-bound, and qualified, pool. Reaching out to help motivate and prepare more students for college is a long-term investment that will pay off for higher education and for the nation.

There are some outstanding models of precollegiate intervention programs in which colleges have taken the initiative to collaborate with schools and communities.[8] But much more dramatic commitments are needed to achieve diversity on campus and do right by minority and low-income students. "If we do affirmative action in grade 3, we won't have to do it in grade 13," Cliff Adelman has quipped (quoted in Gladieux 1996, 8). He couldn't be more right.

A boost to such efforts could emerge, ironically, from the rollback of affirmative action. Affirmative action as we know it may be scaled back, restructured, or even abandoned because of legal challenges and state ballot initiatives. Techniques and terminology may change but, as necessity is the mother of ingenuity, surely new strategies will evolve to advance the same broad goals of campus diversity. One example may be the University of California's response to its regents' decision to end race preferences in admission (and subsequent approval of Proposition 209 by California voters). The university has adopted a systemwide "new directions for outreach" program and has committed $60 million to the effort (Outreach Task Force 1997).

Perhaps new forms of affirmative action will evolve—reaching disadvantaged schools and populations, those in the inner city, those with educational handicaps, those with academic potential but poor preparation—without using racial or ethnic classifications. Minorities and underrepresented groups nonetheless would surely benefit, as would society.

Institutions likewise have a stake and a responsibility in ensuring that more students who arrive on their campuses persist and complete degrees. Again, this is a matter of enlightened self-interest for colleges. One university has estimated that it costs more to recruit students than to keep them. The institution invests an estimated $1,400 to recruit each of its incoming freshmen, and for every student who leaves after a week, month, or even a semester, that investment is lost.

Again, there are some effective models out there, including student orientation, advisement, mentoring, and support programs designed to boost student persistence and degree completion.[9] But much deeper and wider commitments are needed.

Many years ago, former U.S. Commissioner of Education Harold Howe (quoted in Gladieux and Wolanin 1976, 28) asked, "Do institutions serve the needs of students, or is it the other way around?" It was a rhetorical question, with an everlasting ring.

NO SILVER BULLET

Most of what we have said in this chapter has been common sense. Everyone knows that financial aid is not enough; that to equalize college opportunities for the poor requires more fundamental, complementary strategies. But debates on student aid policy tend to be insular. It's easier to focus on program mechanics, eligibility formulas, delivery systems, and funding levels for the aid programs—all of which are important but often obscure the larger challenge.

This chapter also only scratches the surface of a complex social issue. The roots of unequal educational opportunity are deep. There appear to be huge and growing disparities in the capacity of K–12 educational systems to prepare young people for the world beyond high school. Higher education, much less student aid as a financing strategy, cannot by itself redress social deficits and imbalances that appear to threaten our country's future. But neither can colleges stand apart. All of us—policymakers, educators, analysts, citizens—are challenged to try to make a difference.

NOTES

1. This report from the Department of Education's Office of Educational Research and Improvement found that women are significantly underrepresented in engineering, physical sciences, computer sciences, and mathematics fields, while over-represented in the social sciences.

2. The Census estimates are particularly volatile for minority groups due to survey methodology: figures are based on self-reports of ever having enrolled in postsecondary education, and they include everyone in the age group, including recent immigrants, which may especially alter the college-going picture for the Hispanic population. The Census figures also, no doubt, include 18- to 24-year-olds who may show low income but are recently emancipated from middle- or high-income households, skewing the picture of enrollments by income.

3. The UCLA/ACE American Freshman Survey is conducted annually by the Higher Education Research Institute at UCLA, sponsored by the American Council on Education. The survey, first administered in the mid-1960s, provides community colleges, four-year colleges, and universities a cost-effective method of collecting comparative data on their entering students for use in institutional decision-making,

research, and assessment activities. In 1998, over 700 campuses and 350,000 survey respondents participated in the survey.

4. The rates cited here, in contrast to those reflected in Figure 11.5, are for students attending four-year institutions. Figure 11.5 incorporates *all* beginning postsecondary students.

5. The College Board's EQUITY 2000 program is a mathematics-based school reform strategy that grew out of similar research. At EQUITY 2000 school districts, students are required to complete Algebra I by the 9th grade and geometry by the 10th grade and are provided with safety net programs (such as Saturday academies) to help them succeed.

6. Over 92 percent of all 8th-grade students in 1988 expected to go to college, as did 88 percent of all low-income students.

7. MPR Associates, Inc., the contractor that wrote this report for the U.S. Department of Education, developed a four-year college qualification index for NCES based on high school GPA, senior class rank, NELS 1992 aptitude test, SAT and ACT scores, and academic course work.

8. Programs like the University of North Carolina's MSEN program (grades 6–12); California's MESA program (grades 4–12); and Xavier University's ChemStar, BioStar, and MathStar programs (high school) have had great success in motivating and preparing underrepresented students for college. These college/community partnerships work.

9. Some prominent examples include: the Emerging Scholars Program (ESP) based at the University of Texas at Austin, which utilizes peer groups and interaction to form strong, cohesive study groups that encourage academic excellence and problem solving; the Supplemental Instruction program developed at University of Missouri–Kansas City (UKMC) and now in place at over 1,100 campuses across the country, providing tutoring-like experiences for students on campus; and the University of South Carolina's Freshman Seminar Program (entitled University 101) originally developed to help retain African American students through their freshman year.

REFERENCES

Adelman, C. 1997. "Diversity: Walk the Walk, and Drop the Talk." *Change* July/August: 34–45.

Carnegie Commission on Higher Education. 1968. *Quality and Equality: New Levels of Federal Responsibility for Higher Education.* New York: McGraw-Hill.

College Board. 1973. *Toward Equal Opportunity for Higher Education.* Report of the Panel on Financing Low Income and Minority Students in Higher Education. New York: College Board.

Council of Chief State School Officers. 1996. *Content Standards, Graduation, Teacher Licensure, Time and Attendance: A 50-State Report.* Washington, DC: Council of Chief State School Officers.

Fenske, R. H., C. A. Geranios, J. E. Keller, and D. E. Moore. 1997. *Early Intervention Programs: Opening the Door to Higher Education.* Washington, DC: The George Washington University.

Gladieux, L. E. 1996. "'A Diverse Student Body': The Challenge of Equalizing College Opportunities." *The Journal of College Admission* 152/153: 4–9.

Gladieux, L. E., and T. R. Wolanin. 1976. *Congress and the Colleges*. Lexington, MA: Lexington Books.

Hauptman, A. 1998. "Achieving the Initial Purposes of the Pell Grant Program." In *Memory, Reason, and Imagination: A Quarter Century of Pell Grants*, edited by L. E. Gladieux, B. Astor, and W. S. Swail. New York: College Board.

Johnstone, D. B. 1986. *Sharing the Costs of Higher Education*. New York: College Board.

King, J. E. 1996. *The Decision to Go to College*. New York: College Board.

Kipp, S. M., III. 1998. "Demographic Trends and Their Impact on the Future of the Pell Grant Program." In *Memory, Reason, and Imagination: A Quarter Century of Pell Grants*, edited by L. E. Gladieux, B. Astor, and W. S. Swail. New York: College Board.

Kramer, M. 1998. "Linking Access and Aspirations: The Dual Purpose of Pell Grants." In *Memory, Reason, and Imagination: A Quarter Century of Pell Grants*, edited by L. E. Gladieux, B. Astor, and W. S. Swail. New York: College Board.

Levine, A., and J. Nidiffer. 1996. *Beating the Odds: How the Poor Get to College*. San Francisco: Jossey-Bass.

McPherson, M., and M. Schapiro. 1998. *The Student Aid Game*. Princeton: Princeton University Press.

Mortenson, T. 1998. "Educational Opportunity by Family Income 1970 to 1976." *Postsecondary Education Opportunity* September.

Nettles, M., L. Perna, and C. Millett. 1995. "Pursuing Broader Participation and Greater Benefit from Federal College Student Financial Aid." In *Financing Postsecondary Education: The Federal Role*. Washington, DC: U.S. Department of Education.

Outreach Task Force for the Board of Regents of the University of California. 1997. *New Directions for Outreach*. Oakland, CA: University of California.

Rendón, L. I. 1997. "Access in a Democracy: Narrowing the Opportunity Gap." Paper presented at the Policy Panel on Access, National Postsecondary Education Cooperative, Washington, DC, September 9.

Swail, W. S. 1995. "The Development of a Conceptual Framework to Increase Student Retention in Science, Engineering, and Mathematics Programs at Minority Institutions of Higher Education." Ed.D. dissertation, The George Washington University.

Tinto, V. 1997. "From Access to Participation." Paper presented at the Policy Panel on Access, National Postsecondary Education Cooperative, Washington, DC, September 9.

U.S. Bureau of the Census. 1997. *Current Population Survey*. Washington, DC: U.S. Bureau of the Census.

U.S. Department of Commerce, Bureau of the Census. 1993. *Current Population Reports*. P20–476. Washington, DC: Government Printing Office.

U.S. Department of Education, National Center for Education Statistics. 1995. *Programs at Higher Education Institutions for Disadvantaged Pre-college Students*. Washington, DC: Government Printing Office.

———. 1996a. *The Condition of Education 1996*. Washington, DC: Government Printing Office.

———. 1996b. *Descriptive Summary of 1989–90 Beginning Postsecondary Students: 5 Years Later*. Washington, DC: Government Printing Office.

———. 1997a. *Access to Postsecondary Education for the 1992 High School Graduates*. Washington, DC: U.S. Department of Education, National Center for Education Statistics, 1997.

―――. 1997b. *The Condition of Education 1997*. Washington, DC: Government Printing Office.

―――. 1997c. *The Digest of Education Statistics 1997*. Washington, DC: Government Printing Office.

―――. 1997d. *Reading and Mathematics Achievement: Growth in High School*. Issue Brief (December). Washington, DC: National Center for Education Statistics.

U.S. Department of Education, Office of the Secretary. 1997e. "Mathematics Equals Opportunity." White paper prepared for the U.S. Secretary of Education. Washington, DC: U.S. Department of Education.

U.S. Department of Education, Office of Educational Research and Improvement. 1998. *Women and Men of the Engineering Path: A Model for Analyses of Undergraduate Careers*. Washington, DC: Government Printing Office.

CONCLUSION

Jacqueline E. King

Many of this book's authors suggest that the overarching goal of student aid has shifted from access to affordability. Most observers of higher education, if not all, agree that college affordability has become a central policy goal. Certainly, major new programs have been enacted recently at both the state and federal levels that are clearly targeted toward improving college affordability for middle-income students and their families. As D. Bruce Johnstone states in the introduction, "the principles that have underlain the American 'system' of financial assistance and tuition policy seem to be unraveling."

What has caused student aid policy to unravel? There is no single answer, but this volume suggests several hypotheses that, together, help to explain why policy goals have shifted, and what we in higher education might do to adjust to the new realities and preserve the student aid programs we value.

A. Clayton Spencer, in her chapter on the "new politics" of higher education, shows that polling and public relations have moved higher education policy into the national spotlight. Paying for college is a "hot-button" issue among middle-class voters. President Bill Clinton has long known this, from his days as a governor, and has used policy initiatives such as the federal direct student loan program and the Hope Scholarship tax credit to respond to the fears expressed by many middle-class voters that their children will not experience the upward mobility they have enjoyed. Congress has jumped on the bandwagon and now concentrates almost exclusively on the needs of middle-income students, providing need-based aid to low-income students almost as an afterthought.

This same "new politics" helps explain why politicians have focused a great deal more attention recently on not only the prices colleges charge but the basic cost structure of higher education. According to Spencer, families, colleges, and government are no longer viewed as partners in providing educational opportunity. If anything, colleges are viewed as the enemy, constantly raising their prices to capture parental and governmental resources. As a result, both state and federal legislators have taken a watchdog approach to higher education, looking for ways in which colleges and universities are not providing good value for the dollar, or for ways they might change their operations to become more efficient.

Jerry Sheehan Davis and Joseph D. Creech paint a different picture. They suggest that the fabric of student aid policy is unraveling because the system has become too complex; a source of frustration rather than of motivation to students and families. Sandy Baum and Michael Mumper support this hypothesis, describing the complexity of two major aspects of the financial aid system: need analysis and guaranteed student loans. Policymakers may have focused so intently on creating equity and efficiency in student aid that they lost sight of the value of clarity and of the importance of financial aid as an incentive to students to aspire to college and work hard in high school. Public opinion polling and focus groups conducted by the American Council on Education suggest that, because most people do not understand the system, they tend to assume that it holds no benefits for them (Ikenberry and Hartle 1998). This is especially true among low-income parents and those with no college experience; they are most likely to throw up their hands at the complexity of financial aid and assume that no money is available for their sons or daughters.

To Creech and Davis, the GPA-based Georgia HOPE Scholarship (and its imitators in other states) is a logical and positive reaction to a system that has grown too difficult to navigate and understand. Parents and students in Georgia know what the requirements are for earning a HOPE Scholarship: any student who maintains a certain GPA in specified courses receives a scholarship equal to in-state tuition at the University of Georgia. While many grants may go to upper-income families who do not really need the money, that may be a worthwhile price to pay for a student aid program that is motivating students to work hard and aspire to college.

Lawrence E. Gladieux and Watson Scott Swail add a third explanation for the shift from access to affordability in student aid policy. They explain that even after years of expenditures on need-based student aid, only minimal improvement can be seen in the college-going rate of low-income students (compared with middle- and upper-income students) and almost no change in the rate at which these students attain degrees. The data in John B. Lee's chapter portray this issue in the starkest possible terms: high-ability, low-income students are no more likely to attend college than low-ability, high-income students. In general, students from the lowest income quartile are still about half as likely to attend college than those from the highest quartile.

Gladieux and Swail assert that this is because student financial aid alone cannot solve the problems of differential educational and social opportunity. Students from poor urban and rural areas face academic and attitudinal barriers that are much more difficult to surmount than the financial barrier of paying a tuition bill, crucial as that may be. Overcoming these academic and attitudinal barriers requires improvements in the schools, counseling and mentoring by caring adults, and interventions with families and communities to promote high academic aspirations for all students. Such programs are much more expensive, complex, and difficult to do well than simply handing out financial aid.

In 1972, the TRIO programs of academic support and counseling were written into the same section of the Higher Education Act as Pell Grants because policymakers understood that student aid alone could not overcome the many debilitating effects of poverty. Because providing these kinds of services effectively is difficult and expensive, TRIO has never received the funding needed to serve a significant proportion of low-income students, even though it has always enjoyed bipartisan support in Congress. Today, TRIO serves less than 10 percent of the eligible population. In addition to TRIO, a patchwork of state, local, private, and college-sponsored programs provide counseling and academic support to low-income high school and college students, but even taken together, these programs fall short of meeting the need for such services.

One cannot be certain that Pell Grants, and other need-based grant programs, would have been more successful if greater efforts had been made to address the academic and attitudinal barriers to college attendance. Still, had need-based student aid been accompanied consistently by improvements in K–12 education and the academic support and counseling services provided by TRIO, it seems likely that low-income young people would have a better record of college attendance and completion. Policymakers may be abandoning the goal of access, in part, out of frustration with this persistent gap in educational attainment. At the very least, the inability of student aid advocates to point to a documented record of success has limited support for these programs over the years. In part, it is the advocates themselves who are to blame. They have promoted Pell Grants and other need-based programs as the means of creating educational opportunity—with little or no hard evidence to support that claim—when, in reality, these programs alone were never sufficient to attain such a goal.

If the student aid system is unraveling, and if we in higher education would like to maintain many aspects of it, what can we do? What options do we have? While there is no way to turn back the clock to the "good old days" when access was the central policy goal, there is a lot we can do to preserve a system of student financing that addresses access as well as affordability. In general, this means becoming more responsive to public opinion, more sophisticated and aggressive in our lobbying, and more effective in our efforts to reach low-income students.

First, colleges and universities must become more proficient at using the tools of the new politics—focus groups, polling, and other market research techniques that monitor public opinion, as well as toll-free telephone numbers, the Internet, and other high-tech lobbying methods. Since policymaking is increasingly tied to public opinion, it is imperative that higher education understand how it is viewed by the public so that it is able to muster grassroots support for core programs. This is not entirely new territory. When Congress threatened to cut the in-school interest subsidy on student loans in 1995, the higher education community formed the Alliance to Save Student Aid; established a toll-free number for students, parents, and university personnel to call their congressional representatives; and demonstrated that there is strong support among students for that program.

Second, if affordability is the public priority, higher education cannot expect to maintain publicly funded programs devoted to access unless voters are satisfied that their concerns about affordability are being addressed adequately. In other words, once we have learned what the public is concerned about, we must be willing to take action to address those concerns. ACE's recent research has found that the public is worried about the long-term cost spiral in higher education, is frustrated and confused by the complexity of student aid, and is misinformed about college prices (Ikenberry and Hartle 1998). These findings suggest that higher education must rein-in costs and keep tuition increases minimal, streamline and simplify the student aid system, and do a better job of educating the public about paying for college. Public opinion often shifts and changes, so higher education must continually monitor public opinion and exercise caution in crafting responses to what might be fleeting concerns. However, since politicians *will* pay attention to public opinion and offer policies and programs that ostensibly respond to the public, higher education ignores public opinion at its peril—and at the peril of the need-based student aid programs it values.

Third, higher education generally, and student aid advocates in particular, must do as much as possible to bolster the college participation and success rate of low-income and minority students. This is important both to create a record of what need-based aid can accomplish when paired with other efforts and to demonstrate higher education's commitment to equal educational opportunity. In Washington, a simple first step would be to devote considerably more effort toward lobbying for increased funding for the TRIO programs.

However, most of the work on overcoming the academic and attitudinal barriers to college must happen at the local campus level.

Of course, most colleges and universities already work to improve local schools and provide mentoring, tutoring, and other services to low-income students at middle schools and high schools, in addition to spending millions on need-based student aid. These efforts tend to happen in isolation, however, in a jumble of small programs. Researchers have found that faculty who work just down the hall from one another often are unaware that they are running overlapping outreach programs in the local schools (Fenske et al. 1997). Higher education must coordinate and publicize its outreach efforts for maximum effect. For example, colleges in a particular city might band together to produce a single citywide outreach program that could be publicized widely through the local media. Not only are such efforts generally more effective, they are more likely to garner the attention of the public and politicians and to demonstrate that higher education's commitment to access is more than mere lip service.

Even if higher education were to invest all its energy in support of access, however, affordability as a policy goal is here to stay. Higher education must direct its efforts in support of both goals. The time is past for wringing our hands about the demise of access. The time has come to acknowledge affordability as a permanent, legitimate goal of public policy and to take a new, smarter, more proactive approach to protecting and enhancing need-based aid.

REFERENCES

Fenske, R. H., C. A. Geranio, J. E. Keller, and D. E. Moore. 1997. *Early Intervention Programs: Opening the Door to Higher Education*. ASHE-ERIC Higher Education Report, Volume 25, No. 6. Washington, DC: The George Washington University, Graduate School of Education and Human Development.

Ikenberry, S. O., and T. W. Hartle. 1998. *Too Little Knowledge Is a Dangerous Thing: What the Public Thinks and Knows about Paying for College*. Washington, DC: American Council on Education.

INDEX

by Virgil Diodato

Page references with f, n, and t indicate figures, notes, and tables, respectively.
Examples: 168f, 195n7, and 167t.